Women, Power and Political Systems

EDITED BY MARGHERITA RENDEL
WITH THE ASSISTANCE OF GEORGINA ASHWORTH

ST. MARTIN'S PRESS NEW YORK

Library of Congress Cataloging in Publication Data
Main entry under title:

Women, power, and political systems.

"A selection from the papers presented at the
meetings of the Sex Roles and Politics Research Committee
(then Study Group) of the International Political Science
Association held at the University of Essex and at the
International Congress of IPSA in Moscow in August 1979"
— Pref.
   Includes — index.
   Contents: Women, power and political systems/
Margherita Rendel — Women and citizenship/Judith Stiehm
— Women's role in the formulation of public policies in
Brazil/Fanny Tabak — [etc.]
   1. Women in politics — Congresses. 2. Women's rights —
Congresses. I. Rendel, Margherita N. II. Ashworth, Georgina.
HQ1236.W64   1981   305.4'2   81-5330
ISBN 0-312-88769-8   AACR2

CONTENTS

List of Tables

List of Figures

Preface

Acknowledgements

TABLES

FIGURES

PREFACE

The contributions to this volume are a selection from the papers presented at the meetings of the Sex Roles and Politics Research Committee (then Study Group) of the International Political Science Association (IPSA) held at the University of Essex and at the International Congress of IPSA in Moscow in August 1979. All the meetings were attended by scholars of many nationalities and from all geo-cultural regions of the world. Whether the theme of our discussions was law as at Essex or development as in Moscow the emphasis of our discussions fell, not surprisingly, on the role of government in maintaining or modifying patriarchal societies. The papers testify to the development of the study of women (Women's Studies) in political science. By taking women as the centre of concern, while not of course excluding men, the papers deepened our understanding of political systems.

The Research Committee is not alone in its concern for developing work about women as a subject in political science. Other organisations also interested in such studies are the Workshop on Women of the European Consortium for Political Research, the Sex Roles and Politics Study Group of the Political Studies Association of the United Kingdom and similar bodies in other national political science associations. Furthermore, UNESCO has commissioned a special study of teaching and research, in higher education, related to women in political science and law. This study will be published later in the year.

The Research Committee is continuing its work and welcomes co-operation with organisations and individuals sharing our interests.

Margherita Rendel
Chairperson,
IPSA Research Committee on Sex Roles and Politics
University of London Institute of Education

ACKNOWLEDGEMENTS

We wish to thank all those who participated in our discussions both at Essex and in Moscow for their contribution to sessions that were enjoyable as well as illuminating. Margherita Rendel is also grateful to Georgina Ashworth, Basil Bernstein, Margaret Deyes, Judith Evans, Eva Gamarnikow, Toni Lovenduski and Jean Woodhall for many helpful comments and suggestions.

We also wish to thank Yvonne Briggs, Pat Culshaw, Rosemary Hoggarth, Pat Moore, Marian Smedley and Kate Tierney for their skill in producing a clear manuscript from much amended drafts.

MR
GA

1 WOMEN, POWER AND POLITICAL SYSTEMS

Margherita Rendel

The most serious omission of political science in its treatment of
women has been its failure to deal with women in the political system
as a whole. By political system is meant, for the purposes of this
discussion, the ways in which power and powerlessness are distributed
(and legitimated) in society and all that flows from that distribution, as
well as the institutions and processes traditionally thought of as
forming the political system. The power of the powerful rests, after
all, on the powerlessness of the powerless, and on the labour and
resources that power can extract from them. It is a mistake to suppose
that the powerless are always totally without power, but the price that
the powerless have to pay for what little power they do sometimes
exert is disproportionately high. Without an understanding of the role
of the powerless, how is it possible to understand the power of the
powerful? Or the nature of the political system? Among the powerless,
women are disproportionately numerous.

In this chapter, I shall attempt to set out some of the ways in which
the subject of women and politics could be examined and why such
approaches are important. Then I shall review briefly how the subject
has been treated by political scientists so far and the critiques that
have been made of this work. I shall then show how the chapters in
this book contribute to filling some of the gaps; it will be seen that
their arguments are directly relevant to issues of public policy. Among
the most serious and extensive omissions from political science are
studies of the family and the labour market. These omissions distort
the understanding both of women and politics, and of the political
system as a whole. The misunderstandings are serious in their effects on
the policies of governments both in developing countries and, in
different ways, in developed countries.

The Political Importance of the Family

The neglect of the family by political scientists, apart from studies of
political socialisation, has been commented on by various feminist
writers, for example Boals (1975). It was not always the case. Political

thinkers (admittedly not the same as political scientists) from Plato onwards have had plenty to say about the political importance and political role of the family. Historically, the political significance of the family is apparent. In many European countries, the state grew out of the household of the king,[1] whose household offices formed the original great offices of state.[2] The familial base of public power gave scope for the wives, mothers and daughters of men holding what we should now call public office to exercise the functions of such office as proxies. They were rarely able to hold office in their own right (Stopes, 1894; Stenton, 1957; McNamara and Wemple, 1974). At some periods, abbesses were at least a partial exception (Stenton, 1957; McNamara and Wemple, 1977). A few daughters, mothers, sisters and widows succeeded or were appointed to high political office. Something similar seems to happen at the present time in the succession of widows as 'male equivalents', for example in the House of Commons, House of Lords,[3] US Congress, the second dáil of the Irish Free State (McCracken, 1958; Currell, 1974; Kirkpatrick, 1974), even occasionally to premiership.[4] Although such women may accede to power through family connections, they have to promote their careers and *maintain* themselves in power through the same means open to others, both men and women. Rare is the woman who, like Eva Perón, achieves and maintains her own political power on the basis of family connection but without ever holding elected or appointed office (Navarro, 1977).

Mistresses of powerful men have occasionally been potent political figures. At first sight they appear to be using another version of the familial base for access to politics. I would suggest instead that they are using their lovers as patrons. Perhaps the most important means of securing promotion in political life is through patronage. It is often suggested that the need for patronage causes particular difficulties for women when those who can be patrons are men; in some countries these difficulties can be overwhelming (Jahan, 1976). It can, of course, be argued that patronage is a kind of familial base. This is to confuse understanding by metaphor. Family has, and had more extensively in the past, a legal base of formal legal rights and obligations relating to control over property and persons.[5] Patronage has no such legal base.

As in political life, so in economic activity and the public domain generally where women had access to crafts and trades through family connections. This is still true at the present time: a sizeable proportion of those few women who do achieve high positions in industry and commerce do so by reason of family relationship (Fogarty, Allen, Allen and Walters, 1971a, p. 142). For those without family connections, patronage is what matters (Kanter, 1977). But in politics at least, family may facilitate access to patronage. However by the end of the Middle Ages, gild rules in some crafts excluded widows and daughters from succeeding their husbands or fathers (O'Faolain and Martines, 1973, p. 170), and capitalist organisations which removed production for the market from the home prevented women from sharing in the economic activities of their husbands and fathers (Clark, 1919). The Agricultural and Industrial Revolutions replaced family with wage labour and separated the home from the place of production. By the first quarter of the nineteenth century, men's trade unions had excluded women from many industrial trades and occupations (Lewenhak, 1977). The exclusion of women from education and the civil death imposed on married women meant that women lacked competence, in both senses, to act in the public domain, that is, in activities based outside the home. To summarise, women acceded to power in the past and still do so by reason of family relationship. This route was blocked by disqualification and changes in economic structure. Disqualification has now been removed. The need for patronage both in political life and in the public domain remains.

The family is politically important for other reasons too. It has been perceived as a miniature state. Thus in England the provisions of the Statute of Treasons of 1352 made the murder of her husband by a woman or his/her master by a servant,[6] but not vice versa, petit treason for which the penalty was to be burned alive and the offender's property to escheat to the victim's heirs. Filmer (1949 edn) argued that not only the state but society as a whole was the family writ large. That family was a patriarchal family descended from Adam who had absolute power over all his descendants.[7] Filmer's arguments were important because they represented the views of the Jacobite Tories, and because patriarchialism was still strong in spite of the growth of liberal and constitutionalist ideas. The husband/father governed the family, disciplined its members, provided for them and represented them to the outside world. Such ideas have remained alive in the twentieth century. Many constitutional documents describe the family as the fundamental unit or group in society. Comparable provisions are to be found in a number of international documents, both of UN organisations and of regional organisations.[8] This is not to suggest that the family is seen only as a political unit and clearly there are good reasons for safeguarding the rights of individuals to join together to found a family. I am concerned to establish that the family is also a political unit, and is in this century and at the present time recognised as such by those engaged in politics. That this is so is made abundantly clear in Chapters 7 and 8.

Universal suffrage has, in principle, made the adult individual the smallest political unit. However, legally and economically, the family, consisting of husband, wife and dependent children, tends in practice to remain the basic unit. This unit is in many ways made to replicate the hierarchical structure of the state. The husband/father is allocated the role of head of the family and of the household and is, in principle, responsible for the maintenance of its members.[9] In practice, the state allows him the power to enforce his authority. The husband was and often still is entitled to obedience from wife and children, an obedience which can still be enforced through their economic and often also legal dependence on him. The husband/father, head of the family, has in the past been legally entitled to use 'reasonable' force to impose his wishes (including sexual demands) on his wife,[10] and in practice is often still able to do so. The unwillingness of the state to interfere effectively or at all in the past and the difficulty of securing effective protection in the present[11] almost gives a *de facto* legitimation to the monopoly of force by the husband/father (Hanmer, 1978). Weber noted that the state had a monopoly of the legitimate use of force.

The family replicates the state in other ways as well as in having a system of authority backed ultimately by force. It has a system of stratification relating both to deference (Barker and Allen, 1976b, p. 10; Bell and Newby, 1976, pp. 156 and 166; Whitehead, 1976) and also to living standards. Stratification and the husband's power are reinforced in various ways. Many women do not know how much their husbands earn and have no right to know. Even cost-of-living increases in the husband's earnings are often not passed on to the wife for housekeeping, still less for personal expenditure. Wives seldom share in the luxurious expense-account living and travel of some business and professional men. The internal stratification of the family also reflects the division of labour within it. The wife's function is to reproduce and service the family, and to service its head, all in exchange for her keep (Delphy, 1977 edn) and an occasional treat.

However, the state's attitude to the status of women in the family is ambivalent. The state both reinforces the authority of the husband and recognises the rights of the wife/mother as an individual citizen. The ambivalence to some degree corresponds with the separation of state and society. Women are recognised as citizens for the purposes of public life, but in society generally and by the state as wives/mothers who are subject to the authority of their husbands. Much effort is devoted to maintaining the family in being with the husband at its head through revenue law, social security legislation and practice and other social services (Wilson, 1977). Indeed in Britain the cohabitation rule[12] seeks to create a family where none exists and often where none is intended. In France, too, women and men are judged as 'good' or 'bad' citizens according to their compliance with these 'family' norms, so that the 'goodness' of a man as citizen and husband is determined by whether he is conscientious as an employee, and of a woman as citizen and wife by whether she takes care of her children and refrains from spending any money on even minimal pleasures for herself. If she does, then she is usually punished and discredited by being deprived of the custody of her children (Barker and Allen, 1976a; Dezalay, 1976a; Delphy, 1977 edn). Similar criteria are applied by the judiciary in Britain (O'Donovan, 1979).

The political system is a battlefield where women have gained some victories which help them to use the machinery of the state for their own advancement in society.[13] Women's emancipation can be seen as an attempt to break up the family as a political unit and to replace it with a direct relationship between the individual woman and the state (Stacey, 1980). In talking about the state we are in fact talking about a collection of institutions which are to a greater or lesser extent integrated with each other but which are also open to control by groups within society.[14] Because these institutions exercise important powers, often monopoly powers, influence and control over the state or its institutions are attractive prizes. The state's 'attitude' to women (or indeed to other groups or interests) therefore reflects at any one time the past and present strengths and institutionalised gains of the many contenders for power.

The state is also itself a political entity. In this capacity it has an interest in maintaining the patriarchal family. The reproduction of the population has always been of interest to states and a large and healthy population has been seen as a source of strength both for peace and war. Bacon (1922 edn) considered that 'The principal part of greatness in any state is to have a race of military men.' Population has been particularly important in relation to warfare in order to ensure a good supply of soldiers. It is men, not women, who constitute armies; some of the implications of this are explored in Chapter 2. Workers to man the fields, mines, factories and counting houses are no less necessary. Policy in relation to population has therefore always been important to governments, whether that policy has been pro-natalist or, as more recently in some cases, anti-natalist. The punishment of both suicide and abortion were justified on the grounds of depriving the state (king) of the direct and indirect services of an individual.[15] Population policies take many forms; they can include grants for births, the availability or not of contraception and abortion, support for or hostility to employment and education for women. These policies have borne far more on women than on men as Chapter 8 shows, inevitably perhaps, because of the biological division of labour in reproduction.

The social division of labour for rearing the next generation is not inevitable; nor is the reason for the existing division quite as apparent as is commonly supposed. Population policies and the obligation placed on women to rear children have contributed to limiting women's opportunities for political activity (Currell, 1974; Flora and Lynn, 1974, p. 38, Lynn, 1979, p. 407). The factors which make it possible to use almost exclusively women for rearing as well as reproduction deserve far more attention than they have so far received from political scientists.

The policy of enforcing the dependence of women on men and imposing on men the obligation to maintain women and children has the effect, outside subsistence economies, of reinforcing men's dependence on paid employment. However, the majority of married women in many industrialised societies in fact support themselves and contribute to the support of their families through their (paid) employment (Land, 1976a). None the less, the family can still be used to harness men to employment because of the low level of women's wages, and women's low wages encourage them to secure a higher standard of living through marriage. Employees are necessarily dependent on their employers for the further reason that in highly industrialised countries there may be few or no other means of obtaining subsistence. The employer may therefore be able to extend control widely over the activities of employees. The political importance of such control should be obvious but has scarcely been considered by political scientists.

The servicing of the labour force raises additional issues. First, it is the male labour force that is serviced and, secondly, it is largely the female labour force that performs this task unpaid, as well as servicing itself, and often in addition to work in the paid labour force. The division of labour within the family ties women to the task of servicing. In the particular cases of the diplomatic service and the armed forces, women are under an ill-defined obligation to perform unpaid additional services for the male servants of the state (Callan, 1975).[16] In a similar way, the wives of publicans, clergy and senior managers (Whyte, 1963; Kanter, 1977) are treated as an extension of their husbands.

The servicing functions (which are additional to those of reproduction and child-rearing) absorb time and energy which militate still further against women's capacity and opportunity to participate in political activity. That domestic duties interfere with women's political activity has been noted by political scientists and accepted; it has seldom been treated as problematic. The virtual *de facto* exclusion of one-half of the population from political activity as a result of the policies on which the state's war-making capacity rests is not sufficiently considered and is certainly not examined in the way other policies of the state are generally examined.[17] Thus one of the foundations on which the strength of the state rests is largely unscrutinised by political scientists. The traditional 'true greatness' of the state demands the consecration of women to these tasks. The family is the institution through which this consecration and the reproduction of the population as a whole are organised. Through the family, individuals are 'incorporated'[18] in groups performing functions for the state. Calling the banns for marriage is, as it were, for the woman a special kind of call-up paper.

Women are compelled to carry out these functions on these terms because they are made to be dependent on men through the family, through their disadvantageous position on the labour market or their relegation to a secondary labour market (Barron and Norris, 1976b).

The Political Importance of the Labour Market

The case of economic institutions is different from that of the family. Political scientists have long concerned themselves, although with fluctuating degrees of interest, with such matters as a state's access to raw materials, trade routes, and the structure and control of industry and commerce. These concerns have been reflected in the study of the economic bases of international relations, state control over economic activity and the debate over nationalised industry.

Comparable attention has not been given by political scientists to the labour market, by which I mean the selection and promotion of individuals or groups of individuals who sell their labour services. The omission is unfortunate since the operation of the labour market has considerable political consequences. This is especially true in industrialised countries where the majority or overwhelming majority of the population is directly dependent on wage labour for a livelihood. Before industrialisation and in non-industrialised countries, ownership of property, especially a modicum of land, could ensure at least a bare subsistence. In industrialised countries, this subsistence is ensured, if at all, by a job or social assistance. But an employee's right to his or her job or to social assistance is not recognised and protected by the courts in the same way as the ownership of land.[19] In non-industrialised countries poll taxes and other devices have been used as a lever to generate a supply of wage labour, and have thus replaced a subsistence by a partly monetised economy with very important consequences for the balance of power between men and women, since it is men rather than women who are drawn into the monetised sector (Boserup, 1970). In the section which follows I am chiefly concerned with the political consequences of the market for wage labour.

Outside state socialist countries, it is largely employers who determine the conditions on which men and women can sell their labour, although both the state and employees through trade unions exercise varying amounts of control or influence. The employers' power is based essentially on the legal ownership of property and the right of initiative in dealing with it is based directly or by delegation on that ownership. The result is that control over property is applied also to control over labour power to work the property. Also, employers are fewer in number and can usually combine more easily than those dependent on selling their labour.[20] It should be noted in passing that these two characteristics also strengthen employers in their dealings with the state, since the state is committed to upholding the rights of property and there are, of course, good reasons why some property rights should be protected.

The right of initiative gives employers scope for many different types of action. In contrast, the effective power of employees is limited to withdrawal of labour and the variants of it, such as work to rule, go slow, overtime ban, withdrawal of goodwill, all of which carry costs for employees. Employees are not able, for example, to determine the price, quantity or quality of the goods or services they produce, the structure of the employer's organisation or even what is produced. The power of employees is at most limited to influence, sometimes very substantial, over the price of their labour and the conditions under which they sell it. Many employees do not effectively influence even that either individually or through their trade unions.

Because employees are dependent on the employer for their livelihood, the employer's power is far-reaching and can extend far beyond control over the performance of the labour service bought and the conditions under which it is performed. Employees commonly have to

comply with the employer's demands and the state expects their first
loyalties to be to the employer. An employer's control may extend
from apparently trivial matters, such as dress, to secrecy over the nature
and scope of the business, including trade secrets. Thus clauses in
contracts of employment disabling a former employee from seeking
employment with a competing employer, within a specified
geographical area, for a specified period of time or in a particular type
of work are lawful. The courts in the United Kingdom have been
concerned first with safeguarding the employers' interests and only
secondly with the need of employees to be able to earn a reasonable
living.[21] Even more remarkable is the failure of the courts, again in
Britain, to use the opportunities offered by legislation and considerations of public policy to protect from dismissal employees seeking the
employer's compliance with legal requirements such as safety regulations.[22] Race and sex discrimination and unfair dismissal cases also
provide many examples of a similar failure. The interpretation of the
role of the state or of different organs of the state such as the courts in
such cases cannot be discussed here. For the purposes of this chapter,
it is sufficient to note the weakness of the employee(s) *vis-à-vis* the
employer(s).

The price and conditions under which labour power is sold are of
interest to the state. Employers can largely determine the standard of
living and the health of a great part of the population. Poor wages and
long hours of work under bad conditions in practice almost invariably
mean poor housing and nutrition causing endemic bad health and
stunted growth. Women are disproportionately numerous and disproportionately concentrated in such industries, and especially in wages
council industries[23] and in home-working (Low Pay Unit, 1974 and
1980; Trades Union Congress, n.d. *c*. 1978; Hakim, 1979). Such
conditions impair the ability both of women to bear healthy infants
who will grow into healthy adults and of men to develop a physique
adequate to the demands of military service, as the United Kingdom
found in both the Boer War and in World War I.[24] It falls to the state
by the provision of services and cash allowances to mitigate or correct
the deficiencies caused by low wages and poor or dangerous conditions.
This is a form of subsidy channelled by the state to the employer:
where the system of taxation is regressive, the burden is borne by
employees twice over through low wages and through taxation.

Poor material conditions concern the state for the further reason
that they cause discontent and unrest ultimately leading to the need to
use police and troops for repression. The cost of this repression arising

from employers' power in the labour market is borne by the state in a number of ways. In the first place, organs of the state are brought into conflict, possibly violent conflict, with sections of the population. Secondly, the government risks losing respect, authority or even control. Thirdly, the financial cost of such activities, although borne ultimately by the population through taxation and borrowing, is covered immediately by the public funds at the disposal of the state. It would appear then to be in the state's interest that all its citizens should 'live in convenient plenty, and no servile condition'.[25] Authoritarians and absolutists, on the other hand, might well welcome or even engineer unrest in order to legitimate repression.[26] Either way, the political importance of the labour market is clear.

My assumption is that the state, taken as the bureaucracies, politicians and political institutions with their personnel, traditions, ethos, ways of operating and the powers at their disposal,[27] is an entity with interests that are independent of those of employers, and that it is not simply a tool of employers. On this assumption, it is very much in the state's interest that the mass of the people should live in 'convenient plenty' and in 'no servile condition'. If they do, they can form a counterweight to the power of employers and help to maintain the state as an independent entity. The mass of the people can form this counterweight by their participation in political activities and their use of political processes: moreover, empirical data from several countries tend to show that individuals with a higher level of education, better jobs and a higher standard of living are more likely to participate, and, in particular, are much more likely to hold the more powerful elected and appointed offices (see also p. 3).

Employment gives access to political power in a number of ways. First, individuals are recruited to the higher levels of government bureaucracies, many of them direct from tertiary education onto career ladders leading to positions of power. Secondly, individuals are recruited in a similar way to private commercial and industrial bureaucracies whether these are trading organisations or pressure groups. These individuals may come to exercise political power both through their dealings with the state and through their influence on those dealings resulting from their control over resources and services that the state needs. Individuals from such bureaucracies are appointed to offices in the state or to advisory or consultative posts giving them direct and frequent access to those who formally make political decisions.[28] Equally the state uses such appointments in order to influence the advice it will receive. As there are thousands of such posts and appointment to the majority of them depends on experience obtained in paid employment or self-employment,[29] they also provide an opportunity to distribute minor and occasionally substantial political power and prestige through the labour market.

The other channels of access to political power are political parties, of course, as well as trade unions, and family and personal connections. Family connections have already been discussed briefly, as have personal connections or patronage (see p. 6), and no more will be said about them here. Political parties offer power both through access to public office and in the party organisation itself. The power offered by trade unions is akin to that offered by other pressure groups. In contrast to the public and private bureaucracies, political parties and trade unions recruit much more widely and heterogeneously and therefore offer a route to power to those who lack high-level educational qualifications. Since fewer women than men obtain higher education, or higher education relevant to political or economic activity, one might expect that they would be more likely to reach positions with political power through political parties or trade unions. But this tends not to be the case. In political parties women, especially those in national legislatures, tend to be better educated than their male counterparts in the same party (Currell, 1974; Kirkpatrick, 1974; Koonz, 1976), and the power-base of trade unions lies predominantly in male-dominated manual industries. At all levels and in virtually all channels of access to political power women are few in number and proportion. Not only are there few women who hold political office, there are few who have access to positions of political influence because they do not have the experience which is at present a qualification for appointment. Consequently it is that much more difficult for women to bring influence to bear on policies which directly affect them, for example the law relating to abortion, or on policy generally.[30]

Women, as we have seen, are disproportionately numerous in poorly-paid jobs, in low-paid industries, in part-time and in temporary jobs, in small rather than large undertakings, and they are relatively poorly trained and less likely to be skilled. The demands of their families and social pressures compel many to interrupt paid employment.[31] Women's position in the labour market is much below their level of achievement in the educational system, even taking into account the smaller numbers of girls and women at the higher levels.

Education and the Labour Market

Access to different levels of employment is largely influenced but not
determined by access to education and training, as many studies of
social mobility and its relationship to education have shown (for
example Halsey, 1980). Though not so closely studied as class differences, the differences in access to education resulting from race and sex
are at least as important. For members of these disadvantaged groups
employment opportunities are not commensurate with their
educational achievement, as is shown in Chapters 3, 4 and 5. However it
is clear that educational achievement provides a minimum qualification
for selection to elites, particularly in societies where educational provision is limited, as Chapter 4 makes clear. The educational system acts
to make available for the more powerful positions a number of individuals some of whom will be selected by a process of patronage and co-
optation. The interlocking between education, employment and political power means that those with power have an interest in selecting
those who will conform and rejecting others equally qualified. The
process of being selected itself encourages conformity (Kanter, 1977).
Women are visibly different from those in positions of power, however,
and can therefore less easily be seen to conform. The educational
system acts to select those who shall have access to the better forms
of employment and to exclude the rest. This is a political function. It
is separate from and additional to the political functions exercised
through the content of the official and hidden curriculum which provides one of the forms of ideological control within society.

The official and especially the hidden curriculum are such as to discourage the majority of pupils from entering the competition for selection. Not all social groups receive the same educational opportunities in
relation to ability (however that may be defined) even when educated
in the same classes. Differential treatment of different social groups
within the same institution has been most clearly demonstrated with
regard to sex. Girls are not given the same opportunities as boys: they
are directed towards different subjects and rewarded for different types
of behaviour (Frazier and Sadker, 1973; Department of Education and
Science, 1975; Wolpe, 1977; Byrne, 1978; Deem, 1978 and 1980). The
official curriculum, the hidden curriculum and the content of education
itself all perform a function of selection that has political consequences
(Barbagli and Dei, 1969). Thus merely to permit access to educational
facilities does not ensure equal opportunity in either education or
employment in any type of society, as several chapters show. In short it

is not accurate to claim that career is open to talent. But much of the rhetoric of the liberal democratic state asserts just such an openness. The disjunction between rhetoric and practice may lead the victims to blame themselves or it may alienate them from the state and indeed from society as a whole and from themselves.

In state socialist countries the position is in some ways at least rather different. The political importance of the labour market is clearly recognised. The state maintains an effective control over both education and the labour market and is able largely to determine the level of wages and the distribution and availability of trained and qualified labour. State socialist countries in furthering their ostensible commitment to increase women's participation in social production have been able to increase dramatically the numbers in higher education and especially the proportion of women in scientific and technical subjects (Wolchik, 1980). As a consequence the numbers and proportion of women in the labour force and in the non-traditional sectors of the labour force are relatively high and their success contrasts with the distribution of women in education and the labour force in both Western and Third World countries.

However women have not been more successful than elsewhere in reaching positions of power. Chapter 7 discusses the ways in which women in Czechoslovakia have attempted to remedy this. One common explanation is that women in state socialist countries bear an even heavier burden of domestic work than do women in advanced industrialised states because they lack domestic equipment and services. The limitations of these are discussed in Chapter 9.

Conditions in Third World countries are more varied, as Chapters 3, 4, 5 and 6 show. Direct and indirect colonialism have everywhere disadvantaged women. Girls have had far less access than boys to any sort of education. Consequently many older women are illiterate. The inadequacy of educational provision, especially at secondary level, is a legacy of the colonial past that is especially disadvantageous to girls and blocks the normal progression to further and higher education and training. The discrepancy between the two sexes is particularly marked at the intermediate levels in both education and employment in some Third World countries (Giele and Smock, 1977). On the other hand, women in some countries have been relatively successful in gaining access to higher professions and sometimes to politics. Traditional concepts of women's proper role may effectively restrict women's continuation of a career or employment; also that employment may make little difference to women's position in the family as Chapter 5 shows. Layne (1979) discussing Jordanian women employed in factories makes substantially the same point. The burden of domestic work and the greater amount of agricultural work that tend to fall to women as a result of modernisation may make it virtually impossible for women to derive any benefit at all from so-called development, as Chapter 6 shows.

Three Labour Markets

Such factors, together with reproduction and the assumption that child-rearing must be linked with child-bearing, affect the ideological and cultural assumptions about women's employment and consequently their position in the labour market. Since the labour market and the related educational system provide access to many positions of power within the state, the operation of the labour market is clearly a matter of concern for all states. However, the labour market is not one homogeneous whole. Barron and Norris (1976b) and other sociologists have shown that there is a dual labour market. It might however be more accurate to think of three labour markets: the man's labour market, the woman's waged labour market and the woman's unwaged labour 'market'. Much of what I have said applies to the man's labour market. The woman's waged labour market, as others have shown, provides a reserve of labour power that is used in both capitalist and socialist countries to make good any inadequacy in the supply of male labour. It also serves to divide actual from potential employees and to set men against women.

The woman's unwaged labour market is often called the marriage market. It consists of marriage and analogous relationships where women's labour, sexual and reproductive services are exchanged for clothes, board and lodging — the domestic duties of reproducing the male and female labour forces and of servicing the former. For middle-class women especially, the duties include socialising and contributing to the education of the young (Bernstein, 1977) and, for some women, as we have seen, acting as assistant to the husband in his job. Some authors, chiefly sociologists, have explored some of the economic and sociological consequences of these divisions of the labour market, but the political implications have not been explored. As we have seen, in marriage especially some women are performing work for no more than their keep; economic weakness and dependency, and sometimes violence, keep them in this position. This is tantamount to unfree status. What *are* the political implications of a substantial proportion of the population being maintained in a *de facto* unfree status? The lessons to be drawn from slave societies are scarcely encouraging.

In some ways and at least until the present, people are the state's 'currency'. The state depends on them for military strength and for the labour to provide arms and economic support. Just as states must control currency, so they have an interest in labour markets and therefore labour markets are a necessary subject for political scientists.

Women and Political Science

I have set out two serious omissions from the discipline of political science, both of which are particularly relevant to an understanding both of the political system as a whole and of the role of women in it. It is my contention that the omission of women contributes to a misunderstanding of the political system as a whole. However, political scientists have not totally ignored women. As we shall see, when they have considered women, not only have they too often misinterpreted the data but they have also shown a partial view of political activity.

More has been written about women and politics in voting studies than on any other aspect of women and politics (Jaquette, 1974). These studies have been subjected to severe criticism in their handling of women by Bourque and Grossholtz (1974), by Goot and Reid (1975) and by Evans (1980b). Although some political scientists are revising their views and some make women of central importance, for example Mossuz-Lavau (1979) and Mossuz-Lavau and Sineau (1980), it is worth summarising the criticisms of the studies because the interpretations expressed in them still have wide currency and not only in political science.

Bourque and Grossholtz categorise the faults of methodology and interpretation under four headings: 'Fudging the Footnotes', that is making statements which the sources cited do not substantiate; 'The Assumption of Male Dominance'; 'Masculinity as Ideal Political Behaviour' and 'Commitment to the Eternal Feminine'. They note the contradictions in the interpretations offered by political scientists for the data presented, as well as inadequacies in the data itself. Goot and Reid who offer the most comprehensive survey of the literature (and the longest bibliography) criticise the definitions, the theory and the methods. Many political scientists apparently believed that 'a state's claim to being a "democracy" is in no way impaired by its withholding the vote from women altogether' (p. 6). They draw attention to the inconsistencies, contradictions and double standards of the explanations offered, and of the failure to see that there is more than one possible explanation for a particular set of data. They conclude:

> like most 'value-neutral' research, much of the work we have reviewed simply assumes the dominant values of the dominant groups of society. The values taken for granted here are the values of the (male) researchers operated in a male-dominated society in which they too are among the beneficiaries (p. 35).

Both Goot and Reid and Bourque and Grossholtz find 'socialisation' (probably the second most written about aspect of women and politics) an inadequate explanation of women's supposedly lower political part-icipation; the differences between men and women are not big enough in mass activities, such as voting, to be consistent with a view that politics is a man's world. Indeed Evans (1980a) argues that such differ-ences as may exist between the level of men's and women's political participation in voting are likely to disappear (p. 212). Evans is concerned with just what the differences are. She concludes that the findings about the husband's influence are uncertain (p. 214) and that it cannot be said that women are more likely to vote right-wing than men (p. 216): more precise and detailed data, and more subtle inter-pretation are required. The different attitudes of different groups of women need to be explored (p. 221). Earlier data from Scandinavia show that the following factors are associated with high political activity for women: high education, residence in an industrialised area, white-collar occupation, working outside the home, higher social class and politically very active mother, but probably residence in an indus-trialised area is the most important and education the least important variable (Holter, 1970, pp. 100-5). Some political scientists, however, have until recently been so far from studying particular groups of women that, as Bourque and Grossholtz found, they do not mention women at all in their studies of political participation (p. 227).

They also found that there was no attempt to treat systematically the virtual exclusion of women from leadership roles (p. 257). As they correctly observe: 'Control is exercised over access to the important roles in the political system so that women are excluded' (p. 263). Duverger (1955) commented on the opposition shown by men to women's political participation at every level. Holter (1970), using Scandinavian data, noted the hostility shown by men to women in politics and, using German data, the different standards applied to men and to women participating in politics. Indeed there are relatively few studies of women elites in politics, apart from studies of women legislators.

The structure of power and the working of the political system is perceived by many of the political scientists reviewed in a narrow and tendentious way. They use their view of what politics ought to be about to assail women's concern with reform. Goot and Reid comment:

> politics appear to be restricted to material interests jockeying for advantage in a tough-talking world of wheeler-dealing, cost-benefits and compromise. A masculine world. Women's 'demands' are seen as soft, unimportant, at best unreal; women are dumb to the 'needs' of politics (p. 31).

Political interests use such a misleading view of politics for their own ends. Political scientists, by accepting such a view, confuse our understanding of political activity, and support some rather than other political interests. Evans asks: 'Do women in some part anyway consider themselves apolitical because areas which concern them, and which are indeed important parts of the political debate, such as education and health, are frequently presented as being above "politics"?' She also notes the calls to 'keep education out of politics' and the slogan 'Patients before Politics' in the campaign for private medicine (p. 221). Such a view leads to a circular interpretation: what concerns women is not political, and what is political concerns only men.

Yet Holter, Bourque and Grossholtz, and Evans agree that there are differences in the political behaviour of men and women. Holter suggests that men and women may have different motives for political activity, that men are fighting for interests or dominance and women are concerned with helping others. She also found that women who were politically active tended to score high on tests of submissiveness (pp. 112-13). Bourque and Grossholtz say:

> Paradoxically, it is the discipline's treatment of these differences which demonstrates the problem. What we see in the treatment of women is a symptom of a larger problem in the discipline — a willingness to either avoid questions of power and justice by blaming the victims, or to substitute explanations based on social norms while at the same time ignoring the political system's role in the maintenance of these norms (p. 261).

They ask: 'What happens to our understanding of political life and our very definition of "politics" if we assume that women are as interested in and competent to exercise political power as men? (p. 264)'. The chapters which follow should help to answer this question.

Women join organisations (Holter, 1970; Verba and Nie, 1972; Lansing, 1974; Andersen, 1975) and are active in them, and they are active in social movements. Some of these bodies are no doubt 'political' in that they act on the political system, but they are concerned with topics often perceived as being apolitical (Evans, 1980a), for example bodies demanding pedestrian crossings, play-groups, Sunday opening for municipal swimming pools, restricted licensing hours for night clubs, better bus and train services, refusal of planning consents for betting shops, and so on. Such political activities, frequently a part of women's activity, have seldom been the subject of the political scientist's interests unless and until they become institutionalised as pressure groups.

The omission is especially unfortunate as it cuts off effective study of how and why the powerless come to have a scrap of power, and how and why that power comes, or not, to be institutionalised,[32] that is, before becoming established as pressure groups. We need to know more about the formation and institutionalisation of groups and especially about the consciousness-raising process that makes possible the formation of a group in the development of a pressure group from a social movement. Such knowledge is important for the study of women in politics because women's activity in movements can and does have a politicising effect. Thus Hertz (1977) has shown that women below the poverty line, the least political of women by all norms of education, class and level of employment, were politicised in the USA by their experience in the Welfare Mothers Movement, and fought for their needs by insisting on their status and rights as citizens instead of accepting the role of client, dependent on administrators and welfare workers. The Women's Movement in the USA sprang out of the Civil Rights and related movements.[33] If a higher proportion of men than women moved on into conventional politics, as may have been the case, then why did this happen? And if women did not because the political system is not responsive to their needs and demands, does not that tell us something about the political system?

The omissions may reflect the 'snobbery' of political scientists in paying relatively little attention, in comparison with national and inter-national politics, to local government and local politics where women are more visible. It may also reflect the unwillingness of many political scientists to include within the scope of our discipline movements that are not concerned with the exercise of public power, and activities that are not conventionally defined as political. In any case little political science is written from the viewpoint of the powerless. It is written from a viewpoint nearer the powerful. The political scientist writes as if at the Prince's elbow.

Much of the literature that discusses women in a political context or in connection with power is sociological, anthropological or social-psychological in its inspiration. This applies to methodology, whether participant observation or the use of large-scale surveys with question-naires and concern with variables of class, family background, education and socio-economic status. Such questions are among the central concerns of political sociology. They are not, however, the only ways in which women and politics can be considered, as the chapters which follow will show. It is not, I suspect, accidental that relatively more work has been done in political sociology than in other branches of political science. Women are perceived as part of the social structure and not as part of the structure of power; as being rather than doing (de Beauvoir, 1949), and hence as part of sociology, psychology, anthropology, rather than of political science.

Earlier in this chapter I have drawn out from sociological data about women, the family and the labour market factors which are important for understanding the political system as a whole, and there-fore directly relevant to political scientists. The study of women more than the study of class illumines the distribution of power within society because the study of women must necessarily consider the role of the family which produces and reproduces, and maintains both the supply of military men and the supply of labour in general.

The study of women also helps to unify knowledge that has been fragmented into separate academic disciplines. Much of the separation is arbitrary but carries with it power and authority for academic institu-tions and particularly for those at the top of such institutions (Bernstein, 1971, p. 63). The fragmentation encourages a habit of seeing issues in isolation from their context; indeed disciplinary boun-daries make a virtue of such tunnel-vision. These limitations make scholars and scholarly work less useful or relevant to governments and international organisations than they might otherwise be. Research in women's studies has shown both the limitations of traditional discip-lines and the gains in understanding from an integrated and interdis-ciplinary approach. A UNESCO Committee of Experts stressed these points:

We are in complete agreement on the necessity for women's studies to be both interdisciplinary and multi-disciplinary, since the specificity of the conditions of women encompasses all disciplines. Women's studies, like other studies of an interdisciplinary nature, question the concept and structure of knowledge contained within the disciplinary boundaries and the power of those who define these boundaries and what comes within them. The same can be said for women's studies within disciplines. By their interdisciplinarity and in raising such points, women's studies could help bring about a restructuring and re-unification of knowledge and scholarship at present increasingly fragmented, despite the fact that much of the most fruitful development is taking place between the boundaries of established disciplines (1980).

Women and Development

The value of an interdisciplinary approach and the dangers of omitting women are clearly demonstrated in development policy. Ester Boserup (1970) was the first to document systematically the adverse effect of development on women. In many developing countries with shifting agriculture, women undertake the greater part of the field work and raise the subsistence crops. Where there is plough agriculture, men undertake a larger proportion of the field work, but in these areas women's agricultural and domestic work is still essential to the survival of the family. Women spend many hours each day fetching water and collecting firewood. Preparing harvested food for storage and consumption, and pounding grains by hand when there is no mill take many hours each day (Giele and Smock, 1977; Palmer, 1977; Rogers, 1980). Even where women are secluded, they may contribute economically to the family, for example by carpet-weaving.

The principal responsibility for feeding and clothing the children often rests with women. These responsibilities tend now to rest even more with women than in the past because it is the men who have migrated to towns where Western governments and economic institutions have wished to employ them (Boserup, 1970). Traditional societies use complex and sophisticated networks of relationships, rights, and control over resources and especially land which ensure that women have access to the means of carrying out their responsibilities. The women have considerable leverage against the men, who often have fomally dominant positions (Rogers, 1980). The day-to-day system can therefore be seen as one of checks and balances in many, though not all, traditional societies. It is scarcely appropriate to talk of 'owner-ship' of land in this context.

Development planners have largely taken Western industrialisation as their model. As Nash (1975) observes, they have:

> applied norms established in the large-scale capital-intensive sectors of the developed world as the logic for the industrial order in the rest of the world. These have been summarized as follows: (a) large-scale organization (b) linked to world-wide economy with (c) urban centres of some size (d) characterized by diverse occupational struc-tures (e) and an educational system to feed this structure (f) with a wage structure that reflects supply and demand of various occu-pational skills (g) a labour market mechanism to sort out, distribute and redistribute workers (h) managers and managed with rules governing the relationship (i) industrial discipline for individual and group (j) a State strong enough to govern industrialism (k) and 'acceptance of these imperatives by men who live in the industrial order'.[34]

The assumption is that the benefits of development will 'trickle down' to those at the bottom. Boserup (1970), Palmer (1977), Rogers (1980) and others have shown the adverse effects on women of such policies.

Rogers also shows the mechanism and policies that produce these effects. The view of gender-roles and of women current in Western industrialised societies has been accepted without question until very recently as suitable, indeed desirable, for all societies everywhere as a necessary base for social progress. This preference is shown in the home economics programmes so severely criticised by Nash (1975) and Rogers (1980). It has been assumed that traditional family structures and the attitudes of women block change. Measures have therefore been taken both under colonial administrations and under development plans to transfer land subject to a multiplicity of rights into the absolute ownership of one individual. The individual selected is almost invariably the male, who is assumed to be the head of a nuclear family. He is often regarded as the managerial decision-maker for the land farmed, even if he is a migrant worker who does not, in fact, work the land. Access to agricultural extension training schemes, agricultural machinery and equipment, new varieties of seed, credit and so on is almost always limited to the male managerial decision-maker. Women are deprived of their rights as cultivators and hence of access to cash.

Furthermore new methods often involve more work on tasks, such as weeding, traditionally done by women and which the men refuse to do. Their leverage against the men is diminished and they are reduced to the status of an unpaid worker, wholly dependent on the husband (Rogers, 1980). Thus a patriarchal nuclear family is imposed legally and economically on very different systems.[35] At the same time, the sanctions that in Western countries make the patriarchal nuclear family sometimes moderately viable are not, and probably could not be, imposed. We have already seen the role of the family in organising a hierarchical and authoritarian society.

The shift to the male is also reflected in the statistics, in the automatic allocation of the term 'head of household' to a male and in the definition of work. Even so, female-headed households are numerous in Third World countries (Birdsall and McGreevey, 1978).[36] Virtually all women's work is excluded and, even when included, it may be valued at two-thirds of the time actually spent, whereas men's work is fully counted (Rogers, 1980). Women's work of less than twenty hours a week or intermittent work may also be excluded.

These defects in development plans can be accounted for in a number of ways: false logic in assumimg that the conditions associated with the economic development of Western Europe and North America are always a necessary condition for development, compounded by cultural imperialism and ethnocentric views of what is desirable. All these lead to an arrogant disregard of the knowledge, experience and skill of local women who have, after all, maintained their families for generations. Tunnel-vision, which is carefully inculcated in our systems of advanced education and training, tends to make development planners context-unaware. (Field-independent is the euphemistic phrase often used for this defect.) This training tends to have the further consequence of encouraging too great a reliance on authority and too little capacity to adapt professional skills and training to local opportunities.[37]

Rogers (1980) stresses the bitter conflict between the sexes which the changes are bringing. Men treat women with contempt; women show their resentment at the way they are treated and their hatred towards the men who exploit their labour and deny them access to the means of independence and advancement. But is this so entirely different from the situation in Western developed countries? Could it be that developments in Third World countries now could throw some light on developments in industrialised countries in the past?[38]

Planners are often dismayed to find both that men are unresponsive to their plans and that women oppose them. The evidence suggests that men are interested in schemes that give high cash returns on the investment of labour or resources. The women oppose schemes which deprive them of control over land and resources, of access to cash, and which increase their burden of work often to an intolerable level. The men, however, gain in power to control their wives, an end which is often explicitly supported by planners (Rogers, 1980, p. 101), as well as obtaining absolute and irresponsible (that is accountable to no one) control of the land. The evidence also shows that women are very interested indeed in obtaining access to agricultural training opportunities and are willing to apply what they learn for much smaller returns than the men. Planners however seem slow to absorb these lessons and act upon them. They have sometimes seemed primarily concerned with securing the subordination of women to men, but there are some signs that these attitudes are beginning to change.

Women are ill-placed to protect their interests at governmental and planning level for a number of reasons. The burden of maintaining families falls on them while it is men who migrate to the towns. In areas such as Latin America where women rather than men migrate to towns, they have access only to the lowest-paid jobs, chiefly domestic service. Because of their role in agriculture as well as the discriminatory attitudes of past colonial administrators, the effects of which have not yet been fully corrected, women's access to education was and still is much less than that of men. There is frequent talk about integrating women into development, but development is being built, as many authors have shown, on women's unpaid and unacknowledged labour. It would be more fitting for attention to be directed at integrating women into political processes and thereby giving them power and a full share in decision-making.

For a capitalist economy, the absolute owner of land has advantages. There is a single interest in the land and a single individual to deal with. It is easy for the large capitalist to acquire land which can be used for a variety of purposes as seems most profitable: cash crops for export, building, sport or pleasure. There is no guarantee that such land will not be depopulated[39] or that it will be cultivated with a view to the needs of future generations. The land can be used for purposes of competition of whatever sort with other landowners. To ensure that it is used in order to make provision for those who live on it requires limitations on the power of ownership. Such limitations can be secured through government controls which make, as we have seen, the state a site of conflict. They can be secured by private legal limitations, for example trusts which separate legal from beneficial ownership, but such devices can be of only limited application and effectiveness.

Alternatively, limitations can be imposed by networks of rights and obligations. Such a solution raises the question of why it should be necessary to change the system of ownership and control in the first place. However such a solution, if followed, would require that much higher priority be given to local organisations, universal education and egalitarian ways of arriving at decisions. Chaney, Simmons and Staudt (1979) consider some aspects of how networks might function. As Chapter 10 of this book shows, networks are relevant also to developed countries, particularly as many of the dominant groups in the world, which are hierarchical, authoritarian institutions organised for competition that is frequently mutually destructive, are controlled from developed countries.

Towards Filling the Gaps in Our Knowledge and Understanding

Is it a necessary condition for women to share more effectively in decision-making that they should share also in the most destructive of all forms of competition, namely war? It may be that a willingness to exercise power is a *sine qua non* for being taken seriously by policy-makers. Stiehm in Chapter 2 considers the implications of the exclusion of women from military combat. Her chapter is based on work she has done on the effects of the admission of women to military academies in the United States. The traditional position, enshrined in documents such as the Geneva Conventions, excludes the use of women in warfare. This might be thought proper from every point of view, since women are thought to be naturally more pacific than men, a view challenged by Beard (1971 edn) and others. More important, perhaps, is the fact that women are needed as bearers of succeeding generations. It might then be thought that mothers would receive benefits comparable with those of ex-servicemen but that is not the case. Furthermore, lack of military service was a reason given for excluding women from the franchise and from public office (Rendel, 1977a; Harrison, 1978). There is something special, it seems, about participation in military service which is different from mere service to the country or work, or activity useful to the country. Stiehm examines the reasons given why women cannot be engaged in combat duties and finds them inadequate. She asks what it would mean to men if women were also warriors? Women can demonstrate their femininity by bearing a child, but men

cannot demonstrate their masculinity in a comparable manner.[40] A
further question that I would ask is why human beings need to demonstrate either masculinity or femininity since they have so many and such
varied qualities and abilities that they can demonstrate in other ways.

Access to decision-making is what counts in assessing political
participation. In highly centralised countries, such as Brazil, those who
do not have access to decision-making positions are especially disadvantaged. Furthermore, in non-democratic countries, the normal measures
of political participation, such as voting behaviour or membership of
the legislature, are of little value. In Chapter 3 Tabak shows that
although modernisation has not by itself ensured women's participation, United Nations campaigns, such as International Women's Year,
have compelled the government to give some thought to the position
of women and have legitimated the demands made by women themselves. Both liberty and legitimating support increase women's political
participation.

In Chapter 4 Awosika concentrates on the links between education
and employment. She reinforces Tabak's view that modernisation and
development do not necessarily increase women's participation. She
also indicates the numerous other factors that do influence it, and
points out the vicious circle between lesser education for girls, poor
employment prospects and dependence on a husband leading to a justification for not educating girls; if women are to regain their traditional independence, they also need child-care facilities to replace the
help previously provided in the extended family.

Like Tabak and Awosika, Abadan-Unat in Chapter 5 notes the
adverse effect in Turkey of economic development on women's opportunities for employment. She also demonstrates the connection
between women's family background, their education and the jobs they
move into. Like others, she concludes that education is not enough to
change attitudes. Ataturk's reforms provided a legal base for participation by women in the public domain. However, when government
policies ceased actively to support the advancement of women after
1946, there was no counterweight to traditional family pressures.
Women are subjected to contradictory and complex double standards
and seen as both sexually vulnerable and asexual.

Sachak in Chapter 6 takes these themes further. She shows the inter-
relationship between government policy, development, some forms of
self-help, the sexual division of labour and familial roles of women, and
some of the practical policy implications of a discipline-bound view of
problems and solutions. She notes definitions of employment in

practice tend to apply almost exclusively to urban areas and particularly to public employment with the result that development policy, which is largely employment policy, is distorted. In her research, she and her colleagues asked both women and men in the villages studied about their employment and what facilities would most assist them. While the differences between younger and older men do not challenge the assumptions of planners, the replies of the women were very different. Concepts of men's work and of women's work make it difficult to implement policies of rural development.

In state socialism as in Third World countries, women bear a heavy burden of domestic work. The governments of state socialist countries have made the ending of discrimination against women in education and employment an important aspect of their policy. In Chapter 7 Wolchik analyses the attempts of women in Czechoslovakia from 1964 onwards to secure attention for women's actual needs as opposed to their legal status. In other state socialist countries the same problems have arisen. For example, in the German Democratic Republic, the issues have been dealt with in fiction (Einhorn, 1980). In the Soviet Union it seems that ways are being considered of meeting women's domestic needs by providing communal services.[41] These issues have, however, been at the centre of another debate: whether women are more likely to achieve liberation in state socialist countries or in capitalist countries. Jancar (1979) argues that women need to be able to organise independent pressure groups to get their needs met. Her opponents argue that policy directives by the state can better secure the necessary changes.

In these various countries with differing social and economic systems, and in different ways, the links between reproduction, family, education, employment and power none the less have certain resemblances. Kickbusch shows in Chapter 8 that each gain by women to improve their position is countered by yet another obstacle. Her analysis suggests that women will not be able to obtain 'a right to themselves' although they may obtain more rights; the key to women's oppression lies therefore in patriarchy rather than in capitalism. Industrialisation and capitalism created the housewife and a subservient role which enables 'the clodhopper . . . to exercise his share of the power equally with the highest nobleman' (Mill, 1869). Government (and private) policies — reproduction policy — ensure that family labour always remains women's first and overriding responsibility. Kickbusch suggests that self-help might provide a means of modifying this system. In a very different context and perhaps with more limited aims, Col in

Chapter 10 explores some of the ways in which self-help might operate.

It is often assumed that some of these difficulties could be overcome by technological developments. In Chapter 9 Rothschild shows that the contrary is the case, a view shared by Rose and Hanmer (1976a). Technology, she argues, helps capitalism to lock women further into subordination within patriarchy. She defines technology to include management and organisation as well as machines, and invites us to compare women's relationships to reproduction and housework with the alienated position of the industrial worker. Physical drudgery has been replaced by psychological draining as the housewife is expected to be the universal emotional prop. It is men and indeed women's children (Leonard, 1980) who gain from the comfort of a pre-capitalist environment to which has been added all modern conveniences. Rothschild thus gives empirical support to Kickbusch's theoretical analysis. Furthermore, the worship of technology for its own sake and the conception of technology as the domination of nature tend to depreciate humane values in favour of depersonalised, alias rational, considerations within narrow, alias relevant, boundaries. Examining the effect of technology on women's domestic labour and its relationship to capitalism and patriarchy raises these political issues.

The activities and work of women are one of the factors missing from the frame of reference of most planners and policy-makers. The next three chapters consider what makes for change. Col discusses the ways in which women by their own actions and through their own networks can increase their influence on policy and its implementation. More women competing for jobs and influence might exacerbate still further the ferocity of the struggle for survival and lead to a Hobbesian struggle of each against all. The traditional conservative right-wing policy of relegating women to the home maintains not only the competitive struggle but also the hierarchical, authoritarian structure of society. Women with experience in feminist networks which are informal, anti-hierarchical and anti-authoritarian will want 'flatter' organisations and a less authoritarian style of management or government. This would mean a shift from a competitive route to the top to a co-operative sharing of talents. It would be a political development of the first magnitude.

Sinkkonen and Haavio-Mannila examine what women MPs in Finland have done, how they have done it and the relationship of their activities to the women's movement in general. They show clearly that women MPs have done more than men MPs to advance women's interests. Secondly, they find that the fewer the women proportionately, the less they accomplish. Kanter (1977) discusses the problems of token women and Rendel (1978) the factors which influence how many are enough to be effective. Sinkkonen and Haavio-Mannila relate both the strategies and the content of measures affecting women to the concerns of the women's movement. For women to seek equality with men leaves them, as Kickbusch points out, with formal access to jobs, but at the cost of the double shift or double burden which is so oppressive to women in state socialist, capitalist and developing countries. To equalise sex-roles means extending the struggle for women's liberation to the relations between individual men and women, especially within marriage and the home. For such a struggle to be successful it is not so much the outstanding achievements of tiny elites that is required, but small gains by thousands of individuals in everyday affairs. For this, mass consciousness-raising is needed, and structural as well as personal solutions.

Laws to advance women and to prevent discrimination are of limited use if judges restrict their effect by narrow interpretations. The judiciary and especially the higher judiciary is in all countries overwhelmingly male. Do women judges, like Sinkkonen's and Haavio- Mannila's women politicians help women? This is the question which Cook addresses in Chapter 12. She found that men, far more than women, did not live up to the feminist views they claimed, and concludes that it is worthwhile for women to support the appointment of women judges.

As Cook observes, women's roles are legal as well as cultural. Hence legal rights, whether or not they give us a right to ourselves, are necessary. The political activity of women is essential for gaining those rights. Mezey and Mezey (1979) were able to show for the USA that the more 'feminist' the legal environment, the higher the participation of women and the more acceptable are women politicians. The removal of disqualifications on women may however be consistent with the continuance of discrimination (Rendel, 1975, p. 73). To end discrimination, promotional legislation is needed. In Britain the value of promotional legislation was clearly stated by the Race Relations Board (1967, para. 65) and reiterated by the Home Secretary when setting out the government's proposals for sex discrimination legislation (Home Office, 1974, para. 19). There is then a zig-zag progression between the advancement of women and constitutional and legislative provisions. For women to reach powerful positions and to be able to act on behalf of women, they need the support of a strong and active women's movement. I have suggested that the failure of political scientists to study women in all ways relevant to politics and of politicians to include them in economic and other concerns derives in part from seeing fragments of reality within predetermined boundaries: women, as we have seen, do not fit within the definitions that help to make the boundaries. A holistic view that includes women would increase the understanding of political scientists and the effectiveness of politicians and planners.

Notes

1. The word 'king' derives from Old English 'cyning', 'cynn' — kin, race etc. See *Shorter Oxford English Dictionary*, 3rd edn (OUP, Oxford, 1965),

2. For example, in the early fourteenth century, the Wardrobe was a department which has a great deal to do with military and other expenditure: see F.W. Maitland (1970, p. 98). Other offices such as the Exchequer and the Chancery established their independence much earlier.

3. Fifty-two women have been created life peers; for about one-quarter the promotion was a tribute to their husbands (*Dod's Parliamentary Companion*, supplemented from the House of Lords Information Office).

4. For example, Mrs Bandaranaike; Mrs Indira Gandhi succeeded her father.

5. For example, rights of wardship, marriage, dower, curtesy, inheritance and disinheritance, guardianship, custody, domicile and so on.

6. A lay person or cleric who killed his/her Bishop was also guilty of petit treason. The distinction between petit treason and murder was abolished in 1828.

7. 'For as Adam was lord of his children, so his children under him had a command over their own children, but still with subordination to the first parent, who is lord paramount over his children's children to all generations, as being the grandfather of his people' (Filmer, 1949 edn, p. 57).

8. Examples include the Canadian Bill of Rights, 1960; the Federal German Grundgesetz, 1949; the 1964 Constitution of the United Arab Republic; the Italian Constitution; the Universal Declaration of Human Rights, 1948; the Declaration on Elimination of Discrimination against Women, 1967; the International Conventions on Economic, Social and Cultural Rights, and on Civil and Political Rights, both 1966; the European Convention on Human Rights, 1950; and the Social Charter, 1961.

9. In England and Wales the husband's responsibility derives from common law going back into the mists of time. For various reasons it is often impossible for the wife to enforce this obligation.

10. The husband has a right to the sexual services of his wife. 'The wife *submits* [italics in the original] to her husband's embraces because at the time of marriage she gave him an irrevocable right to her person' *per* J. Hawkins, *R* v *Clarence* (1888) 22 QBD 23 at 54; and 'for she has no right or power to refuse her consent' *per* B. Pollock at 64. It follows that a husband cannot legally rape his wife since the absence of consent must be proved for rape to be established. It is however assault if the husband uses force.

11. In the first place it was hard to secure recognition of violence by men against wives or cohabitees as violence and not as 'just a domestic tiff'. There have been two main types of difficulty in enforcing legislation against battering: those of enforcing injunctions and court orders against husbands; those of enabling women to establish their own livelihood and housing separately from their husbands.

12. The cohabitation rule provides that a woman can be denied social assistance benefits if she is deemed to be living with a man and therefore receiving

financial support from him. For example, women in their seventies have been deprived of benefit because they have had a male (and young) lodger in their house.

13. Consider interdepartmental rivalries and the complaints made by governments of all political complexions that the civil service is not responsive to their policies. Mediaeval English kings had similar problems as the great offices of state developed their own bureaucratic procedures and routines.

14. It is no part of my purpose here to enter into a discussion of the nature of the state, a discussion which has been undertaken by many others and recently, for example, by Ralph Miliband and Nicos Poulantzas.

15. ' . . . and, as the suicide is guilty of a double offence; one spiritual, in invading the prerogative of the Almighty, and rushing into his presence uncalled for; the other temporal, against the King, who has an interest in the preservation of all his subjects; the law has therefore ranked this among the highest crimes, making it a peculiar species of felony, a felony committed on one's self' (Blackstone, *Commentaries*, Book 4, para. 189, Chitty (ed.) (Lippincott, Philadelphia 1893)). However neither Frederick Pollock and F.W. Maitland, *The History of English Law*, vol. 2 (CUP, Cambridge, 1923), p. 488, nor W.S. Holdsworth, *A History of English Law* (Methuen, London, 1923) give this explanation but instead refer to the extension of the notion of felony to suicide because the property of the suicide was forfeit, like the property of a felon.

16. Officers' wives are expected to perform certain welfare and supervisory services *vis-à-vis* the wives and families of other ranks.

17. Some work is now being done on this subject, for example, Lahav (1977); Klebanoff (1979) and Yuval-Davis (1980).

18. Compare the statement of Maurice Hauriou (1927): 'Les masses démocratiques ont besoin d'être encadrées. Elles le sont par l'administration et par les partis politiques' (1927; p. 48). To which I would add the family.

19. In Britain, employees' rights to their jobs or right to work is occasionally recognised by the courts, for example by Lord Denning, The Master of the Rolls, 'I have said before, and I repeat it now, that a man's right to work at his trade or profession is just as important to him as, perhaps more important than, his rights of property' (*Nagle* v *Fielden* [1966] 2 QB 633 at 646); and by legislation for the first time in the Industrial Relations Act, 1971. The relevant provisions have since been modified and re-enacted three times.

20. The nineteenth-century Combination Acts in Britain which forbade associations or unions 'in restraint of trade' worked against employees, but had little effect on employers who discussed and decided common policy on social occasions.

21. One of the leading cases is still that of *Warner Bros Pictures Inc* v *Nelson* [1937] 1 KB 209, where Miss Bette Davis was enjoined from engaging in employment as an actress with another film producer until the unexpired period of her contract or three years, whichever was the shorter, had elapsed. The court refused to award damages against Miss Davis and held that she was not forced to a choice between performing the contract or starving, because she could earn her living in some other way, though not so lucratively. In more recent cases: a restraint upon a milkman against serving customers he had served during his last six months of employment was held reasonable; a tie of 12 years or more during which a garage had to accept all its supplies from one company was held too long, but five years was considered reasonable.

22. In *Chant* v *Aquaboats Ltd*, Times Law Reports, 9 February 1978, a woodworking employee was held not to be engaged in trade union activities when he organised a petition against allegedly dangerous woodworking machinery with his trade union's support, because he was not a trade union official. In cases such as

this, the courts can be seen as using their powers to ensure the supremacy of employers despite possibly contrary provisions in legislation.

23. Wages Councils are statutory bodies which fix minimum wages and holidays for those industries with low wages and where the two sides of industry are either not organised or are insufficiently organised to provide effective collective bargaining. The minimum wages fixed are substantially below the national average and are not effectively enforced.

24. The Inter-Departmental Committee on Physical Deterioration was set up after the Boer War and reported in 1904. The Black Report on the provision of health services (1980) raises similar questions and draws attention to the rising rate of neo-natal mortality.

25. Francis Bacon wrote: 'And herein the device of King Henry the Seventh . . . was profound and admirable, in making farms and houses of husbandry of a standard, that is, maintained with such a proportion of land unto them as may breed a subject to live in convenient plenty, and no servile condition' (1922 edn, p. 82).

26. E.P. Thompson in *The Making of the English Working Class* (Gollancz, London, 1963), discusses the evidence for such an interpretation of the actions of the Liverpool ministry after the Napoleonic Wars.

27. See also p. 15 above. It is impossible as well as unreal to offer categorical definitions: institutions have more than one aspect and individuals wear more than one hat.

28. See the vast literature on pressure groups and a much smaller one on advisory bodies, or *l'administration consultative*.

29. In written answers to Parliamentary Questions asked in June 1974 by Mr Edward Bishop MP of 11 ministers responsible for making appointments to advisory and legal bodies, four replied that they were seeking to increase the numbers of women. The remainder replied with variants of 'women of suitable experience and ability are invariably considered' (Hansard, 17 June 1974, Co. 13). In general, women are fewer than 10% on these bodies.

30. Labour women MPs in the British House of Commons have been subjected to an additional burden of work that threatens to restrict their other activities because of the need to oppose the repeated attempts to reduce the availability of abortion by amending the relatively liberal 1967 Abortion Act.

31. Guy Routh, *Occupation and Pay in Great Britain, 1906-60* (NIESR, Cambridge University Press, Cambridge, 1965), B.N. Seear, *Re-entry of Women to the Labour Market after an Interruption in Employment* (OECD, Paris, 1971), Hunt (1968) and Hakim (1979) very fully document these points. Routh shows furthermore that the number and proportion of women skilled workers has fallen since 1901. Seear and Hakim include international comparisons.

32. Studying the powerless is expensive when it involves survey work. Thus the opportunities for political scientists to engage in such work will depend on access to funds and this may in turn reflect the standing of the discipline in the academic community as well as the preferences and priorities of those distributing funds. Access to knowledge is dependent on the *form* of the data. More attention should be given to ways of getting round such difficulties.

33. Freeman (1975), who is a political scientist, gives an excellent analysis of the development of the Women's Liberation Movement in the United States.

34. Quoted by June Nash (1975) from Clark Kerr, 'Changing Social Structures' in Wilbert Moore and Arnold S. Feldman (eds.), *Labor Commitment and Social Change in Developing Areas* (Social Science Research Council, New York, 1960), p. 340.

35. Christine Obbo in 'Victorian Laws, Ganda Women and Development', paper presented to the Round Table of the International Political Science Associa-

tion Study Group on Sex Roles and Politics held at the University of Essex, 6-8 August 1979. Obbo showed the rather ambiguous significance of Christian marriage in Uganda. Rogers quotes other sources for a similar view in relation to other countries.

36. Nancy Birdsall and William P. McGreevey (1978) quote data compiled by Mayra Buvinic and Nadia H. Youssef in 'Woman-headed Households in Third World Countries; an Overview', 'Women in Poverty: What do we Know?' Belmont Conference Center, Eltridge, 30 April-2 May 1978 which shows that in some countries as many as 40% to 46% of households are female-headed and that percentages from between 15% and 26% are commonplace.

37. Rogers (1980), p. 93) cites the insistence of some home economics instructors on the value of expensive imported oranges as a source of vitamin C to the exclusion of local fruits which actually contain more vitamin C.

38. In many countries, whether developed or developing, there is evidence of men's attempts to control both women's economic activities and their sexuality, and the contempt for and brutality towards women in pursuing these attempts.

39. The nineteenth-century Highland clearances are a notorious and shameful British example.

40. In a paper to the Women's Research and Resources Centre, London, in 1978, Mary O'Brien argued that the difficulty for men of proving paternity of a particular child partly explained attitudes to women.

41. The intention is to provide more communal domestic services in order to reduce the work falling on women.

Bibliography

Andersen, K., (1975) 'Working Women and Political Participation', *American Journal of Political Science*
Bacon, F. (1922) *Essays*, P.E. and E.F. Matheson (eds.), Clarendon Press, Oxford (originally published in 1625)
Barbagli, M. and Dei, M. (1977) 'Socialisation into Apathy and Political Subordination' in Karabel and Halsey, pp. 423-32
Barker, D.L. and Allen, S. (eds.) (1976a) *Sexual Divisions and Society: Process and Change*) Tavistock Publications, London
—— (1976b) *Dependence and Exploitation in Work and Marriage*, Longman, London
Barron, R.D. and Norris, G.M. (1976b) 'Sexual Divisions and the Dual Labour Market' in Barker and Allen
Beard, M. (1971) *Women as Force in History*, Macmillan and Collier Macmillan, London (originally published in 1946)
Bell, C. and Newby, H. (1976b) 'Husbands and Wives: the Dynamics of the Deferential Dialectic' in Barker and Allen, pp. 152-68
Bernstein, B. (1975) 'On the Classification and Framing of Educational Knowledge', Ch. 5 in B. Bernstein (ed.), *Class, Codes and Control, 3*, 2nd rev. edn, RKP, London; also appears in M.F.D. Young (ed.), *Knowledge and Control*, Collier Macmillan, London, 1971
—— (1977) 'Class and Pedagogies: Visible and Invisible' in Karabel and Halsey, pp. 511-34.
Birdsall, N. and McGreevey, W.P. (1978) 'The Second Sex in the Third World: Is Female Poverty a Development Issue?', paper prepared for the International Center for Research on Women Policy Round Table, Washington, DC (21

June)

Boals, K. (1975) 'Political Science: Review Essay' in *Signs, 1*, 1, 161-74

Boserup, E. (1970) *Women's Role in Economic Development*, Allen & Unwin, London

Bourque, S. and Grossholtz, J. (1974) 'Politics an Unnatural Practice: Political Science looks at Female Participation', *Politics and Society* (Winter), pp. 225-66

Byrne, E. M. (1978) *Women and Education*, Tavistock Publications, London

Callan, H. (1975) 'The Premiss of Dedication: Notes towards an Ethnography of Diplomats' Wives' in Shirley Ardener (ed.), *Perceiving Women*, Dent and Halsted Press, London

Chaney, E., Simmons, E. and Staudt, K. (1979) 'Women in Development', background paper for the US Delegation World Conference on Agrarian Reform and Rural Development, FAO, Rome

Clark, A. (1919) *Working Life of Women in the Seventeenth Century*, Cass, London

Currell, M. (1974) *Political Woman*, Croom Helm, London

de Beauvoir, S. (1949) *Le Deuxième Sexe*, Gallimard, Paris

Deem, R. (1978) *Women and Schooling*, RKP, London

—— (ed.) (1980) *Schooling for Women's Work*, RKP, London

Delphy, C. (1977) *The Main Enemy*, Women's Research and Resources Collective, London (originally published 1970)

Department of Education and Science (1975) *Curricular Differences for Boys and Girls*, Education Survey no. 21, HMSO, London

Dezalay, Y. (1976a) 'French Ideology in Working Class Divorce' in Barker and Allen

Duverger, M. (1955) *The Political Role of Women*, UNESCO, Paris

Einhorn, B. (1980) 'Women in the German Democratic Republic: Reality Experienced and Reflected', paper presented at the Political Studies Association Annual Conference at Exeter

Evans, J. (1980a) 'Women and Politics: a Re-appraisal', *Political Studies, XXVIII*, 2, 210-21

—— (1980b) 'Attitudes to Women in American Political Science', *Government and Opposition, 15*, 2, 101-14

Filmer, Sir R. (1949) *Patriarcha*, Peter Laslett (ed.), Basil Blackwood, Oxford (originally published in 1680)

Flora, C. B. and Lynn, N.B. (1974) 'Women and Political Socialization: Considerations of the Impact of Motherhood' in Jaquette

Fogarty, M.P., Allen, A.J., Allen, I. and Walters, P. (1971) *Women in Top Jobs*, Allen & Unwin for PEP, London

——, Rapoport, R. and Rapoport, R.N. (1971) *Sex, Career and Family*, Allen & Unwin for PEP, London

Frazier, N. and Sadker, M. (1973) *Sexism in School and Society*, Harper and Row, New York

Freeman, J. (1975) *The Politics of Women's Liberation*, Longmans, New York

Giele, J.Z. and Smock, A.C. (1977) *Women: Roles and Status in Eight Countries*, John Wiley & Sons, New York

Goot, M. and Reid, E. (1975) *Women and Voting Studies: Mindless Matrons or Sexist Scientism?*, Sage Publications, Beverly Hills, Calif.

Hakim, C. (1979) *Occupational Segregation*, Department of Employment Research Paper no. 9, HMSO, London

Halsey, A.H. (1980) *Origins and Destinations: Family, Class and Education in Modern Britain*, Clarendon Press, Oxford

Hanmer, J. (1978) 'Violence and the Social Control of Women' in Gary Littlejohn,

Barry Smart, John Wakeford and Nira Yuval-Davis (eds.), *Power and the State,* Croom Helm, London

Harrison, B. (1978) *Separate Spheres,* Croom Helm, London

Hauriou, M. (1927) *Précis de Droit Administratif et de Droit Public,* 11th ed., Sirey, Paris

Hertz, S.H. (1977) 'The Politics of the Welfare Mothers Movement: A Case Study', *Signs, 2,* 3 (Spring), 600-11

Holter, H. (1970) *Sex Roles and Social Structure,* Universitetsforlaget, Oslo

Home Office (1974) *Equality for Women,* Cmnd 5724, HMSO, London (September)

Jahan, R. (1976) 'Purdah and Participation: Women in the Politics of Bangladesh', paper originally presented to the Conference on Women and Development, Wellesley College, Mass.

Jancar, B.W. (1979) *Women under Communism,* Johns Hopkins University Press, Baltimore

Jaquette, J.S. (ed.) (1974) *Women in Politics,* Wiley, New York

Kanter, R.M. (1977) *Men and Women of the Corporation,* Basic Books, New York

Karabel, J. and Halsey, A.H. (eds.) (1977) *Power and Ideology in Education,* OUP, New York

Kirkpatrick, J. (1974) *Political Woman,* Basic Books, New York

Koonz, C. (1976) 'Conflicting Allegiances: Political Ideology and Women Legislators in Weimar Germany', *Signs, 1,* 3, part 1, 663-83

Lahav, P. (1977) 'Revising the Status of Women through Law: The Case of Israel', *Signs 3,* 1, (Autumn), 193-209

Land, H. (1976a) 'Women: Supporters or Supported?' in Barker and Allen, pp. 108-32

Lansing, M. (1974) 'The American Woman: Voter and Activist' in Jaquette

Layne, L. (1979) Jordanian Women Wage-Earners: Policy and Change', paper presented at the International Political Science Association Congress in Moscow

Leonard, D. (1980) *Sex and Generation: A Study of Courtship and Weddings,* Tavistock Publications, London

Lewenhak, S. (1977) *Women and Trade Unions,* Ernest Benn, London

Low Pay Bulletin, Monthly, Low Pay Unit, London

Low Pay Unit (1974) *Low Pay and Wages Councils,* a memorandum to the Secretary of State for Employment (June)

—— (1980) *Minimum Wages for Women* (September)

Lynn, N.B. (1979) 'American Women and the Political Process' in Jo Freeman (ed.), *Women: A Feminist Perspective,* 2nd edn, Mayfield, Palo Alto, Calif., pp. 404-29

McCracken, J.L. (1958) *Representative Government in Ireland: A study of Dáil Éireann. 1919-1948,* OUP, London

McNamara, J.A. and Wemple, S. (1974) 'The Power of Women through the Family in Mediaval Europe: 500-1100' in Mary S. Hartman and Lois Banner (eds.), *Clio's Consciousness Raised,* Harper & Row, New York, pp. 103-18

—— (1977) 'Sanctity and Power: the Dual Pursuit of Mediaeval Women' in Renate Bridenthal and Claudia Koonz (eds.), *Becoming Visible: Women in European History,* Houghton Mifflin, Boston Mass., pp. 90-118

Maitland, F.W. (1970) 'Memoranda de Parlemento 1305' in E.B. Fryde and E.E. Miller (eds.), *Historical Studies of the English Parliament,* CUP, Cambridge

Martindale, H. (1938) *Women Servants of the State, 1870-1938,* Allen & Unwin, London

Mezey, S. and Mezey, M. (1979) 'Feminist Attitudes and Government Policy', paper presented to the IPSA Round Table, Essex in August

Michel, A. (ed.) (1977) *Femmes, Sexisme et Sociétés,* PUF Paris

Mill, J. S. (1869) *The Subjection of Women*

Mossuz-Lavau, J. (1979) *Les Jeunes et la Gauche*, Presses de la Fondation Nationale des Sciences Politiques, Paris

—— and Sineau, M. (1980) *Les Femmes Françaises en 1978: Insertion Sociale Insertion Politique*, Rapport pour le Cordes, Paris

Nash, J. (1975) 'Certain Aspects of the Integration of Women in the Development Process: A Point of View', UN E/CONF. 66/BP/5 (9 June)

Navarro, M. (1977) 'The Case of Eva Perón', *Signs, 3*, 1 Special Issue on Women and National Development (Autumn), 229-40

O'Donovan, K. (1979) 'The Male Appendage — Legal Definitions of Women' in Sandra Burman (ed.) *Fit Work for Women*, Croom Helm in association with Oxford University Women's Studies Committee

O'Faolain, J. and Martines, L. (eds.) (1973) *Not in God's Image*, Fontana/Collins, London

Palmer, I. (1977) 'Rural Women and the Basic-Needs Approach to Development', *International Labour Review, 115*, 1 (January-February)

Race Relations Board (1967) *First Annual Report*, HMSO, London

Rendel, M. (1975)'Measures to Combat Discrimination against Women in Higher Education', *Women in Higher Education*, Staff Development Unit, London, pp. 68-80

—— (1977a) 'The Contribution of Labour Women to the Winning of the Franchise' in L. Middleton (ed.) *Women in the Labour Movement*, Croom Helm, London, pp. 57-83

—— (1977b) 'Women and Feminist Issues in Parliament', paper presented to the European Consortium for Political Research in Berlin

—— (1978) 'Women as Political Actors: Legal Status and Feminist Issues', paper presented to the ECPR in Grenoble

Report of the Inter-Departmental Committee on Physical Deterioration (1904), 3 vols., Cd 2175, Cd 2210, Cd 2186, HMSO, London

Rogers, B. (1980) *The Domestication of Women*, Kogan Page, London

Rose, H. and Hanmer, J. (1976a) 'Women's Liberation, Reproduction and the Technological Fix' in Barker and Allen, pp. 199-223

Stacey, M. (1980) 'The Division of Labour Re-visited or Overcoming the Two Adams', paper presented to the British Sociological Association Conference

Stenton, D. (1957) *The English Woman in History*, Allen & Unwin, London

Stopes, C. C. (1894) *British Freewomen: their Historical Privilege of Exercising the Franchise*, Swan Sonneschein & Co., London

Trades Union Congress TUC, London, *Homeworking* (n.d., *c.* 1978)

UNESCO (1980) *Research and Teaching Related to Women* 'Evaluation and Prospects', Final Report and Recommendations of Committee of Experts, SS-80/CONF. 626/9, Paris (20 May)

Verba, S. and Nie, N. (1972) *Participation in America*, Harper & Row, New York

Whitehead, A. (1976b) 'Sexual Antagonism in Herefordshire' in Barker and Allen

Whyte, W. (1963) *The Organisation Man*, Penguin, Harmondsworth

Wilson, E. (1977) *Women and the Welfare State*, Tavistock Publications, London

Wolchik, S. (1980) 'Ideology and Equality: the Status of Women in Eastern and Western Europe', *Comparative Political Studies* (Winter)

Wolpe, Ann-Marie (1977) *Some Processes in Sexist Education*, Women's Research and Resource Collective Publications, London

Yuval-Davis, N. (1980) 'The Bearers of the Collective: Women and Religious Legislation in Israel', *Feminist Review, 4*, 15-27

2 WOMEN AND CITIZENSHIP: MOBILISATION, PARTICIPATION, REPRESENTATION

Judith Stiehm

Introduction

Reading about national development and visiting nations undergoing development has provided me with the contrast necessary to see my own nation and its institutions in a new way. The abstract issues discussed here are rooted in the US experience. The application of my arguments to other countries will be left to the reader. The arguments are not conventional. Indeed, the reader's first response may be to dismiss them because they contravene a taboo as fundamental as that against incest. That taboo prohibits the use of women in military combat.

Fundamentally, the argument is that the state's defining function is that of managing society's legitimate force. Yet women are everywhere forbidden to use that force. The result is that they are everywhere less than citizens no matter what the law says and no matter what their self-perception. Further, as *de facto* pacificists, women provide (i) justification to and (ii) victims for society's 'executioners' (Camus, 1960). Thus women play a crucial but only peripheral role in the political process. Nevertheless, women cannot escape responsibility through civic passivity.

All governments are rooted in public opinion, in citizen consent, whether that consent is explicit or tacit.[1] My point is that women have a responsibility for government even if they only condone it. If they support a government they should participate in it; if they do not, they should resist it. Participation necessarily includes acting as representatives and accepting liability for military and/or police duties. Resistance can involve traditional or non-traditional, violent or non-violent means.

The State and Political Man

Max Weber's definition of the state as the institution holding a mono-poly on the legitimate use of force within a specified geographical area is widely accepted — at least as a basis for discussion. The nature of 'political man' is an equally familiar subject to political thinkers. Sometimes scholars assume that 'political woman' is subsumed in that discussion; sometimes they assume she is not; sometimes such assumptions are explicit; sometimes they are only implicit.

In many countries women are legally defined as citizens; they pay taxes and they are permitted to vote; they are mobilised on behalf of their own or others' interests; they participate in political campaigns; they support and advise their political representatives (Columbia Human Rights Law Review, 1977). However, they only rarely *are* representatives. This has led to a certain amount of debate about the claims for pictorial and symbolic representation, especially as opposed to a formal or actual representation (Pitkin, 1967). In the first the whole is miniaturised; in the second the whole is summarised; in the third rules are followed and one could easily be 'represented' by some-one one detests; in the fourth one's actual wishes or, perhaps, needs are represented. The composition of continuing governments is often defended on formal grounds; challenges made on symbolic or actual grounds are often hard to prove and so government critics who are pictorially excluded sometimes emphasise that critique while assuming that actual (and perhaps symbolic) representation will be enhanced if persons who look like them serve as their representatives. While the pictorial argument has achieved some credibility as it relates to racial and ethnic groups, it has rarely worked for women; perhaps this is because so much representation is geographically based and women are not geographically concentrated.

Some effort has also been made to explain women's absence from elected and appointed offices. Some, of course, give 'nature' as an explanation; others point to careers interrupted by child-bearing, to women's lack of legal training and/or to male prejudice. If we go back to Weber, however, another possibility emerges. That is that the basic and monopoly function of the state is to exercise force for, with and on its citizens. If women will not, cannot, or if it is thought that they will not or cannot exercise that force, they become poor candidates for any office with coercive responsibility. Generally the US public seems to find women most acceptable as officials when they serve as judges; they are also acceptable in legislative bodies where they may help to provide a budget for and make rules about the coercive forces (the police and the military); they seem to be least acceptable as executives, and officials who must implement policy by personally giving direction (Harris, Lon, and Associates, 1972).

Everywhere the executive and the military are closely tied. The

United States President is Commander-in-Chief of the Armed Services, yet he is still thought of by most Americans as a civilian, and civilian control of the military is fundamental to our political ideology. Even so, our first president, George Washington, was a revolutionary general; other ex-generals have easily moved to the White House (Grant, Eisenhower); and President Carter graduated from the US Naval Academy. Links between the government, the military and the defence industry have been demonstrated time and time again, and men like General Alexander Haig have moved from the Army to the White House, to NATO as though each were but a part of a single institution. The tie between the military and the government exists at a homely level, too. By law, veterans are given employment preference in federal employment in most state governments, and even in municipal governments. Preference may involve initial hiring and/or promotion, may be limited to a certain time period, or may be used only to break a tie. However, in one of the most extreme cases of preference, the state of Massachusetts provides for absolute preference for all veterans who can pass the civil service examination, and the constitutionality of this law was upheld by the US Supreme Court in June 1979.[2] In this case a woman had argued that because so few women were accepted into the military the effect of the law was to discriminate against women; she lost.

The general practice for federal jobs is to give veterans five bonus points. Illustrative results of this practice are: (i) on a correctional officer examination given in Atlanta, Georgia, a woman scored first; after veterans' preference points were awarded she was ranked 81st; (ii) a non-veteran woman scored 100th on the air traffic control examination in Dallas; after preference points were awarded she was 147th (US General Accounting Office, 1977). The point is, no matter how meritorious, non-veterans cannot expect to compete with veterans for desirable government positions. The military itself affords employment to those who adopt it as a profession and education to many who serve only for a limited time. Yet this is often forgotten in assessing a nation's employment and training opportunities and the inaccessibility of both to women is often forgotten as well. Moreover, provision for a society's other needs are drained by the allocation of resources to a male-dominated military in both developed and developing countries.

Since 1960 military expenditures in the developed nations have fallen relative to (i) Gross National Product (GNP) and (ii) GNP *per capita*. They have increased dramatically (although unevenly) in developing nations (Sivard, 1978: 10). The point is: the more preponderant the military, the more important it is to participate in it if one is to be a full citizen.

Finally, no military confines its activity to international disputes. The military can act to control civilians if the government so requests. Further, apparently civilian governments are often a military legacy, i.e., former military leaders who now rule as civilians, and often the military simply becomes the (all-male) government.

The Military and Women

Most women have little interest in or concern about the military. Perhaps this involves a taboo against the use of violence by those charged with infant nurture. Perhaps it involves a deep-rooted desire on the part of women to believe that defence is men's business and that men *can* provide security (Edelman, 1964). It should also be noted that men do not want women involved in military affairs. Perhaps this is because the burden is so heavy that it is made acceptable only when it is linked to manhood — to the belief that only men can fulfil the role.

On the other hand, women do participate in war and police action because they cannot escape the organised violence of men's culture. They are always among the victims of war and of civil disorder as well. Even if they would prefer to remain aloof they cannot. American women especially cherish the illusion that conflict is a controlled, geographic event — one to which men may go while women stay away. This is because American forces have not fought a sustained engagement in the US for more than a century. What citizens of other nations know is (i) that noncombatants die in great numbers, and (ii) that even women fight when the war is in their own country. Women fight as guerrillas, in the reserves *in extremis*. They also use violence as individuals and illegally. (Indeed, the last two attempts at assassinating the President were made by women.) The only thing women are barred from doing, then, is participating in official, collective, paid, trained, planned, technical and honoured violence. They are not permitted full participation in winning offensive military action, or in the peacetime military where institutional rewards are safest and real. They are most certainly excluded at the highest ranks where the roles of military and political leaders merge and where decisions are most likely to be kept secret on the grounds that the enemy must not know, although in fact the enemy does know, and it is only the citizenry of both (all) countries which does not.

There has been increasing interest in women's military role in the US in recent years (Stiehm, 1980; Binkin and Bach, 1977). While there is a link between this interest and the women's (or feminist) movement, of more importance are demography (a decreasing number of eighteen-year-olds) and the abolition of the draft (brought about by a curious alliance between liberals opposed to the draft and the Vietnam War, and then President Richard Nixon and conservatives who found it hard to fight a war with draftees opposed to it). Much of the analysis of American women's military role has been done by economists who examine the availability and utilisation of bodies and skills. They also assume the continuance of current policy (that women will not be assigned to combat), even though that policy severely restricts the number of women who can join the military and even though it restricts women's career opportunities. Thus, although women in the US military increased in number from 45,000 in 1972 to 110,000 in 1976 (1.9 per cent and 5.0 per cent of the total), and although 80 per cent of the (kinds of) jobs are open to them, and although 40 per cent of the women have entered 'non-traditional' fields, women remain marginal and their career possibilities restricted (Binkin and Bach, 1977). Little work has emerged so far concerning the psychological, social, political and moral implications of restricting, permitting or requiring women's military service. In this chapter some moral and political questions are raised, but a full analysis of psychological and sociological considerations must be put off to another time. To defer consideration is not to suggest that they are unimportant; it is to say that the connection between the military and government, between defence and politics, is close, and that exclusion from one may result in *de facto* exclusion from the other.

Again, women, like the poor of every country, are mobilised by governments, and are often invited to participate as ratifiers. However, their full participation, as representatives of the people, is not desired. The exclusion is deliberate. And now a caveat. When one is excluded, there is a tendency to insist (if one is able) upon inclusion. Yet if one insists that women must not be forbidden to participate in any aspects of government whatsoever, one must not fail to examine the forbidden. Perhaps it needs modification; pehaps it should be ended.

One must not simply say 'me too'. One must try to escape the conventional framing of an issue. For example, when some Israeli officials argued that a curfew for women was desirable in order to protect them, instead of arguing that the same rules must apply to women and men, Golda Meir is said to have mused that a curfew might in fact be a good idea, but that it should be for men — who were the predators — not for women, the victims. Instead of simply saying that women should do what men do too, the variety of possibilities must be examined. Perhaps the problem is not one of women's lack of interest, but of men's proneness to aggression and violence especially between the ages of 18 and 26. If a tendency to violence exists and is heightened in all-male institutions like the military, if men's 'dangerous tendencies' during their 'dangerous period' are increased and not just channelled in the military, would women's presence make a difference? One guesses that the presence of only a few women would not temper men's behaviour but highlight it. But what would be the effect of equal numbers? Or of an all-woman military? Or of a policy of permitting men to appear in public only when accompanied by a woman or a child under the age of six? Again, one must assess forbidden institutions thoroughly. It is too easy to say 'we too'!

Women and Combat

Even those who believe women should serve in the coercive services often believe that they should not serve in combat. This view is widely spread and strongly held. This means that it must be taken seriously (see also Stiehm, 1980).

The principal theme of those opposing women in combat seems to be that women should not be subjected to the suffering of war. Americans are peculiarly susceptible to this argument because our experience has been that men can, and do, pack their bags and travel long distances in order to 'go to war'. In the recent past an exemption for American women was possible. Thus officials are serious when they argue against the use of women because women should not suffer, and when they say women especially should not suffer the ordeal of being a prisoner of war (POW). Some go on to say that it is not that they especially wish to avoid the ravishing of women, but that they are worried that such ravishment would affect the judgement of male decision-makers. Indeed, they argue that the worry caused by the possibility of women becoming POWs is in itself sufficient cause for keeping women out of combat. But is women's suffering so special and does it affect men so much? Isn't it likely that women would find female distress more distressing than men if only for empathetic reason? Isn't it possible that men's aversion to women's suffering is based on men's feeling that the very existence of a suffering woman somehow implies that men have failed to protect her? Isn't the pain men feel the pain of failure?

In war men on both sides hurt women on the other side regularly and terribly. It is clear from this that a desire to avoid hurting women does not control military behaviour. At best men do not want 'their' women hurt (Treadwell, 1954).[3] In fact men do not object to having women in combat so much as they object to having women on *their* side. This is important. It means that even if some women are physically able and are so moved by logic or by their sense of justice as to insist upon sharing war's risk, their offer will probably be refused. Most men do not want women's assistance in the waging of war.

Chivalry is not the only reason men are reluctant to have women fighting by their side. In a tight situation they do not want to depend on individuals whom they perceive as small and weak.[4] Probably everyone in combat would be comforted if their compatriots were larger and stronger than they, and men's chances of having a (physically) bigger 'buddy' do increase if women are eliminated as combatants. Nevertheless, physical size is not required for combat effectiveness as the US was reminded of in Vietnam.

More important to victory than physical size is organisation, co-operation, commitment and pooled effort (Arendt, 1970). Since relatively small but well-motivated men have fought effectively, one might think that women, too, could be effective combatants. However, many argue and argue strongly that mixed-sex units by definition cannot achieve cohesiveness (Bogart, 1969).[5] The presence of women is said either to produce sexual rivalry and jealousy between male group members; or it is said that while men can maintain their unity, in order to do so, they will have to exclude or isolate the women (Wolman and Frank, 1975; Kanter, 1977). The thrust of these arguments is that women should not be in combat because if they are there men perform poorly. The problem, then, might be said to lie more with men and their psychology than with women and their physiology. The problem may also be that male leadership lacks the skills necessary to fuse a heterogeneous group of individuals into an effective, purposeful unit.

There is, I suspect, another motive underpinning arguments against the use of women in combat. Think for one moment of a male versus female tennis match.[6] Usually the male wins. Often women are thought to hold back — to fail deliberately to win (even if only unconsciously). A less investigated but surely operative tension is the male's strong need not to be beaten by a women. Now if one competitor's goal is to demonstrate competence or equality, while the other's need is to demonstrate superiority, they are not engaged in the same competition. For one it is a zero-sum game; for the other it is a non-zero-sum or even potentially a co-operative game. What might this mean in a combat situation? If men feel great pressure to beat women opponents, it might mean that an all-male force facing an all-female or mixed-sex unit would outdo itself. To the motives felt equally by both sides would be added the negative motive of not wanting to be beaten by women. This could lead men to accept excessive costs. It is easy to see that soldiers would wish to avoid giving such an incentive to their enemies — that they would not want to encourage a foe to any 'unnatural' effort. After all, soldiers much prefer an enemy which has the option of surrendering to one which prefers death.

Margaret Mead once suggested that the reason women do not take part in offensive warfare is that they are *too* vicious and *too* violent (Mead, 1967; Truby, 1977). Women do wield weapons in the immediate defence of the home (land), however. They engage in the last-ditch, no-holds-barred warfare appropriate only to the most dire situation, and inappropriate to the ritualised kind of warfare which must be practised if the human race is to survive. In contrast, men, Mead noted, are schooled, disciplined and trained to rules of warfare which check unrestrained violence. Men are not so foolish as to fight to the finish; they fight for more limited objectives such as the establishment of hierarchy and the creation of order. They, therefore, can be trusted to use violence because they will also stop using it at the appropriate time.

Others have also observed that women participate in defensive warfare. One reason, of course, is that when the war is at home the choice literally becomes one of being a victim or of fighting back. Thus the use of women may signal desperation. It has also been argued, however, that the use of women signals fierce commitment, and, moreover, that it signals an uncompromising certainty of the justness of one's position (Quester, 1977). Apparently women legitimate an enterprise; by their presence, by their participation, they sanctify a cause.

If this is the case, one can understand why political leaders attempt to mobilise women in times of domestic as well as foreign crisis. Women are more than a reserve to be tapped at a critical point in a struggle if, by their presence, they demonstrate that consent (or the 'mandate of heaven') has been withdrawn or withheld from one contender, and that the other deserves moral endorsement. In domestic affairs the presence of women in the streets may be an indicator of coming victory. Women do not seem to engage in equal numbers on both sides of a conflict.

When they fill the streets of Accra, Santiago or Tehran, they signal the ultimate winner. When women participate in demonstrations or other forms of endorsement, observers are sometimes led to believe that something new has happened, and that women will not only continue but will increase their participation. This is not necessarily so. Even when new opportunities are offered (or even required as in Algeria where women were made liable for the draft) previous norms are likely to be reinstated once the crisis is past. It seems the norms were not changed, they were only suspended (Stiehm, 1976 and Dodd, 1973).

In exploring the issue of women and combat it seems clear that men's psychology underpins many of the arguments which are framed as though the issue were one of women's physiology. Morever, even the discussion of women's possible loss of 'femininity' may, in fact, be about men's concern for their 'masculinity'. Experts state that an individual's gender identification is established early and is stable (Money and Erhardt, 1972). Why then do some authorities fear that women will 'lose their femininity' by participating with men in what have been male-only activities? Why are these authorities mostly men? Is it possible that women do not worry because they are secure about their identity — because they do not feel they will lose something by adding a new activity to their repertoire? Is it possible that men's identity is less stable — that it depends on oppositrness — that they become confused when what is supposed to be oppositeness — that they become

Apparently men *do* feel that they lose their masculinity when women do what they do. They are not flattered by imitation; they do not feel more but less manly; in fact, they sometimes describe themselves as 'castrated' or the woman who imitates them as 'castrating'. There are no analogous terms used when men imitate women. Scorn may be felt for the house-husband, but he is not accused of being a mutilator. Perhaps this is because men cannot do what only women can do — give birth, but women can do men's reserved role — give protection.

A curious difference between 'masculine' and 'feminine' behaviour should be noted. Women seem to be at their most passive, dependent, ornamental, in short 'feminine', in the presence of men. For the most part women make decisions, work and study in men's absence.[7] Thus in the (highly unusual) mixed-sex work situation, when women behave competently (as they do when supervising house decorations and alterations or when organising a teenage camping expedition, for instance), women understand themselves to be acting 'naturally', because they often act in this way (although not usually in a sex-integrated situation). They experience no sense of 'loss'. However, men, who usually see women only socially (e.g. when they are being their *most* 'feminine'), do not understand that women can be quite comfortable in effective roles, even when their being effective makes men feel uncomfortable.

With men the situation is reversed. While they are gentlemanly in the presence of women, men are more likely to feel themselves 'really' men in all-male groups. There they demonstrate their relative strength, take risks, brag and sometimes behave as if out of control. Since horseplay, vulgar language and over indulgence diminish in the presence of women, sex integration is felt by men as inhibiting and demasculinising. Thus, because men feel they 'lose their masculinity' in mixed-sex groups, it may be natural (although erroneous) for them to attribute a similar feeling to women. Women may also feel inhibitions in a mixed-sex group, but for them the direction of change is toward *enhanced* 'femininity'. The key may be that both men and women feel compelled to be their supposedly 'essential' selves before the more-valued male audience.

How might these phenomena affect the capacity of men and women to serve in combat? Let us assume women's instrumentality is increased when women behave as they would behave in an all-female group. Then, if resources, supplies, respect, challenge and all other items are equal, women would conceivably do better in an all-female unit. For them the advantage of the mixed-sex unit would be that 'all other items' would be more likely to be equal. For men the effect might be different. First, men might be more realistic and instrumental in a mixed group where braggadocio was tempered by responsibility. However, in combat, the irrational, sacrificial, non-face-losing emotional drive to show oneself 'a man among men' can produce acts of outrageous valour which would be lost in a mixed group.[8] The antics of a hero often look foolish, even childish, to the practical-minded, and it might be that men would be less excessively masculine and 'heroic' in the presence of women — that they would reduce their flamboyant and risky behaviour and thus the noble acts which cost the individual too much, but which drive combat forward. In sum, it seems that an integrated situation might enhance female performance for practical reasons and decrease male performance for psychological reasons.

Let us push the psychological argument one step further and begin by supposing that men need to feel masculine and women feminine. If a woman's femininity, her uniqueness, lies in her capacity to bear children, she needs to demonstrate that capacity only once and that demonstration is absolutely definitive. It is good for all time and for all audiences. For men the proof of manhood is more difficult and unsure. Sadly the only observable, unique role men have in society is that of warrior — a role that is risky, unpleasant and often short in duration. During peacetime men lack any certain way of proving that they are men. There is no initiation feat such as a lion to kill and a pelt to wear which might prove them to be men. Instead, like Hobbes's natural man, they must continually prove both that they are adult and that they are not women. Women's uniqueness is clear and sure, then; men's is problematical. In fact, masculinity could be described as ephemeral, fragile and dependent on women not being the same as men. It may be, after all, that it is women who are biologically defined (as life-givers) and it is men who are the second sex (and who monopolise the role of life-takers). Thus, it is men who must 'find themselves' and who depend on women's 'otherness' to prove that they are men. If women were to enter combat, then, men would lose their special identity, the one which is uniquely theirs, and as male-defining as child-bearing is female-defining. It is even possible that if the role of warrior no longer defined a 'man' its undesirability would become so apparent that no one would be willing to accept it. Amelia Earhart suggested as much when she said, 'The trenches, combat service in the air, transport jobs in advanced positions, and even the other, less brilliant arenas of activity in the theatre of war, are the last remaining strongholds of men. I suspect that men might rather vacate the arena altogether than share it with women' (Hamill, 1976).

Protection and Defence

In her *Living* Charlotte Perkins Gilman wrote: 'A stalwart man once sharply contested my claim to this (my) freedom to go alone. "Any true man," he said with fervour, "is always ready to go with a woman at night. He is her natural protector.""Against what?" I inquired. As a matter of fact, the thing a woman is most afraid to meet on a dark street is her natural protector' (Gilman, 1975). More recently Susan Brownmiller has argued that the crime of rape is 'a conscious process of intimidation by which all men keep women in a state of fear' (Brownmiller, 1976).

   These analyses suggest that the roles of protector and predator are closely linked: that a woman (or group of women) is (are) protected by a man (or group of men) who is (are) in turn perceived as a threat to other women who are in turn protected by other men who are considered a threat to the first woman (women) (Dodd, 1973).[9] As women are not trained or permitted weapons to defend themselves each requires a protector and these protectors can easily begin to practise a protection 'racket', that is to extort payment for the protection they offer. Similarly, it could be argued that a professional military offers protection to one set of civilians from a second military which is in turn offering protection to a second set of civilians from the first military. Both sets of civilians (like women) pay a substantial price to their protectors, and, ironically, both may be as likely to suffer violence from their protectors as they are to suffer it from their enemy's military!

Within a society, then, is it possible that the relationship between the military and civilians is analogous to that between men and women? If there is conflict within such a relationship what outcome should be expected? To be politically equal should each element seek to protect and dominate, or is it enough simply to be able to defend oneself? Further, can one defend oneself if one has no capacity either to threaten or use force? Pacifists would answer, 'yes', to the last question, but pacifism is rooted in a renunciation of force not in a lack of access to or lack of capacity for it. Also, pacifists seek to wield the power of truth or unity, they do not seek to avoid power. They stand forth, they do not ask others to give them protection. They stand for justice and risk confrontation. They do not expect peace without danger and even suffering (Stiehm, 1972).

The real point is this. Women have been associated with peace movements since the days of Aristophanes's *Lysistrata*. A very few have made the pacifist commitment made by an equally small number of men. Most women, however, have been happy to speak for peace while relying on men for protection. Similarly, while they have mobilised for political campaigns and celebrations, and participated in balloting rituals, they have been satisfied (i) to let men serve as their representatives and (ii) to let men continue their monopoly on the exercise of society's force. By acquiescing in the latter women have made themselves less credible and less eligible for that full citizenship which involves serving as a representative. The right to vote has been closely associated with military service. During the American Civil War male slaves joined northern military forces and used that contribution as an important part of their pressure to gain both their freedom and the vote. Women's claims to legal rights have also been most successful after war service. In both America and the United Kingdom the vote followed World War I; in France World War II marked an important shift in the direction of equality for women. In countries like Algeria rights were bestowed in a postwar era of gratitude even though the culture was not, in fact, ready for the change (Stiehm, 1976). Even today many aliens find that the easiest way to obtain US citizenship is to join the US military.

Many social relationships are asymmetrical — husband-wife, parent-child, employer-employee, teacher-student — but in theory citizens in a democracy are equal *vis-à-vis* their government, even though government officials may in theory be 'the best' equal citizens. Still, there is one question which always needs asking much as we would prefer to forget it: 'Who guards the Guardians?' Some have suggested God or natural morality, but most modern political thinkers have (with one explanation or another) opted for 'the community' whose members are said to enjoy some semblance of equal rights and equal power.

Not since the Middle Ages has it been suggested that adult men needed to seek the personal protection of another citizen. Yet even today little thought is given to the assumption that women rightly rely on the protection of a man or a group of men rather than participate in their own defence. Nor do we ask what the cost to society is to have some who protect and some who are protected. It may be that the role of protector is excessively burdensome and even violence-creating. The protector (and one cannot help but think of Oliver Cromwell) may feel justified in doing acts on behalf of others that he would never undertake in his own interest (Niebuhr, 1932).

No one doubts that political participation is closely related to economic class — but even if all men were related to the means of production in precisely the same way, if some identifiable group of men were forbidden to participate in any police or military organisation and for reasons said to be obscure were rarely chosen to participate as a governmental representative, would their lack of full citizenship seem evident? Does not women's lack of full citizenship now seem evident? As objects of protection forbidden to participate in the use of force and rarely selected as government representatives they are diminished regardless of the role they play in production and reproduction.

Rousseau's assertion that men might have to be 'forced to be free' may apply to women as well. One should not expect women to hurry to join a military which may have opened the door a little way. After all, many men do not really want to serve in the military either. Indeed, many are strongly coerced to serve and/or progressively entrapped into service. Men know the military role may be dangerous and that it is also unsatisfactory in that it often cannot protect those they are pledged to protect. Still, men do not usually resist military service. They submit to rigorous and degrading training and sometimes find themselves participating in slaughter, and 'the extensive, violent, bloody or wanton destruction of life; carnage' (Gault, 1971). To refuse their civic duty seems, to them, simply more intolerable than doing it.

Conclusion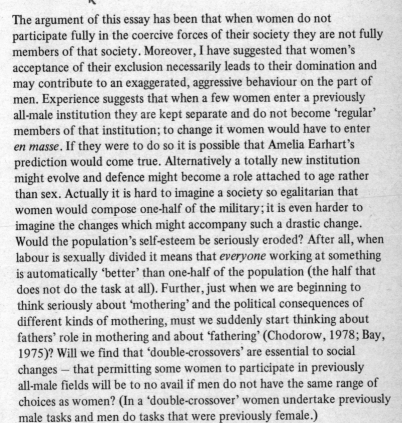

The argument of this essay has been that when women do not participate fully in the coercive forces of their society they are not fully members of that society. Moreover, I have suggested that women's acceptance of their exclusion necessarily leads to their domination and may contribute to an exaggerated, aggressive behaviour on the part of men. Experience suggests that when a few women enter a previously all-male institution they are kept separate and do not become 'regular' members of that institution; to change it women would have to enter *en masse*. If they were to do so it is possible that Amelia Earhart's prediction would come true. Alternatively a totally new institution might evolve and defence might become a role attached to age rather than sex. Actually it is hard to imagine a society so egalitarian that women would compose one-half of the military; it is even harder to imagine the changes which might accompany such a drastic change. Would the population's self-esteem be seriously eroded? After all, when labour is sexually divided it means that *everyone* working at something is automatically 'better' than one-half of the population (the half that does not do the task at all). Further, just when we are beginning to think seriously about 'mothering' and the political consequences of different kinds of mothering, must we suddenly start thinking about fathers' role in mothering and about 'fathering' (Chodorow, 1978; Bay, 1975)? Will we find that 'double-crossovers' are essential to social changes — that permitting some women to participate in previously all-male fields will be to no avail if men do not have the same range of choices as women? (In a 'double-crossover' women undertake previously male tasks and men do tasks that were previously female.)

  While the context and debate assume different forms in different countries, every society must deal with questions about (i) the relationship between women and men, (ii) the relationship between the state and the citizen, and (iii) the relationship between the armed and the unarmed. These issues are fundamental and universal.

Notes

1. John Locke's discussion of tacit consent in *The Second Treatise of Government* comes close to sounding like Henry David Thoreau in *Civil Disobedience*: if one does not actively resist, one supports.

2. *Helen B. Feeney* v *Personnel Administrator of Massachusetts* (1980) 100 S. Ct. 1075.

3. The lengths to which some men go to protect some women from other men are amusing. For example, during World War II some American WACs were zealously protected from their fellow soldiers by having their quarters floodlit and surrounded by barbed wire. The WACs must have felt like POWs (Treadwell, 1954, p. 744)!

4. The average height for males in the US is only 5ft 8ins and for females 5ft 3ins. The difference between average weight is 25 pounds. Thus, there is more difference between males than between males and females. See US Department of Health, Education and Welfare.

5. Similar arguments were once made concerning mixed-race units. Interestingly enough, in this case, some officers favoured integration more than their troops. The officers believed black soldiers were most effective when well dispersed (Bogart, 1969, p. 76f).

6. The King-Riggs Tennis Match of 1973 provoked a complex public response which has never been adequately examined.

7. The behaviour of wives of POWs is an example of this. While alone the women managed their families with competence. When their husbands returned, the women found it difficult to relinquish the authority they had been exercising (see McCubbin and Dahl, 1976).

8. Vietnam War fighter pilots cited the 'craziness' generated in male bar-room bragging as an important part of the willingness to undertake hazardous missions. Glenn Gray (1959) also discusses the communal experience as an appeal of battle.

9. Peter Dodd (1973, pp. 40-54) thoughtfully examines the code of family honour which makes each man's honour dependent (in part) on the reputation of his women kin, and all non-family men a threat to him because of their possible violation of his women.

Bibliography

Arendt, H. (1970) *On Violence*, Harcourt, Brace Jovanovich, Inc., New York

Bay, C. (1975) 'Gentleness and Politics: The Case for Motherhood Reconsidered', *Politics, x*, 2 (November)

Binkin, M. and Bach, S.J. (1977) *Women and the Military*, The Brookings Institute, Washington, DC

Bogart, L. (ed.) (1969) *Social Research and the Desegregation of the US Army*, Markham, Chicago

Brownmiller, S. (1976) *Against Our Will*, Bantam Books, New York

Camus, A. (1960) 'Neither Victims Nor Executioners', *Liberation* (February)

Chodorow, N. (1978) *The Reproduction of Mothering*, University of California Press, Berkeley, Calif.

Columbia Human Rights Law Review (1977) *Law and the Status of Women*, *8*, 1

Dodd, P. (1973) 'Family Honor and the Forces of Change in Arab Society',

International Journal of Middle East Studies, 4

Edelman, M. (1964) *Symbolic Politics*, University of Illinois Press, Urbana, Illinois

Gault, W.B. (1971) 'Some Remarks on Slaughter', *American Journal of Psychiatry, 128*, 4 (October)

Gilman, C. P. (1975) *The Living of Charlotte Perkins Gilman*, Harper Colophon Books, New York

Gray, J. G. (1959) *The Warriors*, Harper & Row, New York

Hamill, P. (1976) 'The Cult of Amelia Earhart', *MS* (September)

Harris, Lou and Associates, *The 1972 Virginia Slims American Opinion Poll* (Harris, Lou and Associates, 1972)

Kanter, R.M. (1977) 'Some Effects of Proportions on Group Life: Skewed Sex Ratios and Responses to Token Women', *American Journal of Sociology, 82* (March)

McCubbin, H.J. and Dahl, Barbara B. (1976) 'Prolonged Family Separation in the Military: A Longitudinal Study' in H.S. McCubbin *et al.* (eds.), *Families in The Military System*, Sage Publications, Beverly Hills

Mead, M. (1967) 'National Service as a Solution to National Problems' in Sol Tax (ed.), *The Draft*, The University of Chicago Press, Chicago

Money, J. and Erhardt, A. A. (1972) *Man and Woman, Boy and Girl*, Johns Hopkins University Press, Baltimore

Niebuhr, R. (1932) *Moral Man and Immoral Society*, Scribner, New York

Pitkin, H. (1967) *The Concept of Representation*, University of California Press, Berkeley, Calif.

Quester, G. (1977) 'Women in Combat', *International Security, 4* (Spring)

Sivard, Ruth Leger, *World Military and Social Expenditures*, 1978 (WMSE Publications, Leesburg, Virginia, 1978)

Stiehm, J. (1972) *Nonviolent Power*, D.C. Heath, Lexington, Mass.

—— (1976) 'Algerian Women: Honor, Survival, and Islamic Socialism' in Lynn Iglitzin and Ruth Ross (eds.), *Women in the World*, Clio Books, Santa Barbara

—— (1980) 'Women and the Combat Exemption/Exclusion', *Parameters*, Journal of the US Army War College (10 June)

—— (1981) *Bring Me Men and Women: Mandated Change at the US Air Force Academy*, University of California Press, Berkeley, Calif.

Treadwell, M. (1954) *The Women's Army Corps*, Department of the Army, Washington, DC

Truby, D. (1977) *Women at War: A Deadly Species*, Paladin Press, Boulder, Colorado

US Department of Health, Education and Welfare 'Weight by Height and Age of Adults', *Vital and Health Statistics*, series 11, no. 4

US General Accounting Office (1977) *Conflicting Congressional Policies: Veterans' Preference and Apportionment vs. Equal Employment Opportunity*, General Accounting Office, Washington DC

Wolman, C. and Frank, H. (1975) 'The Solo Woman in Professional Peer Groups', *American Journal of Orthopsychiatry, 45* (January)

3 WOMEN'S ROLE IN THE FORMULATION OF PUBLIC POLICIES IN BRAZIL

Fanny Tabak

Introduction

Since World War II there has been a certain amount of progress in women's participation in some sectors of political life in Brazil. Within the national economy the female proportion of the labour force in some dynamic branches of industry has even risen. Wider access to higher education and better opportunities for professional training have contributed to increasing the female presence in some important scientific and technological occupations. Although the 'traditional' careers still receive the majority of women entrants, some of the so-called modern occupations, recently introduced in the higher levels of the labour market, have been opened to women. A process of curriculum development in universities accompanying economic growth has also contributed to the increased number of women.

What has been the effect of this rise in the proportion of the qualified female labour force in major sectors of the national economy on the political participation of women in the decision-making process? Several studies of women's political participation based on an analysis of the electoral process have concerned the number of voters, the political affiliation, the proportion of women elected to legislative bodies, parliamentary activity and legal restraints to wider activity. Such studies have provided empirical evidence and have helped us to understand some important aspects of women's political participation, both in advanced and developing countries. More recently International Women's Year, sponsored by the United Nations (UN) in 1975, stimulated a number of projects and studies on themes related to women's participation. Consequently relevant literature has been enriched. Nevertheless, we believe that a deeper understanding of the social condition of women in each country requires further discussion of the empirical results already obtained.

The Methodological Approach

The methodological approach in this chapter needs to be made explicit.
It seems much more appropriate to study the qualitative rather than
the quantitative aspect, as has been the case in some studies on the
orientation of the female vote, party affiliation, election for Parliament
and so on. Elections are only one of the forms of political action. In
the specific case of Latin America, as Jaquette points out (1975), the
problem is not voting but female representation, since in Brazil, as in
many other countries, the illiterate (women and men) do not have the
right to vote. Furthermore, democratic governments are not the rule
and we shall have to work with variables other than voting. An analysis
of women's participation in politics should be based not so much on
electoral participation as on access to the decision-making process and
to the crucial sectors of the economy, on the formulation of the model
adopted for national development, on the real possibility of holding
key positions in government, that is, on participating in public policies
that affect the lives of millions of people. In the particular case of
developing countries where the rate of female participation is
sometimes considerably lower than in industrially developed countries,
it is even more important to study the process of social change and
women's contribution to overcoming underdevelopment.

This chapter examines the role of employment and education —
two important variables — in relation to the political participation of
women in Brazil. More explicitly, it will discuss the distribution of
women in the occupational structure, taking into account the main
changes that have occurred recently and some results of the introduction of new areas of learning and professional training. Economic
growth in Brazil has brought some significant changes in the employment structure related to greater diversification in the secondary sector
and the enlargement of the tertiary sector. To study women's role
in national development it is essential to analyse those changes. On the
other hand, the extension of the public (governmental) educational
system also constitutes a factor of major importance, since it allows the
proportion of highly qualified women in the national economy to
increase.

This chapter will examine the degree of participation of Brazilian
women in high-level decision-making in the public agencies responsible
for the formulation of three subjects of crucial public policy — housing,
urban planning and prices. The National Housing Bank (*Banco Nacional
de Habitação* (BNH)),[1] created in 1964 and largely modified in 1967,

became one of the most powerful institutions, owing to the huge volume of financial resources it controlled as well as its social significance, since thousands of people otherwise deprived of houses are affected by its work. On the other hand, as a result of the accelerated process of urbanisation, there are some big metropolitan areas which lack the facilities to offer employment, houses, education and public services, even at an extremely elementary level, to thousands of people who year after year move into the towns. Finally, uncontrolled inflation has brought an incessant rise in the price of all basic goods and a continuous deterioration in the quality of life for millions of people all over the country.

How far can Brazilian women be considered responsible for the formulation of such public policies? What form did their participation in each of those specific areas take? Did they have a real opportunity to decide at executive level? And how significant was their presence in Parliament? Some general hypotheses can be put forward about women's participation in some crucial sectors of national development in an attempt to evaluate possible changes in their role in Brazilian society.

(i) The expansion of the universities and the development of new careers has led to an increase in the proportion of women in colleges and to the training of a significant number of high-level specialists. We might expect that this would contribute to Brazilian women playing a more important role in politics and assuring them greater participation in the formuation of basic public policies. This would be reflected in a larger proportion of women in positions higher in the hierarchy responsible for public functions, including the highest executive positions and at the head of government agencies.

(ii) Rapid industrialisation and the modernisation of the national economy would probably permit an increase in the percentage of females in some of the dynamic sectors of industry, in the most advanced urban centres and in the big metropolitan areas. The same would apply to some activities (services) that require greater skill.

(iii) The enormous impact of modern mass media, especially television, showing political events at the very moment they take place anywhere in the world, should increase the spread of political information and keep it up-to-date. This might persuade women to put more pressure on their governments for more participation.

(iv) International Women's Year promoted by the UN in 1975, drew the attention of governments to the need to review policies and legislation, and to end legal restraints on the participation of women in the national economy and politics. The World Congress in Mexico in 1975 received formal support from the Brazilian Government. In this context the Brazilian Government have been expected to end the legal restrictions which excluded women from the open competitions giving access to positions in the civil service and state enterprises. A few of these restrictions have been lifted but many remain and women are also denied posts by less formal means.

(v) Even after only four years it is clear that the United Nations campaign has assisted Brazilian women and the feminist movement which developed in Brazil at this time in the fight for equal rights and more political participation.

The Rates of Participation

Latin America has very low rates of female economic activity (12 per cent), although in 1975 the proportion of women in the labour force had risen to 19.6 per cent, according to the results of research conducted by Chang and Ducci (1976). Latin American women were working for between eight and 12 years of their possible working life (15 to 65 years of age), that is, for less than 25 per cent of this period; they were still concentrated in the more traditional sectors of the national economy, engaged in a very small variety of occupations.

Madeira and Singer (1973) point out that women's political participation is determined by the changes that have taken place during the last five decades in the employment structure as a result of industrialisation in Brazil, and it is therefore necessary to examine these changes in some detail. The number of women employed multiplied by 7.5 between 1920 and 1970. The rate of growth was equivalent to 45 per cent during the 1960s, while in industry female employment increased by 53 per cent between 1920 and 1940, and even more (83 per cent) during the 1940s. In the 1950s that rate of growth was reduced, since industrial employment as a whole increased very little, and there was a crisis in the textile industry where women were the majority of employees. In the 1960s the number of women in industrial employment increased by 27.1 per cent, whereas the number of men increased by 88 per cent. Those sectors which absorb more women (textile and clothing) developed to a much lesser extent than metallurgy or transport equipment, where men are mostly employed. The proportion of women engaged in the tertiary sector grew from 24.6 per cent in 1940 to 36.9 per cent in 1970.

Not only women but also men now constitute a smaller proportion in agriculture, although the rate of female employment in small and middle-sized properties has increased. At present, female participation in agriculture is growing not because of modernisation but because of the persistence and enlargement of subsistence agriculture, where female labour constitutes an extension of domestic activities and has very low productivity, and where there is exploitation of women and children.

Female migration to the cities coincided with structural changes in manufacturing which reduced women's entry into industry. The substitution of factory production for industrial crafts has contributed to a diminution in the number of female jobs. The structure of the secondary sector itself has changed, as the most important growth has taken place in the production of intermediary goods and capital goods which absorb a small proportion of female labour. Female employment in industry is changing in qualitative terms, too, since modern techniques require a larger proportion of administrative and bureaucratic services, mainly performed by women. In the tertiary sector, the increase in jobs in the public and private service sectors (*serviços de consumo coletivo*) has enabled women to increase their participation — mainly those who have a high level of education and training — in public health and public administration. Production services have also offered new opportunities for male employment, especially in commerce and finance, where the number of jobs has increased considerably. There is also a qualitative change from the small greengrocery to the supermarket, as women cease to be 'unpaid members of the family' statistically, and become wage-earners.

However the problem is that the number of new opportunities for female employment brought about by economic growth is much lower than the number of women who enlarge the urban population every year. The only available employment is domestic service, which means that these women are not participating in social production. Besides, underemployment, most frequently hidden, grows continuously in the big urban centres. In 1970 a significant proportion, 75 per cent, of all economically active women was included in the categories of subsistence agriculture and paid domestic service. In 1972 from a female labour force of 9,748,000, 27.7 per cent were women from 10 to 19 years of age, of whom only 6.5 per cent were unemployed (Tabak and Toscano, 1976). The *Statistical Yearbook* did not however include in that figure for the labour force the more than 16 million women who worked in 'domestic services', 17 per cent of whom belonged to the same age-group.

The change that has resulted from national economic growth may be seen as having contradictory consequences for the social and economic status of Brazilian women. The disappearance of the need for industrial skills in some branches of the secondary sector and production services has expelled many women from economic activity. On the other hand, new opportunities for integration have appeared owing to the expansion of collective consumption, factory units, and commercial and financial enterprises.

High-level Professionals

In Brazil, especially in science, women are still a minority and hold positions of minor importance, although female participation grew from 9 per cent in the 1940s to 45 per cent in 1973, an increase of 500 per cent in three decades. That expansion was not evenly distributed, since women are concentrated in 'female' careers culturally defined as adequate for them; for example Humanities, Sociology, Nursing, Nutrition and Psychology absorb 70 per cent of the female students. From 1956 to 1973 the proportion of women in Engineering and Medicine grew by only 3 per cent, according to statistics published by the Ministry of Education. Among all graduate students in Engineering, women represented only 0.6 per cent in 1950 and not more than 1 per cent in 1970. In the same year only 26 per cent of all those graduating in Brazil were women.

The professional options chosen by women even today express a reality: the extreme difficulty, owing to sex discrimination, of entering the labour market in some of the careers that hold high social prestige. Pastore (1973) points out that sex discrimination can be considered one of the main reasons why a great number of women turn to a university course that will enable them to become teachers in secondary schools. This explains the process of 'feminisation' of many such courses, which have expanded relatively more than others in different academic subjects. In 1973 the Ministry of Education published statistics on all levels of the national system: these showed that 76 per cent of the total number of teachers were women, while women constituted 49 per cent of the students. If we examine the extent of participation in each of the grades, however, we find that women are 85 per cent of the teaching personnel in primary schools and only 25 per cent in universities. In graduate schools the female proportion is sometimes even smaller among both staff and students; women represented 35 per cent of the students and only 16 per cent of the academics in those schools.

Table 3.1: Percentage of Female Students and Teaching Staff in Sciences, 1973, Undergraduate and Graduate Level

Undergraduate level (Female %)

Subjects	Students	Teaching staff
Biological sciences	43.0	23.0
Basic and technological sciences	26.0	13.0
Agrarian sciences	11.0	22.0

Graduate level (Female %)

	BA	PhD	BA	PhD
Biological sciences	36.0	29.0	19.0	20.0
Basic and technological sciences	21.0	25.0	11.0	4.0
Agrarian sciences	22.0	35.0	0.8	0.4

Source: Ministry of Education, Brasilia, 1973.

The significant proportion of women in undergraduate courses in Biological Sciences, as shown in Table 3.1, or even in Basic and Technological Sciences, should not be considered an indication of substantial female participation in genuine scientific activities. A large number of graduates in such subjects are not research scientists: they only teach the scientific disciplines, and this applies even more to women. On the other hand, the increasing 'feminisation' of such courses can be explained, as already noted, precisely because they are intended to train secondary teachers. Even so, in Physics and Chemistry where the emphasis on research or higher education is more evident, women constitute a much smaller proportion.

The proportion of women members of academic and scientific associations has increased only recently. The Brazilian Society for the Progress of Science, created in 1948 and with over 16,000 members currently on its books, in the first three years of existence had only 67 women specialists, mainly chemists, medical doctors, and secondary and university teachers (Tabak, 1971). Ten years later the number of professions with female representation had risen from 16 to 25. The *Inventory of Brazilian Women Scientists*, published by the National Research Council in 1968, indicated that from a total number of 160 women engaged in scientific work, 23 were physicists, 21 were chemists, 18 were biologists and 13 were botanists. The 1970 general census yielded the information that only 3 per cent of all geologists were women.

The Formulation of Public Policies

After the military coup in 1964 the main feature of the Brazilian political system was an extremely high degree of centralisation of the decision-making process in the hands of the Federal Government. Some public policies which affected the lives of millions of people were implemented during that period. Three examples will suffice.

The first such policy was the creation by the National Congress of a huge institutional structure — the National Housing Bank (*Banco Nacional de Habitação* (BNH))[2] — which handles the very large financial resources resulting from the compulsory deduction of 8 per cent from all workers' salaries. The money collected goes to the Guarantee Fund for Length of Service (*Fundo de Garantia por Tempo de Serviço* (FGTS)), a special fund for providing compensation for dismissal, created in 1967 to replace previous legislation according to which every worker was assured the right to retain his/her job after ten years' work.[3]

Simultaneously, some financial mechanisms were invented which would later have an enormous impact on millions of families. The main declared purpose of the National Housing Fund was to permit those families with lower incomes to buy a house to live in, but during its 15 years of existence the BNH has introduced quite a number of modifications to its original mode of operation. Since it really acts as a bank and requires a return on capital investment, those lower-income families for whom it is intended are in no position at all to pay for the house. The 'monetary correction', a mechanism which readjusts (actually increases) the amount paid by the house-buyers every three months, has made prices exorbitant for thousands of families and caused fear and anxiety to the thousands of women who cannot afford to pay every month. The result has been that the money taken from workers' salaries (billions of cruzeiros) is being used to build luxury houses and apartments, which only the rich can afford to buy. Although the problem of housing is crucially important for every housewife and mother, the government agencies responsible for the changes introduced in the system never permitted women's associations or any sort of popular organisation to participate in any decision which might change the situation in favour of those lower-income families.

The second example concerns urban planning. In Brazil, from the 1960s onwards, the idea of planning has been formally emphasised in government policies. Many different plans, some of them intended to be very comprehensive, were elaborated. Urban planning has been one of the declared main concerns not only of government but also of professional specialists. The evident deterioration in the quality of life in large metropolitan areas, i.e., the capital cities of the 9 more developed Federal States, has resulted from the accelerated process of urbanisation and the concentration of enormous populations. The metropolitan area of São Paulo, for example, currently has a population of over 10 million people. In these circumstances, planning has become an urgent need in order to deal with the disastrous consequences of such chaotic growth.

Nevertheless, the non-participative political model in force in the country for the last 15 years, with all the main decisions made exclusively by the authoritarian central government, has left very little room for local and regional peculiarities to be taken into consideration. Legal uniformity imposed upon the country as a whole has caused serious problems in a country of continental size like Brazil where there are deep regional differences and inequalities. Within a uniform political and institutional framework, decisions concerning the formulation of an urban policy capable of solving the complex problems springing from the lack of basic services and the deterioration in the quality of life of millions of people are always taken in an extremely authoritarian way; again women's associations and other popular organisations have never had a chance of participating in those decisions. There has never been a woman at the head of or at a high hierarchical level in any government agency specially created to handle these problems.

Finally, there is a third area that affects the lives of the millions of housewives who constitute the immense majority of women in Brazil — the prices policy. The Interministerial Prices Commission (*Comissão Interministerial de Preços* (CIP)), created in 1964, is an all-powerful body which fixes the prices of all essential goods and services.[4] However, over a period of many years there has been a continuous increase in the level of prices, particularly for food. Uncontrolled inflation unceasingly contributes to reducing the purchasing power of salaries and the standard of living of most Brazilian families.

The women's organisations have conducted a persistent campaign including demonstrations and petitions against the rise in the prices of goods, and in 1978 special emphasis was given to the issue. However this campaign has been ineffective. The Prices Commission has never had a female representative among its members, so women have never had a chance to take part in any of the decisions taken by that body nor to exercise any serious control over prices in any manner whatsoever. Public statements, made at the beginning of 1979 by the new government, that the first priority would be the fight against inflation were received by Brazilian women with great scepticism, since they doubt whether there is a real political will to end the causes of the problem.

As far as the formulation of public policies is concerned, women have held higher-level posiitons only in education and social welfare. No woman has managed to be nominated to a position higher than that of member of a state provincial cabinet; women in such posts usually have to implement decisions taken at a higher (Federal) level without having any personal responsibility for the policies themselves.

Women in Parliament

In 1946 legislative bodies were legally reconstituted in Brazil after the long authoritarian regime of Vargas from 1937 to 1945. Democratic processes were prohibited after the military coup of April 1964 but some were again permitted after the beginning of 1979. However there has been little political participation by women in elected assemblies, either before 1964 or since 1979, at any level whether local, state or national. Even if we consider the short periods in which electoral campaigns with a certain amount of democratic liberty have been allowed, or when the Congress was allowed to play a less insignificant role, only very few women were elected and their parliamentary performance has not actually helped very much to increase female representation or to increase women's participation in the decision-making process.

One example will suffice. The city of Rio de Janeiro, Federal capital until 1960, was still considered to be an important political centre (many people believe the most advanced) and is thought to show a higher level of political consciousness than elsewhere in the country. Presumably this would apply to women as well and would help to increase female political activity. In fact, the rates of female participation in local legislative bodies from 1947 (when the first election was held after the end of World War II) up to 1978 were very low: in the last period, 1975-8, it came to only 10 per cent as can be seen in

Table 3.2. The total number of women representatives involved was only 14, since some of them were elected several times, one of them continuously since 1947; she is now a member of the National Congress.

Table 3.2: Proportion of Women in the Legislative Assembly of the State of Rio de Janeiro, 1947-78

Legislature	Total no. of representatives	No. of women elected	%
1947-50	49	4	8.1
1951-4	51	2	3.9
1955-8	51	4	7.8
1959-60	53	3	5.6
1961-2	51	3	5.9
1963-6	57	4	7.0
1967-70	56	5	8.9
1971-4	44	4	9.0
1975-8	48	5	10.4
Total	460	34	7.4

Source: State Legislative Assembly Archives, Rio de Janeiro.

It is almost always the opposition parties who selected and supported women to stand for legislative assemblies. In 1947, of the four women representatives in Rio, two were members of the Communist Party, while the other two were also members of non-governmental parties. (The Communist Party in Brazil was founded in 1922 and had existed legally only from 1945 to 1947.) After the military *coup* of 1964, when the previous 10 or 12 parties were compulsorily replaced by one Government and one (ineffective) Opposition party, it was again the Opposition that sent the majority of women representatives to Parliament: 11 out of the 14 women. More important than the number of women elected is the unadventurous use these deputies have made of their mandate. Frequently they have lauded government initiatives, merely asked for information on current events, suggested names for new streets in cities or made proposals concerning immediate problems. The parliamentary activity of these women representatives in favour of equal rights for women and for more political participation has almost always been limited to rather timid requests for the building of a greater number of nurseries, the lowering of the age of retirement for women or to denouncing different sorts of discrimination. Projects oriented to the long-term improvement of national education or raising the standard of living are very seldom addressed in political terms.

It should be noted that in Brazil as in other countries and at all levels it is very seldom that a woman candidate has been elected as a result of her own political activity either among women or in defence of women's rights. The recent political history of the country has shown that many women acquired a seat in Parliament only as substitutes for their husbands who were deprived of their political rights by the military governments after 1964. In other words, as Tabak (1968) has shown, such women deputies were elected thanks to the political prestige of their spouses or relatives who were prohibited from offering their own candidature and not in the least as a result of any personal prestige.

Women elected by a significant proportion of women's votes are still an exception in Brazil in all the assemblies. It was only during the last elections (November 1978) that such support was given to women candidates; the four women elected to the Federal Congress received nearly 2.5 times as many votes as the previous highest number of votes cast for successful women candidates. For this reason that election was more important than others. It was only in 1979 that for the first time a woman got a seat in the Senate, as a replacement for a male senator who had died suddenly. This was 80 years after the Republic was proclaimed in 1889, and 45 years after the right to vote and to sit had become available in 1934. A great number of recently elected women representatives were journalists, lawyers and teachers, and altogether they have received a significant number of votes. Probably as a result of the relatively dynamic activites of some women's organisations since 1975 (International Women's Year), feminist themes were present in many electoral political platforms; almost all the women elected mentioned their intention to fight for equal rights and wider political participation for women.

In 1977 a special commission was appointed by the Federal Congress to conduct an enquiry into the social conditions of women in Brazil. Dozens of reports were presented to that commission by invited journalists, representatives of women's organisations and members of legislative bodies from all parts of the country. Evidence from all quarters concurred in pointing to the same problems that prevent a greater female participation and keep women in Brazil in a situation of inferiority. One of the main problems was the absence of nurseries, although a law had been passed many years ago requiring every enterprise (private or public) employing more than 30 women, aged 16 or more, to provide such a nursery. Indeed the laws intended to protect workers are very frequently evaded by employers. Furthermore, legal restraints are still in force, and sometimes it becomes very difficult — or even impossible — for women to gain access to executive positions in governmental agencies or big industrial and commercial enterprises.

Conclusion

The extent and importance of the political participation of Brazilian women has remained very limited from the 1950s up to the present, no matter how significant the changes in the structure of economic activity may have been or the increase in professional skills. It cannot be said that such participation presents a reasonable pattern compatible with the political importance of the country itself. The representation of women in government or in state-owned enterprises, even when quantitatively large, is relatively insignificant in absolute terms of influence, since it is restricted to certain functions and positions that have as a rule very little or no decision-making power.

In public administration, even at local level, the number of women who are at the head of executive bodies with major responsibility is very small. At provincial and especially Federal levels, women's role is even more insignificant. No woman has ever been a member of the Federal Cabinet or has ever been the president or director of any important state enterprise. In financial and fiscal affairs, in price-control agencies or in those which decide on all crucial public policies, no woman is in a position to take decisions. In the powerful state-owned enterprises like Petrobas (oil), a real economic giant, professionally skilled women were prohibited from entering for many years on the assertion that the work of a geologist was not suitable for them, although many women had graduated in geology. Only a few women have manged to reach some intermediate positions, owing to the fact that their husbands or other close relatives were influential members of the senior executive body. In other words, sex discrimination exists in the public sector of the national economy, although it would be reasonable to expect that in that sector at least a more liberal or democratic attitude would prevail. In spite of all this, the government has signed international conventions which forbid such discrimination and all the constitutions have formally included the principle of 'equal rights'.

The authoritarian regimes that have dominated the country for long periods reached their greatest power between 1964 and 1978 and most certainly did not stimulate a wider integration of women in national politics in Brazil. As in many other countries, Brazilian experience has proved that there is a direct and close association between a regime of democratic liberty and the growth of female participation. Women's organisations, if they are to fight for equal rights against any form of sex discrimination in favour of effective measures to protect the woman worker and her children, and for more political participation, need an environment of democratic liberty to develop their activities. This has existed in Brazil for only very short intervals, for instance from 1945 to 1963 when a Federation of Brazilian Women was organised with affiliated associations in all the more developed states of the Federation and contributed to a great extent to raising the level of political consciousness of many women. A women's newpaper, *Momento Feminino*, published in Rio de Janeiro for nearly ten years, greatly assisted this development.

Female representation in legislative bodies and in the Federal Congress in Brazil during the long historical period examined in this paper has to be assessed very carefully, since parliamentary activity itself was obstructed much of the time and sometimes even annihilated by a highly authoritarian regime. Parliament was deprived of its main functions or could contribute very little to raising women's political consciousness when there was no climate for political freedom.

As all empirical evidence seems to show, the simple facts that the country is industrialising and modernising its occupational structure, and that large metropolitan areas concentrate an ever-growing urban population, are no guarantees of wider female participation. The same statement is true for professional skills: it is not enough to increase the number of high-level technicians in scientific and technological activities of crucial importance to the national economy. Such factors alone are not capable of overcoming existing prejudices and sex discrimination, nor do they ensure that women will have the possibility of reaching positions where they can participate effectively in those levels of political power which really decide and formulate the crucial public policies, which in turn affect the lives of millions of people. On the other hand, it seems inevitable that the main fight will have to be part of a larger social fight, so that not only women but all the other existing minorities finally find their place in society.

Notes

1. The National Housing Bank (*Banco Nacional de Habitação* (BNH)),

funded by FGTS (see n. 3), was created in 1964 as an economic device to collect money from employees to build houses of 'social interest' for lower-income groups, and to enable them to buy houses on a mortgage. Because of inflation the monetary correction was introduced. This has the effect of increasing the amount payable in line with inflation every three months. Often house-owners have to transfer property because they cannot afford the repayments. Therefore flats for the middle-class and luxury flats are built instead.

2. See n. 1 above.

3. The Guarantee Fund for Length of Service (*Fundo de Garantia por Tempo de Serviço* (FGTS)) was created in 1967. The fund collects 8% of wages and salaries and has used some of these funds to finance BNH. Before 1967, employees had effective security in jobs after 10 years' service because very large compensation (double a month's salary for each year of service) discouraged dismissal. Then in 1967, the FGTS was set up. Employees could be dismissed and receive the 8% deposited for them. It became much cheaper to dismiss employees. They could lose their job. Once the money is spent they have nothing. Unemployment is high. Individuals tend to go from one job to another.

4. The Interministerial Prices Commission (*Comissão Interministerial de Preços* (CIP)) fixes prices. It is a body nominated by the Federal Government and composed of representatives of all ministries. It meets the President once a month, and is able simply to raise internal prices. It is illegal to sell above the fixed price, but it happens. In practice the fixed price is a minimum price. The minimum salary, fixed by the government, lags behind the rate of inflation.

Bibliography

Barroso, C.L. (1975) 'A Participação da Mulher no Desenvolvimento Científico Brasileiro', *Ciência e Cultura, 27*, 5

Blay, E.A. (1978) *Trabalho Domesticado: a Mulher na Indústria Paulista*, Ed Atica, São Paulo

Chang, L. and Ducci, M.A. (1976) *Formacion profesional para la Mujer*, Estudios y Monografias no.29, Cinterfor/OIT, Montevideo

Jaquette, J. (1975) 'La Mujer Latinoamerica y la Politica: Paradigmas Feministas, Investigaciones Comparativas por Culturas', *La Mujer en Latinoamerica, I*, Mexico

Madeira, F. and Singer, P. (1973) *Estrutura do Emprego Feminino no Brasil – 1920/1970*, Cadernos Cebrap no. 13, São Paulo

Meuchik, J. (1972) *La Mujer que trabaja*, Ed Grasmica, Buenos Aires

Pastore, J. (1973) *Profissionais Especializadas no Mercado de Trabalho*, IPE, São Paulo

Tabak, F. (1968) 'A Declaração Universal e os Direitos da Mulher', *Revista de Ciência Política*, no. 4

—— (1971) 'O Status da Mulher no Brasil – vitórias e Preçonceitos', *Cadernos da PUC*, no. 7

—— and Toscano, M. (1976) *Inventaire sur la Situation de la Femme au Brésil*, UNESCO, Paris

UNESCO (1970) 'La Femme à l'époque de la Science et de la technique', *Impact-Science et Société, XX*, 1

4 WOMEN'S EDUCATION AND PARTICIPATION IN THE LABOUR FORCE: THE CASE OF NIGERIA

Keziah Awosika

Introduction

In contemporary literature on women's role in the process of development, it is held that the level of development is a major determinant of the extent and nature of women's participation in economic activities outside traditional agriculture. This view is strongly supported by international comparison and researches which show that developing countries in general have a lower degree of female participation in the modern sector of the labour force than the developed industrialised countries (Collver and Langlois, 1962; Durand, 1975). On the other hand, several contemporary studies challenge this view on the basis that historical experience of present-day developed economies renders this notion inconclusive. For example, although some studies suggest that the USA displayed a higher rate of women's participation at a similar stage of development as some developing countries, this does not apply uniformly to all developing countries. The rate of participation is defined as the ratio of labour force to total population while the labour force itself comprises persons employed and unemployed, usually within the 14-55 age-group.

Studies carried out by Nadia Youssef (1974) suggest that some developing countries have rates of women's participation almost as high as some developed countries. For example Jamaica, with a female participation rate of 36 per cent, compares favourably with highly advanced countries such as Sweden and Denmark. Furthermore, there are some countries where high female participation rates are sustained independent of economic development. It is evident that factors other than the level of economic development tend to determine the extent to which women participate in modern activities. Other socio-economic factors such as the age-distribution of society, rural/urban migration patterns, marriage, fertility and child-rearing patterns, prevailing family organisation and societal attitude to female participation in the labour force, female self-perception and conception of work, the structure of industrialisation, educational patterns, the level of literacy and change over time all contribute to determine the level and rate of participation of women in modern activities.

In what follows, education has been singled out as a strong determinant of the rate of female participation in the modern sector of the labour force. This is because education appears to be the only attribute that attracts the potential employee to the employer, if one assumes that other things, such as sex, race and stage in life-cycle, are equal to the employer for a particular occupation. Education is also relevant to the propensity to work, given a desire to utilise professional skills achieved, and in providing a viable alternative to marriage and motherhood. The usual definition of labour-force participation and the problems of measuring it, especially in a developing economy, are examined and then adapted to the Nigerian situation. The basic question considered here is how education can be regarded as a major determinant of women's labour-force participation, given all other factors (some of which have been mentioned above) which help to determine Nigerian women's participation in the labour force. The chapter ends by examining the economic and social implications of trends in education and in the participation in the labour force by women in Nigeria.

Labour-force Concepts

For many countries the labour force is defined as that section of the population which is considered economically active. Thus it includes both the employed and the unemployed, and those who are temporarily not economically active. Since housewives are not considered economically active, they are usually left out in labour-force calculations, as are children, students, apprentices and the elderly. This definition obviously raises some conceptual problems for pre-industrial developing countries where the majority of economic activity is essentially home-based. By treating only 'gainful' employment or monetary activities as economic, this definition will exclude from the labour force women who are producing goods for self-consumption or working in family enterprises from which they derive no direct monetary compensation.

The formalisation of economic activity in industrial societies brings into sharp focus the problem of defining labour-force participation in a pre-industrial developing society. In industrialised countries, the distinction between economic and non-economic activity is arguably clear-cut. In developing countries, however, where unpaid family labour is commonplace, the distinction between household chores and economic activity is still somewhat artificial, depending to a large extent on the subjective judgement of whoever is collecting the data. This definition also tends to understate differences in participation rates between the rural and urban sectors of the economy. In such circumstances, comparing participation rates between developing and largely rural societies with industrial and highly urbanised societies is fraught with conceptual problems (Lucas, 1975; Standing and Sheeham, 1978).

In this study the problems are partly circumvented by concentrating analysis on the modern sector of the Nigerian economy. According to the Nigerian Labour Code Ordinance, the working age is from 15-55 years-old, but in most areas of economic activity, especially in the private sector, this age-range is not strictly applied. Information available on the Nigerian labour force is extremely limited. Apart from the controversial 1963 census (which is the officially accepted census in use) and the 1966/7 *Labour Force Sample Survey*, there are no other comprehensive surveys of the labour force in Nigeria. In recent years, there have been a few surveys carried out by individuals on specific aspects of women in the labour force in Nigeria, but these have been limited to specific areas of the country (Lucas, 1975; Arowolo, 1976; Fapohunda and Fapohunda, 1976). These, and the educational statistics published by the Federal Office of Statistics, form the basis of analysis in this chapter. As has been stated, education is a major determinant of the level and direction of supply for the female labour force. The pace and level of economic development, and the organisation of the economy are presumed to be important determinants of demand for the female labour force.

Nigerian Women in the Total Labour Force

For a clear picture of the position of women in the overall labour force it is necessary to distinguish not only between the rural and urban sectors, but also between the formal and informal sectors of the urban economy. The formal sector consists of the larger and more productive manufacturing and commercial enterprises, government ministries and state corporations, major services such as health, education, the public utilities, and wholesale trade. Characteristically, labour engaged in this sector is relatively highly educated, often unionised and are protected by social legislation. On the other hand, the informal sector consists of small family-based enterprises, retail trading, organised handicraft establishments and petty traders. Many of the labour force are own-account workers employing simple technology and little capital. In many cases the turnover is small and incomes vary in worth and regularity. A major characteristic of the informal sector is the ease of entry and exit; conditions of employment are not governed by any contractual agreements. Moreover, workers in this sector do not necessarily require skills acquired by formal education. It is basically a sector of the economy distinguished by low productivity and low income and an absence of wage-earners.

Evidence from studies carried out in Nigeria and other developing economies, notably in the Middle East and Latin America, tends to support the view that in the process of modernisation women's position in various traditional economic activities was gradually undermined largely because of inadequate preparation for entry into modern productive systems — mechanised agriculture, manufacturing, or administration. Apart from inadequate preparation it should be emphasised that women's role in traditional economic activities could easily be accommodated with their domestic roles as housewives and child-rearers. The modernisation process demands work outside the home environment and under the rigid controls of organised institutions. Men tend to be more mobile and able to migrate to urban centres in search of work. Even in cases where the women migrate to towns, they are hampered by their domestic role on entering the waged labour force, and they therefore remain in the informal sector as petty traders and street hawkers, or in family enterprises and services that would not take them away from home (Little, 1973; Mabogunje, 1975).

Figures in Tables 4.1, 4.2 and 4.3 give a picture of the economic activity, labour force participation and occupational distribution of women. These figures are derived from various sources and should be interpreted with caution; they should be treated as indicating trends in

Table 4.1: Distribution of Employed Persons by Class of Workers and Sex (%)

Class of workers	Male	Female	Both sexes
Employer or own-account worker	59.2	81.4	68.4
Employee	32.2	6.2	21.5
Unpaid household worker	3.5	10.8	6.5
Unpaid apprentice	5.1	1.6	3.6
Total	100.0	100.0	100.0

Source: Federal Republic of Nigeria, National Manpower Board, Federal Ministry of Economic Development and Reconstruction Labour, *Labour Force Sample Survey 1966/67*, vol. 1 (December 1972), p. 21, table 15.

female economic activity and participation rates. Economic activity appears to increase with age and to taper off after the age of 55 (Table 4.2). On the other hand, women's participation rates appear to increase consistently with age while those for men decrease after the age of 45.

Table 4.2: Distribution of the Labour Force by Sex, Age and Participation Rates (%), 15-55 years-old

| Age | Household members by working age | | | Labour-force participation rate | | |
	Male	Female	Both sexes	Male	Female	Both sexes
15-17	7.0	5.6	6.5	45.1	32.4	39.7
18-23	20.2	19.5	19.9	80.4	51.0	65.6
24-9	22.1	24.7	23.1	97.4	62.0	78.3
30-5	19.4	22.3	20.6	99.2	67.4	82.4
36-40	13.2	13.3	13.2	99.4	73.3	87.0
41-5	7.5	6.4	7.1	99.0	79.2	90.8
46-50	7.5	5.6	6.7	97.8	78.4	90.5
51-5	3.1	2.6	2.9	96.0	83.4	91.1
Total	100.0	100.0	100.0	87.2	60.6	74.2

Source: Federal Republic of Nigeria, *Labour Force Sample Survey*.

These rates differ according to regions in Nigeria, although this is not shown in the table. Fragmentary evidence and the 1952/3 census suggest that the female waged labour force is about 34 per cent in the north, 52 per cent in the west and 50 per cent in the east (Lucas, 1975). These differences are explained when the level of educational development and the cultural differences of these regions are taken into consideration.

The occupational distribution of female labour (Table 4.3) reflects the organisation of the economy. More than half of all women workers are classified as sales workers. The overwhelming majority of the remaining 40 per cent are concentrated in only two occupational groups. Of the 14.9 per cent women in the professional group, the majority of them are either teachers or nurses. A survey of professional manpower in selected occupations in 1966 indicates that 5.6 per cent of all doctors, 8.3 per cent of pharmacists and 1 per cent of accountants were women. Women represented only 2.9 per cent of all highly skilled professional groups. There is a very evident tendency for women in modern economic activities to be disproportionately crowded on to the lower rungs of the employment ladder. Educational qualifications are essential for entry, and the higher the level of education, the greater should be the opportunities for high-level employment.

Table 4.3: Distribution of Employed Persons by Major Occupational Group and Sex (%)

Occupation	Male	Female	Both sexes
Professional and related	6.6	2.7	5.0
Administrative and managerial workers	1.3	0.7	1.0
Clerical workers	8.3	1.1	5.3
Sales workers	13.7	59.7	32.8
Miners, quarrymen	0.2	0.0	0.1
Workers in transport and communications	6.6	0.2	4.0
Craftsmen, product process workers and labourers	23.6	16.1	20.5
Service workers	7.3	2.9	5.4
Farmers	32.0	16.6	25.7
Others	0.4	0.0	0.2
Total employed	100.0	100.0	100.0

Source: Federal Republic of Nigeria, *Labour Force Sample Survey*, p. 20, table 13.

Women, Labour Supply and Education

The extent to which educational opportunities are made available to women reflects the attitudes of society towards activities deemed appropriate to women outside the traditional roles in marriage and child-rearing. Figures in Tables 4.4 and 4.5 indicate the level of literacy in rural and urban Nigeria, and also the distribution of enrolments in educational institutions. The 1966/7 *Labour Force Sample Survey* indicates that 62.8 per cent of the urban population were literate. The rate of illiteracy is much higher among women, 50.4 per cent compared with 25.4 per cent male illiterates. Evidence in Table 4.4 suggests that the proportion of males is much greater than of females at all levels of formal education. Above the age of 30, 72.4 per cent of females compared to 36.9 per cent of males were illiterate. The differences in literacy rates are even higher in rural areas.

The data on school enrolment for all Nigeria is incomplete, but the trend suggests that females are concentrated at the primary level of formal education. Secondary school enrolments have been growing, but the rate has been slow considering the expansion of educational institutions in the 1960s. Before Independence in 1960, there were

Table 4.4: Distribution of Persons by Educational Level and by Sex (%)

Educational level	Urban Male	Urban Female	Urban Both sexes	Rural Male	Rural Female	Rural Both sexes
Illiterate	25.4	50.4	37.2	58.0	78.0	68.4
Literate	74.6	49.6	62.8	42.0	21.7	31.6
Roman or arabic script without formal education	19.5	15.5.	17.6	16.6	8.7	12.5
Below primary or standard six	27.7	22.8	25.4	18.0	10.6	14.4
Primary but below school certificate	22.6	10.4	16.8	6.4	2.3	4.3
School certificate below university degree	4.5	0.8	2.7	0.9	0.1	0.5
University degree and postgraduate qualifications	0.3	0.1	0.3	0.1	0.0	0.1

Source: Federal Republic of Nigeria, *Labour Force Sample Survey*.

about 34 secondary schools for boys, most of them established before 1940. On the other hand, there were 24 institutions for girls, mostly established in the late 1940s and 1950s. Enrolments in higher institutions, teacher training colleges, technical colleges and universities are likely to be grossly understated given the rapid expansion of university education in recent years. Again, there are regional differences in the educational levels of women in Nigeria. The northern region with its Muslim ethics did not embark on mass primary education as did the

Table 4.5: Students' Enrolment in Educational Institutions in Nigeria, 1950-69

	First level	Female %	Second level	Female %	Third level	Female %
1950	970,199	22	28,962	11	327	4
1955	1,702,762	30	62,210	17	931	5
1960	2,912,617	37	166,317	21	2,659	7
1965	2,911,742	38	250,917	28	9,378	12
1969	2,345,754	37	222,547	31	9,775	14

Source: UNESCO, *Statistical Yearbook* (UNESCO, New York, 1963 and 1971).

other regions in the mid-1950s. Koranic schools which exist side-by-side with Western-type education did not, as a rule, enrol girls, and mission schools for girls were few. Consequently, female education in the north has lagged far behind the rest of the Federation. Fragmentary evidence suggests that in 1966 only 1 per cent of the female population in the whole of northern Nigeria went to school. However by 1972, in Katsina alone, there were 1,512 girls and 3,556 boys attending school.

Generally, there is reason to believe that girls receive less encouragement than boys to enter higher education. On the whole, girls are taught to consider marriage and children as the primary goals in life. Parents with insufficient means tend to favour education for their sons rather than daughters, because boys are considered to be future breadwinners who must be given the opportunity for education.

Before we relate education to employment opportunities, two other related factors need to be considered: age in relation to educational level level and the content of education. Do the school curricula and the subjects to which special emphasis is given prepare women adequately for employment opportunities? A study of women's occupations in Lagos (Lucas, 1975) revealed that women in the 15-19 age-group prefer to extend their education in order to widen employment opportunities, especially in white-collar jobs. For them, the opportunity cost of withdrawal from the labour force is much higher and they are less likely to withdraw from employment on marriage. Moreover, the Lagos Survey (Table 4.6) also indicates that there is a higher proportion of women over the age of 30 who are uneducated or who have received only primary education. This partly explains why trading (market trading) is carried on mainly by women in the over-30 age-group. In a sample of 220 Accra (Ghana) market women, not one was aged under 30, a situation similar to that in Nigeria. Indeed, a sample survey of 6,000 market women carried out in Ibadan revealed the same preponderance of illiterate market women aged over 30.

In developed countries the age distribution of participation is observed to be 'two-peaked' (bi-modal), with an indentation in the 25-34 age-group and a gentle rise around the age of 40: this distribution coincides with the withdrawal of women from the labour force during the child-rearing period and their joining the labour force after the children have grown up. In Nigeria, as indeed for most of West Africa, the pattern has been different. The rates observed rise until the age of 55, and then taper off, but the peak period for entry into the labour force appears to be between the ages of 25-35. This may result from early marriages, so that by this age women are free of child-rearing and

Table 4.6: Age-specific Participation Rates by Education and Ethnic Groups Among Lagos Females, 1968-73

Education	Age-Group				
1968	15-19 % (no.)	20-4 % (no.)	25-9 % (no.)	30-4 % (no.)	35+ % (no.)
None	55.9 (34)	62.3 (61)	72.7 (88)	88.3 (94)	89.1 (138)
Primary	34.4 (69)	60.0 (55)	66.7 (27)	77.8 (8)	80.0 (45)
Secondary	20.0 (20)	70.0 (30)	78.9 (19)	91.7 (12)	80.0 (20)
1973					
None	49.3 (65)	48.6 (115)	61.8 (131)	71.4 (91)	81.1 (148)
Primary	44.8 (181)	51.0 (206)	58.0 (112)	60.5 (48)	77.8 (68)
Secondary	27.4 (139)	65.1 (129)	75.0 (92)	68.2 (44)	82.1 (28)
Education/Ethnic Group					
None: Yoruba	52.0 (57)	52.8 (87)	70.5 (95)	84.9 (66)	85.2 (121)
Non-Yoruba	—— 33.3 —— (36)		38.9 9(38.9)	36.0 (25)	63.0 (27)
Primary: Yoruba	50.5 (89)	65.7 (128)	65.7 (70)	75.0 (36)	78.2 (46)
Non-Yoruba	38.7 (93)	26.9 (78)	45.2 (42)	—— 50.0—— (34)	
Secondary: Yoruba	27.9 (86)	75.0 (77)	77.7 (63)	70.9 (31)	79.2 (24)
Non-Yoruba	26.4 (53)	52.0 (52)	69.0 (69)	—— 70.6—— (17)	

Source: Re-analysis of 1968 KAP data, 1973 Survey of Women's Occupations in Lagos: see David Lucas, 'The Participation of Women in the Nigerian Labour Force since the 1950's with particular reference to Lagos', PhD dissertation for LSE, 1975.

are ready for the employment market.

How far does the content of education prepare women for professional employment? Such a premium is placed on professional certificates in Nigerian society that both young men and women strive to attain professional qualifications which carry with them high economic and political status. A strong university orientation in the educational system means that the secondary school curricula are very academic and that there are few vocational training institutions. Thus people with secondary school certificates who are unable to go on to university, either for financial reasons or for lack of a place, find themselves ill-equipped and unprepared to fill middle-level occupations. It is no wonder that the Progress Report of the Second National Development Plan (1970-4) lamented the shortage of middle-level personnel in all spheres of the public sector. The position is worse for females than for males. The competitive capacity of women with secondary education in the labour market is weak and many find themselves relegated to clerical positions and the lower levels of the service sector, even after investing so many years in getting themselves educated. Dissatisfaction is manifested in the current trend of women engaging in multiple economic activities in order to gain financial independence. Many prefer to trade part-time while carrying on their normal office work. They would rather do this than go into institutional domestic services (hotel catering, for example) or the nursing profession where the conditions of work are more demanding and relatively lowly paid.

Although education is an important factor in the ability of women to participate effectively in the labour force, the number of women who are given the opportunity to go to school, the content of education and the type of employment opportunities open to educated women are influenced by other social factors. These include religion, pay, the status of intermediate occupations and the demand structure for labour.

Implications of Trends in Women's Education and Participation in the Labour Force

Labour force studies conducted in the USA, the UK and other developed economies indicate a strong relationship between female education and potential in the labour market. The data available for Nigeria support the view that, whether or not educational differences are translated into employment, participation depends upon the labour market and the extent to which economic activities in the modern sectors are sufficiently different from other occupational opportunities available to educated females.

In the modernisation process, some sectors expand rapidly while others contract. In a country where traditional agriculture and family labour predominate, the modernisation of agriculture tends to displace female labour. Similarly, urbanisation concomitant with the development process tends to reduce the female rate of labour participation and to marginalise women's role in the urban economy (Awosika, 1977). From being an independent agricultural worker/trader in the

rural area, the illiterate urban woman finds her activity limited to the
low-paid informal sector; mostly domestic service, home-based crafts
and so forth, which in turn contract as development progresses.

The expanding formal sector — administration, financial services,
large businesses and industry — tend to be male-dominated, largely
because a minimum standard of education is required for entry and
advancement. In addition, there is the way in which female labour is
perceived by potential employers. Hence the rate of absorption of
women into the modern sectors of the economy depends on the availability of male labour: educational qualifications apart, female labour is
at a disadvantage where many equally qualified males are available.

Lack of reliable data over a number of years does not permit an
analysis comparing the growth in education with the growth in the
employment of women; fragmentary evidence does suggest that
education accelerates women's employment rates. As modernisation
proceeds, there should be more job opportunities for trained persons,
and the aspirations of educated Nigerian women are such that more and
more are willing to acquire the skills necessary to enable them to
compete for the more lucrative professional jobs. A survey of Lagos
University women undergraduates (Shoremi and Molt, 1973) indicates
that many prefer to go into the professions new to Africa such as law,
accountancy, banking, medicine or architecture, rather than to join the
civil service or do postgraduate work which may limit them to the
teaching profession. Besides, the former professions afford women a
measure of independence. They become self-employed and employers
of labour. They also enable women to combine their domestic roles
with their professions more effectively.

The propensity for well-educated women to work is accompanied
by the relationship between education, and marriage and fertility
(Arowolo 1976; Fadayami, 1978). Although research indicates that the
effect of education on fertility is slight compared to the uneducated,
the incidence of early marriage is lower among the educated. Factors
such as facilities for child-care and technological innovations to lighten
housework, appear to be strong determinants of educated women's
participation in the employment market. Socially, the new economic
independence associated with increasing earning-power appears to be
winning Nigerian women recognition from their ancestral families and
their marital homes, and has restored to them the status which was almost
lost during the colonial period when the small number of educated
women were inadequately prepared to take on modern jobs. Women
then became financially dependent on their husbands which further

diminished the value of giving education to women.

It is appropriate to conclude this chapter by drawing attention to the need for public policy research into those factors that appear to place limitations on the effective participation of women in the labour force. Once it is accepted that education is a strong determinant of the supply of women into the labour force, public policy should not only ensure adequate provision of educational facilities for women, but also create incentive measures to enable them to participate effectively in development. The training opportunities for middle-level personnel are a case in point: women are not entering nursing schools, and teacher training and domestic science colleges at the desired rate simply because career prospects are not as attractive as in other professions. The Lagos Survey showing that the majority of market women are over the age of 30 and predominantly illiterate, indicates the need for a vigorous adult education and vocational training programme. At secondary school level, there is a need for organised career guidance and counselling for young women who are not going on to institutions of higher learning but joining the labour market directly from school. The historical colonial experience has shown that formal education for women is not enough *per se* to improve their social and economic status. Arrangements must be made to enable women to utilise their education by being effectively employed and adequately remunerated.

Finally, in a world where the extended family and the convenience of its child-care practice are gradually dying out, the provision of nursery schools and child-care centres would go a long way to involve educated women effectively in the work force. It might be added that a nation like Nigeria which is undergoing rapid economic development and suffering a shortage of middle- and high-level personnel will do well to invest in the removal of barriers to effective participation by educated female labour in order to increase the total supply of labour.

Bibliography

Arowolo, O. (1976) 'Female Labour Force Participation and Fertility: The Case of Ibadan City in the Western State of Nigeria', paper presented to the 15th Conference of the International Sociological Association, Togo

Awosika, K. (1977) *Women in Urban Labour Force – Implications for Manpower Planning in Nigeria*, paper presented at the Nigerian Economic Society Conference

Bowen, W. G. and Finegan, T. A. (1969) *The Economics of Labour Force Participation*, Princeton University Press, NJ

Collver, A. and Langlois, E. (1962) 'The Female Labour Force in Metropolitan

Areas: An International Comparison', *Economic Development and Cultural Change, 10*, 4

Durand, J.D. (1975) *The Labour Force in Economic Development: A Comparison of International Census Data*, Princeton University Press, NJ

Fadayami, T.O. (1978) *The Demand for Pre-School Care: An Aspect of the Problems of the Nigerian Working Mother*, NISSER, Ibadan

Fapohunda, O. and Fapohunda E. (1976) *The Working Mothers of Lagos*, Human Research Unit, Lagos

Federal Republic of Nigeria, National Manpower Board, Federal Ministry of Economic Development and Reconstruction (1972) *Labour Force Sample Survey 1966/67, 1*, Manpower Studies no. 11, Lagos

Little, K. (1973) 'Women in African Towns South of the Sahara – the Urbanisation Dilemma' in Irene Tinker and Bo Bramsen (eds.), *Women and World Development*, Praeger, New York

Lucas, D. (1975) 'The Participation of Women in the Nigerian Labour Force since the 1950's with particular reference to Lagos', PhD dissertation for LSE 1975; 'Women in the Nigerian Labour Force', paper presented at the UN/ECA African Population Conference, Ghana, 1971

Mabogunje, A. L. (1975) 'Dimensions of Rural-Urban Migration in Nigeria', paper presented at the Conference on Economic Developments and Manpower Generation in Nigeria

Organisation of African Trade Union Unity (1976) 'African Women Workers: Analysis of the factors affecting Women's Employment', Proceedings of a conference, ECA Training and Research Centre for Women, Addis Ababa

Shoremi, M.O. and Molt, F. (1973) 'Characteristics and Expectations of Lagos University Undergraduates', *Research Bulletin*, no. 6/001 Human Resources Research Unit, Lagos

Standing, G. and Sheeham, G. (eds.) (1978) *Labour Force Participation in Low Income Countries*, ILO, Geneva

Youssef, N.H. (1974) *Women and Work in Developing Societies*, Population Monograph series no. 15, Berkeley, Calif.

5 WOMEN IN GOVERNMENT AS POLICY-MAKERS AND BUREAUCRATS: THE TURKISH CASE

Nermin Abadan-Unat

Introduction

When compared to other cultural areas, predominantly Muslim nations have low rates of reported economic activity, low female literacy rates and low female school enrolment at all levels. For women in these countries, seclusion from economic activities and economic dependency are the norm.

Two types of restrictions operate to affect women's status in Muslim societies. The first includes the legal and religious restrictions and inequalities mentioned in the Quran, Hadith, Sunna and Sharia law codes, and the second is that imposed by the practice of purdah or seclusion (White, 1978). Turkey, however, together with the Soviet Republics of Central Asia and Albania, represents those Muslim countries which following major revolutions have eliminated the Muslim inheritance pattern and introduced secular, civil law into all spheres.

Indeed, for the founder of modern Turkey, Kemal Ataturk and his close collaborators, the abolition of women's inferior status had been a major goal from the beginning of the War of Liberation (Abadan-Unat, 1978a). Ataturk strongly believed that the modernisation of Turkish women could only be realised by the reform of two major institutions: education and law. Thus, in a series of bold strokes, the theocratic edifice of the Ottoman state was destroyed. In 1923 the Ministry of Education took over the administration and control of all religious schools and all their means of support (endowment and funds). The abolition of the Caliphate in 1924 was followed by the closing of all medreses (religious seminars) and other separate schools. In 1928, Article 2 of the first Constitution of the Republic of Turkey, which had made Islam the state religion, was amended to provide for dis-establishment and, in 1937, the principle of secularism was incorporated into the Constitution. In the meantime, the jurisdiction of the Shariat courts were taken over by the lay government.

Through the adoption of the Swiss Civil Code in the new Turkish Civil Code in 1926 and the creation of courts modelled on those in

Western countries, orthodox Islamic laws and their application were discarded. As a result, a series of reforms affecting women's status, such as the establishment of a minimum marriage age and registration of marriage, prohibition of polygamy, abolition of *talaq* (one-sided divorce, pronounced by the husband), recognition of the right to divorce and the enactment of a secular inheritance law, and a civil code replacing all religious laws were effectively carried out.

Parallel to the adoption of the Swiss Civil Code, Article 6 of the Civil Service Law, no. 788 was amended in 1926, so as to secure women the right to be employed as civil servants. Thus, Turkish women, who had already begun to enter public service in 1880 as teachers, were given a sound legal basis for their employment rights.

Turkish women were granted political rights much earlier than women in many European countries. They were enfranchised for municipal elections in 1930 and four years later were given the right to participate in national elections. Thus, secularisation not only meant the adoption of new laws and the sweeping away of the religious elites' traditional power, but it also meant a change in the patterns of authority and in the value system of Turkish society.

The realisation of these legal and educational reforms in Turkey has yielded significant results. Female educational achievements have been great. Female school enrolment at all levels in Turkey is far ahead of all other Muslim countries, with the exception of Soviet Central Asia and Albania (White, 1978). Turkey has produced a greater percentage of women lawyers and physicians than the highly industrialised Western countries such as the USA or France. Similarly, government positions related to high-level policy-making have greatly attracted Turkish women. The ratio of female judges, prosecutors and top rank administrators in government in Turkey outnumbers many of the more advanced Western countries (Abadan-Unat, 1978b).

In this light the chapter aims to find some answers to the following questions: can modifications in the superstructure alone, such as reforms in law and education, produce noticeable changes in the mentality and outlook of women? Do they influence the sex-role distribution noticeably and thus produce a different perception of politics and society? Or, does education as a dependent variable merely determine status and class identification, and thus primarily act as an instrument for social mobility? If so, do equality before the law and expanded educational opportunities facilitate only the growth of the middle class? In order to answer these questions the author has attempted to evaluate the impact of the modernisation of Turkish

women by analysing their role and function in public administration —
the sector which has recorded the highest and fastest growth over the
past 40 years.

The hypothesis adopted here is that, because no systematic effort
has been made in public policy or ideologically to assert the ethical
value and social function of work outside the home, the prime moti-
vating factor for women to enter employment is economic need, and
only in rare cases the quest for social prestige. Consequently, social
institutions such as the family and the powerful mass media, especially
television and its consumer oriented advertisements, have become the
major framework for value judgements and preferences. This is one of
the reasons why women are relatively less interested in training programmes which increase chances of promotion.

Since the transition to a multi-party system, no new definitions of
women's role in Turkish society have been made. On the contrary, the
conservative ideologies of successive governments have caused a tacit
elimination of innovative activity such as intensive efforts to expand
female literacy and women's rural programmes. The most important
factors inducing noticeable changes in the outlook and attitudes of
Turkey's young female generation have been urbanisation, migration
and industrialisation (Kazgan, forthcoming). In this respect, a striking
similarity with Tunisia is to be noted. In contrast to Bourguiba's early
efforts in 1956 towards the adoption of the Personnel Status Code,
which replaced segments of Quranic laws with new statutes, and his
strong support for women's education and political involvement,
Tunisian policies of the 1970s marked an increasing tendency to con-
servatism and a significant reduction in government programmes for
cultural reform and resocialisation (Tessler, 1978). Thus, only indirect
factors such as urbanisation have continued to modernise women.

In order to throw some light on questions specifically pertaining to
women in government service, a brief reassessment of women's position
in economic life seems pertinent.

Women in Economic Life

Although Turkey embarked some decades ago on a programme of
accelerated industrialisation, it still retains some of its basic agrarian
aspects, indeed the major socio-economic characteristic is one of
economic dualism, as defined by Adelman and Morris (1973). Such a
dualism is characterised by the coexistence of low productivity, a

subsistence agriculture sector, along with high productivity in agri-business and the industrial sector. In this type of sectoral disharmony women suffer more economic hardships than men. Classified by the same authors as a 'moderate dualism country', women's share in economic life in Turkey closely follows the pattern of decreasing employment opportunities with growing urbanisation that Boserup so ably described (1970). Table 5.1 gives us a clear picture of the evolution over the last 20 years. It can be seen that no more than 11 per cent of Turkish women are employed outside the agricultural sector. Furthermore, the 1975 census revealed that only 15 per cent of all urban women are employed. More than four-fifths of all urban women are housewives.

Table 5.1: Women in Agriculture, Industry and the Services 1955-75 (%)

Sectors	1955	1960	1965	1970	1975
Agriculture	96.6	95.0	94.1	89.0	88.9
Industry	2.3	2.7	1.5	5.1	3.5
Services	1.6	1.9	2.6	5.0	7.4
Others	0.5	0.4	1.8	0.9	0.2

Source: DIE, censuses of 1955, 1960, 1965, 1970 and 1975.

The overwhelming majority of women working in agriculture are unpaid family members. They represent the major source of 'cheap labour', a significant portion of Marx's labour reserve army. Being lodged and fed free in the parental home, the girls of peasant families secure a sizeable income for their fathers through the 'bride price', which in practice is actually an indemnity paid for the loss of (unpaid) service. In the case of wage-earning female agricultural workers, such as cotton, tobacco and fruit pickers, the discrepancy between male and female wages still persists. Owing to the absence of an effective agrarian trade union organisation, and the absence of voluntary payments into social security for the rural sector, this discrepancy has so far not been eliminated.

Within the industrial sector a trend similar to India (ICSSR, 1975) can be registered. Though total employment in factories has been increasing steadily, women's employment in this sector has decreased since 1965, their share being reduced from 11.5 per cent in 1965 to 3.5 per cent in 1975. (Kazgan, forthcoming). Owing to the absence of comprehensive studies, it could be assumed that this decline is partly attributable to the extent and nature of modernisation methods, and partly to external migration. Industries which have adopted a higher capital-intensive technology resulting in the displacement of labour have found it easier to displace women than men. Furthermore, a significant number of female migrant workers have taken industrial jobs. In Federal Germany alone their absolute number increased from 173 in 1960 to 143,611 in 1975 (Abadan-Unat, 1977). Whether these women would have taken up industrial jobs in their home country remains a debateable issue. In contrast to the general neglect of social policy in the agrarian sector in Turkey, a number of protective labour laws have been adopted in the industrial sector to secure women's social welfare. However, actual implementation of these laws is lacking. Moreover, the number of trade union affiliated female workers is minimal. Only 9 per cent of all women employed in industry in 1977 were covered by social security — a function that is fully dependent on affirmative action by trade unions (Tezgider, 1978). Again as in India (ICSSR,1975), women have increasingly shown a growing interest and determination to enter government jobs. Since empirical studies dealing with the attitudes and behaviour of Turkish women in the executive and judiciary are not available, the author has preferred to make extensive use of the findings of Oya Çitçi's comprehensive survey (1979), embracing a large number of governmental agencies, including all kinds of clerical, administrative, managerial and specialised occupations, and to deduce from these findings some implications applicable to top-ranking women policy-makers.

Turkish Women in Public Administration

During 1938-76, the number of female civil servants in Turkey increased 19 times, while the number of male civil servants rose six-fold. In order to assess this growth, a chronological table listing the various types of government agencies is necessary (see Table 5.2). At first glance one significant feature becomes evident: the greatest concentration of female civil servants can be observed in agencies covered by the general budget, while there is a decline in municipal agencies — the reason being that a great number of recently created municipal agencies are located in rural areas where limited educational opportunities have not permitted women access to government jobs.

When measuring the educational level of these women officials, the first fact to be noticed is their higher level of educational attainment compared with men. While 54 per cent of all male civil servants are only

Table 5.2: Distribution of Female Civil Servants in Absolute Figures and Percentages, 1938 and 1976

Type of administration	1938	%	1946	%	1963	%	1970	%	1977	%
General budget	4.287	8	12.573	15	47.414	20	80.099	22	190.313	27
Annex budget	824	4	3.813	6	3.487	10	3.748	8	7.783	21
State economic enterprise	731	10	2.502	13	15.623	13	26.116	19	48.380	
Local administration	6.874	18	11.140	21	6.178	10	4.838	8	7.829	12
Total	12.716	9.5	30.046	13.5	72.702	16	123.812	19	244.305	25

Note: General budget covers all ministries and administrative agencies in the provinces representing the central government.
Sources: DIE, *Memurlar Istatisgği*, no. 149 (DIE, Ankara, 1938); DIE, *Memurlar Istatistiği*, no. 288 (DIE, Ankara, 1946); DIE, *Devlet Personel Sayımı*, vols. 1-3, nos. 473,503,518 (DIE, Ankara, DIE, *Devlet Memurları Sayımı*, no. 664 (DIE, Ankara, 1970); Devlet Personel Dairesi, *Kamu Personeli Anket Raporları*, vol. 1.

primary or secondary school graduates, 68.5 per cent of women are educated to high school (*lycée*) level or beyond. As other authors have noted, women have to be better qualified for particular posts than men. Thus, there seems to be a rather clear relationship between educational level and non-agrarian employment. According to the 1975 statistics, showing the occupational mobility of girls, 5 per cent of Turkey's primary school graduates, 12.5 per cent of its secondary school, 30 per cent of its high school, 56 per cent of its vocational and 70 per cent of its university graduates were able to find a job in the non-agrarian sector (Die, 1976). In addition, the most qualified female labour seems to be concentrated in the service sector— be it private enterprise or government service; 41 per cent of all women working in this sector have some form of higher education. Although university graduates represent only 1.9 per cent of the total active female labour force, they represent 16.6 per cent in public administration.

Another interesting aspect of women's entrance into the civil service is the fact that, unlike the prevailing pattern in Western countries, there is no visible interruption in the pattern of Turkish women's working life. While in industrialised countries there are two peak periods for participating actively in the public domain, namely the 20-25 and 40-60 age-groups, in Turkey entrance into employment is a kind of apprenticeship before marriage. Those women who remain in employment after marriage, make no interruption at all. Partly owing to the unwillingness of the women themselves, and partly from the country's prevailing structural unemployment and the lack of part-time jobs, there is practically no chance of women returning to employment once they have left to raise a family.

In 1963, 43.9 per cent of all women employed in the public sector were under the age of 30; in 1976 this percentage rose to 55 per cent for the same age-group. The highest percentage of women working in public administration belongs to the 18-24 age-group (Çitçi, 1979). After the age of 25, a definite decrease can be witnessed. Therefore, it is not erroneous to state that the great majority of women serving in public administration possess little commitment; they do not whole-heartedly embrace a career, but work to obtain an additional source of income. This tendency has been confirmed by the Hacettepe Population Census of 1973 which revealed that among those women who gave up their jobs, 35 per cent gave marriage as the major cause, 18 per cent child-raising and 5 per cent the negative attitude of their husbands (Özbay, forthcoming).

With this in mind, one might ask what kind of positions are occupied by women? This question can be answered by evaluating both the distribution pattern of women among the various agencies as well as their occupational activity. The census taken in 1976 by the State Personnel Directorate reveals that the highest number of women working in the government agencies are located in the Ministry of Education (31.6 per cent), similar again to India with a heavy predominance of pre-school and primary school teachers. The second favoured ministry, requiring adequate foreign language knowledge, is the Ministry of Tourism and Information which employs 26.3 per cent of the women. In third place comes the Ministry of Health and Social Assistance with 22.2 per cent, representing once more a government agency with a heavy concentration of 'feminine occupations', such as nursing and midwifery. It is interesting to note that this tendency to work in ministries with specific, female-oriented tasks has increased over the years. Those three ministries were employing 55.7 per cent in 1963, 67.9 per cent in 1970 and 69.1 per cent in 1976 of the women (Özbay, forthcoming).

Overall it appears that women tend to work in occupations from which men are excluded or which have a general social service content, or which require upper-class multilingual training. As to the jobs, the 1976 census reveals that almost half (44 per cent) of the female employees are performing clerical work. The typists and bureau clerks are the most numerous (70.3 per cent), while 1.5 per cent occupy assistant directorships or higher positions.

With regard to professional women, another trend familiar to studies of Third World countries seems to be the rule in Turkey. It is characterised by the following: (i) the percentage of professional women is relatively higher than in capitalist countries; (ii) women are mainly concentrated in metropolitan and urban centres; and (iii) since they seek security and facilities related to their work rather than quick promotional opportunities, they prefer government employment to private practice. Thus, while the total percentage of female lawyers in Turkey is 18.6 per cent, they are over-represented (with 42.1 per cent) in institutions covered by the general budget or classified as state economic enterprises. Similarly the proportion of women engineers in these enterprises is 7.9 per cent – higher than in most capitalist countries.

The reciprocal relationship between education and employment, however, becomes most evident when the distribution of women according to their educational level and labour force participation is examined. Since the growing participation of Turkish women in public administration is essentially the result of long-range educational policies rather than a specific special element of an egalitarian, democratic, nondiscriminatory public philosophy or political programme, its impact has remained instrumental and class-oriented. Apart from the early years of the Republic, when successful, professional *avant-garde* women were presented to the public as model pioneers on the path of the new, Western-inspired civilised society, no political party or government programme has committed itself to improving the status of women other than through small legal changes in favour of urban civil servants. Indeed, after the transition to a multi-party regime in 1946, a sizeable number of political parties have publicly reiterated traditional values, constantly praising the function of housewives and mothers. The findings of the first comprehensive empirical research on Turkish women employed in various public agencies, carried out by Oya Çitçi, furnishes convincing evidence that women enter the public domain with an internal set of values based on an ideal housewife model.

Socio-economic Characteristics of Turkish Civil Servants and Emancipatory Values

Çitçi's sample consisted of 742 women civil servants out of a total of 14,838, representing 15 administrative agencies in Ankara, the capital, each employing more than 500 women (1979), and 68.5 per cent of the respondents of the survey were high school or university graduates. Most of them were from upper-middle-class families and their fathers were employed in liberal professions, business or bureaucracy. More than half of the respondents (52.1 per cent) were married, two-thirds coming from nuclear families. The majority classified themselves as additional breadwinner − only 8 per cent of the women were heads of families. The average number of children was 1.6. Because of the relatively high percentage of low-age children (70.8 per cent), the question as to who is entrusted to take care of them was very relevant. The survey indicates that 63.1 per cent were entrusting their children to their mothers or mothers-in-law and only 12.1 per cent were using the facilities of day-care centres, while another 6 per cent were employing domestic help. Equally important is the fact that 79.2 per cent had no additional household help.

These characteristics determined to some degree the response concerning the function and role of women in society. Although 75.3 per cent consider women's emancipation − here conceived as women's ability to benefit from all legal and educational reforms — quite important, only 5 per cent thought that equality between men and women had actually been achieved. It was felt by 30.2 per cent that men should retain their superiority. This superiority was explained having been sustained for the following reasons:

(i) The patriarchal character of the Swiss Civil Code, which became the Turkish Civil Code. Article 159 limits the married women's 'actual ability' to take employment by requiring her to seek her husband's permission. In case of refusal, the women may apply to the court, and, there, must furnish convincing proof that her prospective employment will serve 'the genuine interests of her family'.

(ii) The persistence of tradition and mores in favour of male supremacy.

(iii) The fact that by-and-large men are the major breadwinners and heads of the family.

Participation in the public domain can produce profound changes in the mentality of women only if the socialisation process for girls places a different emphasis on sex-roles. Oya Çitçi's survey furnishes detailed data indicating that granting equal educational opportunities — even for those who make the best use of them — is ineffective for the majority of women in society as long as 'the family, educational institutions, mass media and books are uniformly reinforcing the traditional outlook emphasising that women have to primarily be good homemakers and mothers'.

This attitude is also reflected in the 1973 Hacettepe Survey, which revealed that only 33 per cent of women would continue to work if they did not need money. Thus, it becomes clear that two-thirds of the married women work to help the family income and tend to stop working as their economic situation improves (Özbay, forthcoming). All these figures indicate that, by and large, Turkish women in employment acquiesce in the dual role of women (first defined by Alva Myrdal) and, without attempting to introduce significant changes into their lives, aspire to return to their traditional functions. On this particular question, the place of residence plays a minor role. Women of rural origins approve of male supremacy by 93.4 per cent and urban ones by 83.6 per cent. Education, however, seems to be a more important factor. Respondents with a primary education approve of this option by 93 per cent and university graduates by only 75 per cent. Nevertheless, the fact remains that three-quarters of all female civil servants attribute a secondary importance to their own employment and career.

On the other hand, these same women give way to some contradictory thoughts and feelings when confronted with a set of alternatives fitted to delineate the ideal way of life for women. Table 5.3 indicates that a negligible percentage of the respondents considers a career life-style as an ideal. The majority would like to achieve self-realisation and the best combination of career life and housework. In other words, if society is ready to provide women with various supportive services and build up institutional assistance, there appears to be a readiness to work outside the home in spite of the traditional climate of opinion that has been outlined. Women want to use their innate abilities and talents but, apparently in the absence of affirmative action and strong organisational support, these women do not find the courage, zest and determination to fight for their rights. The lack of a value system based on a work ethic, encourages many women to make use of the early pension plan. With only partial unwillingness they assume the roles of sex-object and passive homemaker.

This early retirement scheme (Law no. 1992, 3 July 1975) makes it possible for female civil servants to retire after the completion of 20 years of active service. The justification for it has been the stress women have to endure because of their dual role. It is significant that the legislators, instead of introducing unpaid extended maternity leave or broadening various forms of social assistance, have opted for a solution which actually sends women home at an age when they could devote most of their time to work outside the house.

When the Oya Çitçi survey was undertaken the law had not yet been passed, and this early retirement plan was met with great enthusiasm; 80.9 per cent of the respondents indicated their intention to make use of this right. Of the university graduates, 71.9 per cent wanted to give up their career. However, since the passage of the law, only a very limited number of working women have actually used this option. During the period between July 1975 and July 1977 the number of female civil servants who retired after 20 years of work was 2,058, while 24,114 women officials continued to work (Çitçi, 1979). There is a discrepancy between stated intention and actual behaviour which could reflect many factors, particularly the pressure of economic necessity.

Female officials have been conditioned by traditional values to such a degree that, when asked whether they would consider a better job with better opportunities for promotion and higher pay, but requiring longer working hours and absence from home, 74.2 per cent refused to consider such an offer.[1] Oya Çitçi intelligently tried to detect the extent of this 'self imposed' limitation to liberation by gauging the

Table 5.3: Views on the Ideal Way of Life for Women, According to Marital Status, Residence and Education (%)

Women in public administration	To be only a good homemaker	To get a professional education and use it eventually	To be a successful career woman	To combine the roles of housewife and career woman
Marital status				
Married	17.5	16.2	0.2	65.8
Bachelor	12.5	15.2	0.3	71.7
Widow	16.3	9.1	–	75.5
Residence				
Rural	21.7	17.3	–	60.8
Small town	24.4	16.3	–	50.1
Urban	13.4	19.9	0.3	71.1
Education				
Primary	27.9	6.9	–	65.1
Secondary	16.9	17.1	0.2	65.7
University	5.6	14.6	0.5	79.2

Source: Oya Çitçi, 'Türkiye' de Kadin sorunu ve calisan Kadinlar', mimeographed unpublished PhD thesis, Ankara, 1979, Tables 58-60.

behaviour of the respondents with regard to their marriage, use of income, degree of participation and activity in association. With regard to marriage, Çitçi presented a set of alternative solutions almost totally centred around the preponderant role of the family: 60.2 per cent of the respondents declared they had independently chosen their spouse; 11.7 per cent disregarded the choice made by their family and opted for their own choice; 19.5 per cent were married through an inter-mediary or a 'matchmaker', and another 8.6 per cent concluded a pre-arranged marriage. Although about 79.6 per cent said that they made their final decision after a harmonious consultation with their family, only one-tenth actually acted totally on their own.

The attachment of economically active women to their family is also reflected in the interesting survey which Kandiyoti carried out on a sample of two generations among urban women in Istanbul (Kandiyoti, forthcoming). Her findings confirm the trend described above. In her conclusion she states that while the education of the daughters is very high (especially when compared with their own mothers) and their level of employment is not negligible, their ways of meeting their future marriage partners have been quite traditional and their definition of the 'successful woman' is one who reconciles the traditional and modern demands. Kandiyoti indicates that in spite of the considerable degree of social change in the mothers' generation, the daughters have not been able to modify their traditional expectations in any fundamental way, but have just taken on some new roles. This might also explain why puritan values related to chastity are still strongly supported, punishment of adultery with imprisonment is upheld, and the double standard in morality not protested against. While some young Turkish women, belonging to leftist political groups may be strongly in favour of radical change in the economic and social order, they consider a strong stand against sexism irrelevant, alien to the social structure and distracting from the basic social issues.

The close relationship of working women to their families is likewise reflected in the way they use their income; 60 per cent add all, or the major portion of their income to the family budget. In this respect marital status plays a determining role. While only 17 per cent of married women officials spend more than half of their income for their own needs, this percentage reaches 69.7 per cent for unmarried women. As may be anticipated, the amount of income working women contri-bute to the family budget is closely related to the general income of the household.

Another important criterion which might help to establish the degree of emancipation of Turkish female employees is their participation in family decision-making matters. Table 5.4 casts light on the major issues in which women actively take part. As would be expected from the idealised dual feminine role, women have the most say in their traditional stronghold, that is household management. Although the percentage of matters decided jointly is relatively high, there is a kind

Table 5.4: Distribution of Sex-ratio in Decision-making Within Families (%)

Subject	Female	Male	Both sexes
Food expenses	25.7	8.1	66.1
Clothing	18.6	5.7	75.5
Furniture	6.5	4.7	88.7
Social problems concerning womens' professional life	34.9	7.8	57.2
Special problems concerning mens' professional life	—	57.9	41.9
Family size, family planning	3.9	3.9	92.1
Education of children	11.2	2.3	86.3
Household chores	67.7	0.7	31.4
Invitation of guests	9.1	9.4	81.3
Holiday, travel	2.8	5.5	91.6
Political behaviour of women	39.1	12.8	48.0
Political behaviour of men	—	52.0	48.0
Selection of newspaper subscribed at home	10.2	25.7	64.0

Source: Oya Çitçi, 'Türkiye' de Kadin soruna ve calisan Kadinlar', p. 242, Table 100.

of tutelage in settling professional matters solely concerning women. In this domain 7.8 per cent of men are taking the decisive steps.

A slightly higher degree of individual freedom prevails in political matters, although there, too, 12.8 per cent unconditionally accept the political choice of the men they live with (husband, father and brother). With regard to the political participation, namely voting, a number of surveys have shown a definite pattern wherein Turkish women's voting participation is lower than men's — married women are less inclined to vote than unmarried girls or widows, while working women show a greater interest in politics than housewives (Tekeli, forthcoming). Çitçi's survey confirms these findings. Only 64.2 per cent of her respondents admitted to having voted in the last election. Differentiated according to their marital status, 72.9 per cent of the married,

50 per cent of the unmarried and 81.6 per cent of the widows went to the polls. This means that bearing responsibility as 'head of the family' leads to increased civic interest and political participation. As can be expected, education plays the most important differentiating role. While 88.7 per cent of the university graduates voted, only 56.3 per cent of the primary school graduates made use of their citizenship rights.

Finally a few words on the attitudes of women civil servants towards membership of associations. Only 23 per cent of the respondents admitted belonging to any kind of association. Here, membership in a professional association seems to dominate (77.1 per cent). Thus, a number of general tendencies can be summarised:

(i) Irrespective of the positions occupied, both women officials and professional women with higher education adopt a conciliatory, dependent, passive role in the public domain. Their readiness to fight for greater equality and wider liberties for women at large is relatively weak with the exception of those who have a strong political or ideological commitment.

(ii) The importance attached to emancipation is determined by education and place of residence as well as by class affiliation. The urban middle-class families seem to place the greatest importance on emancipatory values.

(iii) Ambivalence towards continuing a career while assuming the role of housewife and mother is the rule rather than the exception.

(iv) The beginning, duration and termination of active participation in government service is more dependent on special conditions (economic needs or child-raising) than on personal feelings and preferences. The highest level of motivation to continue work outside the home seems to prevail among those jobs outside the country, namely among blue-collar and white-collar workers abroad. The dominant climate of opinion in favour of high productivity and a high standard of living in those highly industrialised countries seems to play a determining role for these migrant workers.

(v) Where there is conflict arising from the clash of loyalties, solutions favouring the smooth functioning of family life are preferred.

(vi) The job status of women officials does not automatically increase democracy within the family or political participation. Here again educational level, marital status and class affiliation produce diversified patterns.

Women in the Judiciary and Executive Positions

Can the findings of Çitçi's survey covering a broad range of women civil servants be equally applied to the women elite in the executive and the judiciary? In the absence of empirical findings, we are forced to do some speculative thinking. Law and medicine have traditionally been exclusively male professions. In Western industrial societies very few women have been able to penetrate these strongholds until recently (Epstein, 1970). Yet in Turkey both of these professions have attracted a surprisingly large number of women. One in every five practising lawyers in Turkey is a woman. Again, one in every six practising physicians is a woman. This surprisingly high ratio has not been confined to the middle-range positions, but has also produced a significant number of women in higher positions. In fact, the very first woman judge in the highest court of appeal was a Turk, the late Melahat Ruacan, whose nomination in 1954 attracted worldwide attention and praise. Similarly female judges have been elected as chairmen of sections in the highest administrative court of Turkey, the State Council, for over 20 years. Not only have women been eager to enrol in law schools, but with equal enthusiasm they have tried to be active within the judiciary, as reflected in Table 5.5.

Table 5.5: Sex-ratio Distribution According to Occupations Within the Ministry of Justice (as of 3 February 1978)

Position	Female	%	Male	%	Total	%
Judges	102	3.1	3,172	96.9	3,172	100
Prosecutors	13	0.6	1,891	99.4	1,904	100
Other women employees with non-juridical background	2,525	11.3	19,800	88.7	22,325	100

Source: State Personnel Directorate, unpublished data.

The sex-ratio distribution within the Ministry of Justice reflects a strong male dominance with a slight inclination to admit a few women into top positions. A similar trend can be observed in another traditionally male-oriented ministry, the Ministry of Foreign Affairs. Women became eligible for diplomatic posts only after the promulgation of the new Constitution in 1961, in which Article 12 categorically prohibits all forms of discrimination based on sex, although previously they were not legally prohibited from entering such posts. Here, as in the other ministries, only a few top positions are occupied by women.

Table 5.6: Sex-ratio Distribution According to Occupation Within the Ministry of Foreign Affairs (as of 11 May 1977)

Position	No. of females	No. of males	Total
Head of section	5	63	68
Second secretary	5	20	25
Second secretary (abroad)	6	45	51
Counsellor	1	100	101
Consul	8	48	56
Expert	1	30	31
Administrative asst	49	130	179
Total	75 (14.6%)	436 (85.4%)	511 (100%)

Source: State Personnel Directorate, unpublished data.

The significant difference in male/female recruitment within two traditional/conservative ministries obviously lies in a class-determined educational requirement. Diplomatic service, as well as service in the Ministry of Information and Tourism, requires fluency in a foreign language. These skills are acquired in expensive, foreign-sponsored and financed private schools, available only to the daughters of the upper-middle-class families whose parents consider this kind of education the best investment for a desirable marriage. It is usually these girls, who are not taught the value and gratification of work, that are able to compete with men and get easy access to these positions. However, after the first stage of apprenticeship in the home country, when the time comes for appointment abroad, a surprisingly large number of diplomatic candidates resign. This results from the policy adopted by the Ministry of Foreign Affairs which prohibits the appointment of married couples together in one embassy or consulate. To be a liberated woman, ready to face the many difficulties of professional life alone, requires a new mentality. If this mentality has not been acquired, only a temporary solution such as the appointment of the spouses to nearby cities may be tried, or resignations occur.

By analysing the sex-ratio in the key positions of two other central administrative agencies, namely the Ministry of Commerce and the State Planning Organisation, interesting differences can be observed. The Ministry of Commerce is one of the major administrative units dealing with the male-dominated business world. Thus, the women who

Table 5.7: Sex-ratio Distribution According to Positions in the Ministry of Commerce, 1977

Position	No. of females	No. of males	Total
Asst commercial adviser	2	15	17
Asst commercial attaché	1	8	9
Commercial attaché	1	35	36
Asst rapporteur	6	18	24
Rapporteur	16	89	105
Head rapporteur	1	9	10
Head of section	10	86	96
Adviser	4	18	22
Total	41 (13.2%)	268 (86.8%)	309 (100%)
Other positions	295 (19.6%)	1,180 (80.4%)	1,505 (100%)

Source: State Personnel Directorate, unpublished data.

work in this ministry function are engaged chiefly in research (that is, securing foreign and domestic statistics, summarising reports and making diplomatic contacts) as well as in the usual clerical domain. In the key positions, as in the Ministry of Foreign Affairs, young women with fluency in foreign languages are able to compete with men — once again proving the importance of the connection between education and class affiliation.

In the most recently created central administrative unit, the State Planning Organisation, the situation has improved a great deal in favour of women. Planning is a future-oriented activity requiring constant fact finding, compilation of statistics and the carrying out of predominantly advisory and co-ordinating functions; it seems to appeal more to women than to men. Here, too, some sort of imbalance is evident — the secondary positions related to expertise and specialised planning are fairly well staffed with women, while the strategy-determining positions are still preponderantly occupied by men. This agency appears to be the only one where there is remarkable balance in the ratio between men and women in positions higher than clerical.

It is interesting to note that in those ministries where the heaviest concentration of women in lower positions is to be found — such as Education, Health and Social Assistance — promotional opportunities for women have been very limited. Only 3 out of 27 general directors in the Ministry of Education are women. In the Ministry of Finance, the general director of the treasury is a woman, but other senior positions are heavily occupied by men.

Table 5.8: Sex-ratio Distribution According to Positions in the State Planning Organisation (as of 3 February 1978)

Position	No. of females	No. of males	Total
Head of section	2	10	12
Planning expert	27	58	85
Asst expert	24	44	68
Total	53 (32.1%)	112 (67.9%)	165 (100%)
Other positions	129 (30.3%)	296 (64.7%)	425 (100%)

Source: State Personnel Directorate, unpublished data.

Can one expect that the relatively high number of professional women active in public service will continue, and is it possible to assume that their value judgements differ essentially from the values of their sisters in the middle and low ranks? In view of an overall climate of opinion favouring the traditional social function of women, it would be erroneous to answer in the affirmative. The basic difference between women officials in the higher and lower ranks lies in the nature of their informal activities. The choices of those in higher ranks will be heavily determined by the choices of the upper class, and include especially leisure activities such as sports, card games, attendance at fashion shows as well as charity work and voluntary association affiliation. As pointed out by Vida Tomsiç, a Yugoslav social scientist, the influence of traditional values and ideas concerning the role of man and woman in the family and society has its own obstinate persistence long after the circumstances in which a certain value or prejudice originated have disappeared. This is especially true when the living conditions cannot be changed as quickly and profoundly as legal regulations (for example educational and employment possibilities). Research on the attitudes towards the new status of women in a socialist society shows that people have changed more in theory than in practice. One cannot help but get the impression that some of the new values accepted during the National War of Liberation in Turkey — when women's emancipation was one of the objectives as well as one of the reasons for women's active participation in the revolutionary movement — have been lost in today's practical life. Fighting tradition is a long and complex process (Tomsiç, 1975).

Conclusion

I return to the question posed at the beginning of this chapter: what has been the impact of legal and educational reform in Turkey with regard to women? It can be said that among all Muslim countries, Turkey has definitely been able to achieve remarkable results. But, as underlined by Özbay, class privileges in education particularly affect the female population. Furthermore, education by itself is incapable of equipping women or men with a new outlook on society and its social and economic structure. Education may eventually help to develop a stronger personality, but it does not contribute directly to a new consciousness. The presence of the relatively large number of professional women in the various government agencies has not been sufficient to open up new avenues towards a strong movement for a more egalitarian society. The modernisation of women through education has primarily enlarged the ranks of the middle classes. The increasing interest of women in politics, mostly observed during large-scale meetings and political rallies, has so far remained rather emotional. Women in responsible executive positions have done little or nothing to channel these growing aspirations into new activities, where the female work force could have had a positive effect on production.

Women in the executive and the judiciary are really freed in the public domain from all sex-defined stereotypes. Their performance can be summarised as asexual and totally adjusted to the standard male behaviour rules. Only in the realm of private life does one encounter the traditional, conformist way of life. The degree of self-assurance, gained through work outside the home, permits these women to shoulder this ambivalent way of life.

The number of women participating in public administration could be a misleading indicator of equality, as they are predominantly assuming secondary roles with limited reponsibilities. Systematic efforts and specially designed policies have induced women to appear satisfied with non-demanding jobs and slight responsibilities. The fact that the general right to strike has so far not been granted to civil servants, men and women, has reduced the potential for pressure for specific demands concerning women officials. Justified claims for better working conditions, longer maternity leave, paid maternity leave and the creation of part-time jobs are all demands which have not been expressed through the activities of the associations, but rather through nongovernmental organisations with limited influence.

No doubt the most significant progress has taken place in the level of participation in the professions. In this respect Turkey is displaying the characteristics of 'developing' Third World countries, where women enjoy access to the prestigious professions despite the low rates of participation in the non-agricultural labour market. As Öncü correctly stated, the ready availability of lower-class women as domestics in private homes has significantly contributed to the 'emancipation' of upper-class women to pursue professional careers. Furthermore, the need for qualified personnel has so far encouraged women from elite backgrounds to enter the prestigious professions. Thus, this process is to some extent historically specific.

Looking to the future, it may be expected that the growth in number of both Turkish civil servants and professionals will steadily continue, noticeably in regions with fast rates of urbanisation and industrialisation. But unless the question of female employment in general is treated as a subject on its own merits, and specific policies and programmes developed for urban and rural women, women's role and impact on government affairs will not produce effective changes in society. The essence of efforts to advance the social position of women and their complete integration in development goes beyond the problem of legal and educational equal opportunities. It requires a deep structural transformation of society, a growing awareness of the need to use human resources fully and a strong ideological commitment to fight all forms of discrimination between the sexes.

Note

1. A recent survey of Turkish civil servants shows that fewer women than men move between departments and that a smaller proportion of women than of men are fully satisfied with their jobs. See Omer Bozkhurt, *Türkiye' de kamu büroknasisinin sosyolojik görünumü* (*Sociological Portrait of the Turkish Civil Service*) (Memurlar, Ankara, 1980), pp. 214 and 215.

Bibliography

Abadan-Unat, N. (1977) 'Implications of migration on emancipation and pseudo-emancipation of Turkish women', *International Migration Review, 11*, 1 (Spring)
—— (1978a) 'The Modernization of Turkish Women', *The Middle East Journal, 32*, 3 (Summer)
—— (1978b) 'Women's Movements and National Liberation: The Turkish Case',

paper presented at the 9th World Congress of Sociology, ISA, Uppsala, August 14-19

—— (ed.) (forthcoming) *Women in Turkish Society*, E.J. Brill, Leiden

Adelman, I. and Morris, C.T. (1973) *Economic Growth and Social Equity in Developing Countries*, Stanford University Press, Calif.

Beck, L. and Keddie, N. (eds.) (1978) *Women in the Muslim World*, Harvard University Press, Cambridge, Mass.

Boserup, E. (1970) *Women's Role in Economic Development*, St Martin's Press, New York

Çitçi, O. (1979) 'Türkiye' de kadin sorunu ve calisan kadinlar' ('The Problem of of Women in Turkey and Working Women'), mimeographed unpublished PhD thesis, Ankara

DIE (1976) *1975 Nufus Sayimi*, DIE, Ankara

Epstein, Cynthia Fuchs (1970) *Woman's Place*, University of California Press, Berkeley

ICSSR (1975) 'Status of Women in India', a synopsis of the Report of the National Committee, New Delhi

Kazgan, G.(forthcoming) 'Labour Force Participation, Occupational Distribution, Educational Attainment and the Socio-economic Status of Women in the Turkish Economy' in Abadan-Unat

Öncü, A. (forthcoming), 'Turkish Women in the Professions: Why so Many?' in Abadan-Unat

Özbay, F. (forthcoming), 'The Impact of Education on Women in Rural and Urban Turkey' in Abadan-Unat

Tessler, M.A. (1978) 'Women's Emancipation in Tunisia' in Beck and Keddie

Tezgider, G. (1978) 'Çalişan kadinlarin sorunlari üzerine bir inceleme' ('Problems of Working Women'), Calisma dergisi (October)

Tomsiç, V. (1975) *Status of Women and Family Planning in Yugoslavia*, Ljubljana

White, E.H. (1978) 'Legal Reform as an Indicator of Women's Status in Muslim Nations' in Beck and Keddie

6 CREATING EMPLOYMENT OPPORTUNITIES FOR RURAL WOMEN: SOME ISSUES AFFECTING ATTITUDES AND POLICY

Najma Sachak

Introduction

The problem with the applications of most employment theories is that they rely mainly on formal employment structures. The definition of what constitutes an employed person (relating to hours of work and continuity of job) and a labour force (those who are employed and those who are seeking employment) is relevant only to the needs of formal wage employment which in Tanzania exists mostly in the urban areas. Thus the requirements of urban areas determine policy on wages, prices and taxes. This dominance is evidenced in the better provision of facilities — housing, health, water, electricity and transport — in the urban areas than in the rural areas. In Tanzania, the industrial sector is small and employment within it is increasingly competitive; urban employment tends to be male-oriented and male-dominated. In the rural areas, the definition of employment is even more difficult because the majority of the people are in the informal sector. The

Table 6.1: Dispersion in Wages and Farm Incomes: Tanzania, 1973-5

	Agriculture	Wage	Minimum wage[a]
Average income (Tz sh. p.a.)	3,917	7,160	4,896
% of farmers falling below	40-60	80-90	65-75
% of wage-earners falling below	15-20	60-70	25-33

Note: a. Minimum wage in Dar es Salaam in 1979, multiplied by 2 to reflect family income.
Source: ILO, *Towards Self-Reliance* (International Labour Office, Addis Ababa, 1978), p. 183.

relatively poor standard of living in rural Tanzania is indicated by the dispersion in wages and farm income, shown in Table 6.1. Employment issues have become part of general development policies. In post-independence Tanzania, the most important policies on rural development have been based on the principles of *ujamaa* and the Arusha Declaration,[1] and villagisation.[2]

The Study

The objective of the research presented in this chapter was to find means of creating additional opportunities for wage-employment for rural women by setting up public works-projects in rural areas. There is considerable interest among donor agencies in financing such programmes involving women in Tanzania and other countries.

In Tanzania, the experience in recent years closest to public works projects are self-help schemes and famine relief activities, but in view of the prevailing ideology on (socialistic) development, any community-based development project could conceivably take on the character of a public works scheme. Both self-help and famine-relief projects are organised around communally-provided labour, and tend to concentrate on providing communal services, such as roads, clinics, classrooms and dams, some of which may have a significant effect on production. A road can clear access to a crop-buying centre which may lead to increased production; the provision of a water-supply system may eliminate long wasteful journeys to distant water sources and free labour time for more productive work. Public works programmes are supposedly most effective for these purposes. Self-help projects can be viewed as harmonised communal commitment to the development effort, from one end of the 'work' spectrum. From the other, though, they may well represent indirect taxation paid in labour. There is little tradition of public works as such in Tanzania, and women have seldom been able to enter this sector: there is no comparison with the role of women in public works programmes of the type found, for instance, in India. There are limited opportunities for men, mainly in maintaining roads and marketing crops.

The only way to do this research was to cut through theoretical problems of defining women's labour and to describe the employment situation as it exists at the grass-roots level. The survey was conducted in selected villages in Dodoma Region in Central Tanzania, and was attached to an existing study in Dodoma on the role of women in food production under conditions of famine. The employment study relates to the original study in two ways.

(i) The original programme would provide detailed, sex-

differentiated data on labour used seasonally in various jobs on the
farm and in the home. This could help to identify slack periods, if any,
in the demand for labour for both sexes, enabling comparisons to be
made: it would then be easier to estimate 'employable' labour available. This is an important consideration in planning employment
programmes, especially in areas with long dry seasons, or in famine,
because of the necessity to seek work to obtain food.

(ii) It was expected that the growth of the new capital being
constructed at Dodoma would have increased the prospects of finding
employment in the expanding construction industries and the
supporting 'informal' sector, which attract unskilled and semi-skilled
labour from the rural areas. The hinterland of Dodoma could thus
provide insights into the motives for, and expectations of, migration
for work.

The survey was conducted in six villages in Dodoma Rural District;
they were selected for the original research on the basis of the severity
of famine — Chifutuka, Manzase, Majeleko, Bahi Nagulo, Handali and
Haneti. Initially interviews were conducted at two levels: a 'general'
village interview with the members of the village committee and other
villagers, and separate 'household' interviews, with a representative
male and female member of the household. This was designed to be a
test questionnaire for preliminary study, and only ten households in
each village were interviewed, regardless of the population of the
villages.

The village interview was designed to give an inventory of the village
in terms of the facilities available in health, water, transport and so on
(Table 6.2), as an indication of the existing 'capacity' for providing
wage employment, and to discuss their record of work in self-help and
famine-relief projects, as a rough pointer to the amount of labour and
the time during which this is available for work other than farming. At
the interviews the women present were always fewer than the men, but
were particularly drawn out in the discussions. In content, the
household questionnaires were designed to make only tentative forays
into the whole unknown area of 'formal' employment in the villages.
Whenever applicable, the household interviews for the test questionnaire included those with COMWORKS[3] employees, nurses, midwives
and their spouses.

The next stage for the wider employment study was an interview
with a representative woman in each household on the basis of a 5 per
cent random sample of households in the six villages. This questionnaire
focused on aspects of employment for women who seek work, such as

Table 6.2: Inventory of Facilities Available in each Village

Type of service/facility available	Manzase	Majeleko	Bahi Nagulo	Chifutuka	Haneti	Handali
Health	Rural dispensary	First-aid box c	First-aid box	Rural dispensary	Rural dispensary	Rural health centre a
Water	Water pump; wells	No water pump; wells	No water pump; wells	One water pump	One water pump	One water pump
Status of transport/communication	Off main road to Iringa	Partly main road to Dodoma; tracks	7-8 miles to rail station; 5 miles to main road	By road to 3 nearby places; tracks	Main road Dodoma-Kondoa	Main road to Dodoma; rail station 10 miles away
Education	1 primary school	1 primary school	1 primary school	1 primary school	1 primary school	1 primary school
Trade	1 co-operative shop	1 co-operative shop	1 co-operative shop	1 co-operative shop	1 co-operative shop; 1 beerstore; 1 hotel; 1 butchery	3 beer shops; 1 butchery; 1 co-operative shop
Flour mills/other small industries	None	1 flour mill	1 creamery	None	1 flour mill; 1 creamery	2 flour mills; 1 creamery
Total population of village (October 1978)	2,269	1,788	2,880	1,600	5,000	4,415

Notes: a. Rural health centre: the best health facility available in rural areas – normally has a maternity ward and referral to a hospital.
b. Rural dispensary: the next in scale of medical facilities available – no maternity wards or other wards.
c. First-aid box: the lowest in the scale of medical facilities available – usually, medicine for headaches etc. dispensed at village shop.
Source: Field research, October 1978 and April 1979.

the woman's work history, reasons why women seek work away from their own farms, how basic needs are met and monetised within the household, and the problems and expectations of women who seek work. Most of the data presented in this study are derived from an analysis of this interview with a larger sample of women.

Employment Possibilities in the Public Sector

While community-based development projects take the form of public works schemes, famine-relief projects in Dodoma were mostly extensions of self-help projects. There are no special labour requirements laid down for obtaining food aid, which is now given regardless of the amount of work done. In most cases villagers continue to work on existing self-help projects. In two of the six villages studied, people mentioned that they had undertaken projects (in both cases, building dams) specifically in return for being provided with famine relief, but the amount of food given depended neither on the amount of work nor for that matter on the stipulated minimum food requirements per individual.

There are few wage-earning jobs available in the villages (see Table 6.3). Crop-buying agencies such as GAPEX[4] create a number of clerical jobs but only during the crop-buying season which lasts for about three months in the year. In the service sector, there are a few opportunities for earning a regular income in road maintenance (COMWORKS), teaching (mainly thanks to the implementation of Universal Primary Education), health services and local administration (wards and village secretaries). However, the recruitment for these jobs is done either at the district or regional level, which means that people who fill these posts are not necessarily from the same village. On the whole, the village economy is not geared towards the support of formal employment, but a study of individual cases could indicate the kinds of problems encountered in full-time work.

The main avenues for regular employment for women are in health and education services; as nurses, midwives, dispensary auxiliaries and primary school teachers. At this level, since training qualifies for employment, it is assumed that employment is, in a sense, 'desexed', and problems specific to female workers are seldom considered. In fact the problems for women workers in the villages are often compounded simply because the infrastructure of social and welfare services available to many women workers in the towns does not exist in the villages.

Table 6.3: Structure of Wage Employment in the Study Villages

Village	Primary school and UPE[a] teachers		Dispensary/ clinic workers		Water pump attendants		COMWORKS[b] road & transport maintenance		Veterinary field assts		Local gov – village chairman/ secretary		Total no. of families per village
	M	F	M	F	M	F	M	F	M	F	M	F	
Manzase	5	2	3	1	1	–	1	–	1	–	2	–	572
Majeleko	7	6	–	–	–	–	–	–	–	–	2	–	398
Bahi Nagulo	6	5	–	–	–	–	–	–	–	–	1	–	567
Chifutuka	4	2	2	1	1	–	–	–	1	–	1	–	420
Haneti	9	6	2	2	1	–	8	–	2	–	4	–	1,000
Handali	11	8	11	11	1	–	1	–	2	–	4	–	850

Notes: a. UPE: Universal Primary Education.
b. COMWORKS: Communication and works (mainly employees in road maintenance).
Source: Field research, October 1978 and April 1979.

Wages are low and do not provide for all needs, especially as access to training and cash incomes also raises expectations about life-styles.

Since formal employment opportunities in the villages are very limited, they do not afford much opportunity for judging work relationships between male and female colleagues. This issue was raised wherever appropriate and there does not appear to be much friction at work between male and female employees. The duties at work and wage differentials are put down to differences in training. Access to training itself may well be discriminatory for women. This requires a separate inquiry.

The Employment Situation for Most Rural Women

In the area under study, wage employment was most sought when there was the threat of famine. This period falls well into the dry season, including the next planting season (September/October and December/January) when stocks of food which are mostly meagre have run out. In the pilot study it was found that in one of the villages as many as 55 per cent of the people in the sample had tried to obtain employment during periods of food shortages. The wider survey sampled the number of women employed and the type of work they performed, summarised in Table 6.4.

Table 6.4: Number of Women in Each Village Who Sought Employment and the Types of Jobs Performed

Village	No. of women in each village who have done the types of jobs given below					Total no. of women interviewed in each village
	Farming for others	Minding children; domestic work for others	Nursing	Teaching	Total no. of women who have worked	
Manzase	11	–	–	–	11 (44%)	25
Majeleko	2	6	1	1	10 (47.6%)	21
Bahi Nagulo	–	–	–	–	1 (3.5%)	27
Chifutuka	14	2	–	–	16 (80%)	20
Haneti	8	–	–	–	8 (20%)	40
Handali	11	–	–	–	11 (26.8%)	41

Source: Field research, October 1978 and April 1979.

Farming for other people (at planting, weeding and harvesting peaks for larger farmers) is the main avenue for earning additional income for most rural women. Such work is naturally only intermittently available and income from it may assist in meeting specific needs only, such as for clothes or food at a time of famine. Often work done on other people's farms is in exchange for work done on one's own farm and involves no payment except perhaps in beer. Women who had worked as domestics for other people had usually done so in the nearby towns, probably for periods of 2-3 years.

Carrying water for residents in the larger towns or villages and making and selling charcoal are additional ways of earning income on a casual basis; length of work depends on the number of people to feed, and how much they earn. Information given at village interviews indicates that it is the adult population, regardless of sex, which normally seeks work on a casual basis only; the younger people tend to migrate permanently. Table 6.5 summarises the reasons why women work for others.

Table 6.5: Reasons Why Women Work for Others

| Village | No. of women interviewed who work for reasons given below | | | | Total no. of women interviewed in each village |
	Assisting neighbours relatives[a]	For obtaining food	Other needs clothes, school fees etc.,	Total no. of women who have worked	
Manzase	7	1	3	11 (44%)	25 (100%)
Majeleko	2	3	5	10 (47.6%)	21 (100%)
Bahi Nagulo	–	–	1	1 (3.7%)	27 (100%)
Chifutuka	8	6	2	16 (80%)	20 (100%)
Haneti	–	6	2	8 (20%)	40 (100%)
Handali	1	6	4	11 (24%)	41 (100%)

Note: a. Normally without payment.
Source: Field research, October 1978 and April 1979.

The period of food scarcity tends to coincide with the time for clearing the farm and planting, and therefore famine-relief supplies are nomally provided at around this time. However, the provision of famine-relief can be as sporadic as the food shortages. This may result from the lack of transport to carry food to the village, or lack of information, and many people are forced to look for work elsewhere in order to get food at a time which is crucial for work on their own farms. Often the practice is for the male (head of household) to go away in search of work, while the women stay and work on the land; occasionally instances are found of the partners taking it in turns to find employment. Women do a substantial part of the clearing and preparation of the land for planting, which is traditionally the responsibility of men.

Fewer women can go away to seek work, even during famine, simply because they have children to look after. Women in full-time wage employment in the villages (nurses or midwives) reiterated the problem of the care of children while they are at work. Their hours of work can be unusually long and irregular, and children have to be left in the care of housegirls or older children. The children can be the source of persistent anxiety particularly when they are sick, and women then are often forced to be absent from work. Thus the problem of child-care is the key to women's involvement in productive wage employment.

Self-help projects also draw upon a considerable amount of women's labour. Most of the work on self-help projects, for example building classrooms, teachers' houses and dispensaries, is done during the dry season between July and October. Since much of this work involves brick-making, the dry season is suitable for drying bricks, but water for brick-making poses a problem where there is no piped water, especially in this season when wells and rivers run dry. Fetching water during the dry season involves longer journeys: for women this adds to the normal burden of providing water for domestic needs. However, one of the few instances of men carrying water is when it is needed for such communal projects.

Both men and women participate equally on these projects – work rotas are often organised on a 'street-to-street' basis, each *balozi* (ten-cells leader) being responsible for making available a given number of workers. There is considerable social pressure on people to turn up for work; in fact, in most of the villages fines are imposed by the village committees for failure to do so. These fines can often amount from 5Tz sh. up to 40Tz sh. (approximately US 66 cents up to US $5), depending on how frequently absenteeism occurs.

In an impromptu interview with a group of women at the site of a self-help project (the building of a clinic) in one of the villages, the women were asked whether the need to attend to such communal activity caused additional problems in getting all their other household and farm chores done. The reply was invariably in the affirmative, and one of them commented, 'We have to face these problems every day; I shall have to hurry a little more today.' Women who do not have anyone to look after their babies turn up for work with the babies on their backs. Others may leave them in the care of grandmothers or daughters who can be girls as young as six to ten years-old (Mascarenhas, 1977).

How Basic Needs are Met and Monetised Within the Household

Most rural women operate only at the fringe of whatever monetary economy exists in the village. Their primary responsibility for providing subsistence for the family limits their access to the cash economy and, in turn, to cash incomes within the household. Small amounts of income can be earned only sporadically, as already described.

Since the expansion of employment opportunities for rural women is designed to give women direct and independent access to the returns on their labour, it is important to see how some basic needs are met now. All women interviewed were asked how they obtained money for various purposes and the main responses are summarised in Table 6.6. Women play a relatively significant part in providing necessities, besides food, in the household (see Table 6.7). Men's dominance shows in their greater control of cash resources of the household. Many of the items listed in Table 6.7 are often obtained from the sale of cattle over which men normally have complete control.

Employment and Wage Expectations, and Institutional Support

In the village interview, people were asked about the need for opportunities for employment, the facilities which could provide wage-earning opportunities and the appropriate level of wages.

There were some basic differences in the aspirations for employment between the adults and the younger people, especially between the adults and young men. The adults seemed more certain that farming would remain their main occupation and that extra wage-earning opportunities could be made available when there was a slack period in farming, and during times of famine. The younger people understood employment opportunities to be available or necessary, permanently rather than casually, paying a regular wage every month, though they seemed to be less certain about exactly what kinds of jobs they could do.

There were differences of opinion between men and women about

Table 6.6: How Women Obtain Money for Their Own and Household Requirements

How money is obtained by women	Manzase	Majeleko	Bahi Nagulo	Chifutuka	Haneti	Handali
From husband and/or nearest male kin	21 (84%)	3 (14%)	7 (26%)	5 (21%)	28 (70%)	6 (15%)
Casual work on other farms	2 (8%)	10 (47%)	–	–	–	–
Making baskets, cloth caps	–	–	18 (67%)	–	1 (2.5%)	3 (7%)
Selling milk, ghee (butter-fat)	1 (4%)	1 (4.7%)	–	1 (2.7%)	1 (2.5%)	2 (5%)
Preparing and selling local beer	1 (4%)	–	2 (7%)	3 (12%)	2 (5%)	1 (2%)
Selling crops grown by herself	–	6 (28%)	–	6 (21%)	2 (5%)	3 (7%)
Selling poultry	–	1 (4.7%)	–	–	–	10 (24%)
Selling charcoal and firewood	–	–	–	–	–	6 (15%)
Selling livestock	–	–	–	2 (9%)	1 (2.5%)	–
Petty trading	–	–	–	4 (17%)	4 (10%)	6 (15%)
Total no. of women interviewed per village	25 (100%)	21 (100%)	27 (100%)	24	40 (97.5%)	41 (100%)

Source: Field research, October 1978 and April 1979.

Table 6.7: Summary of Responses in each Village Indicating Who Meets Basic Needs in the Household

Items provided	Manzase			Majeleko				Bahi Nagulo			Chifutuka			Haneti			Handali			
	F[a]	M[b]	Total	F	M	S/D[c]	Total	F	M	Total	F	M	Total	F	M	Total	F	M	S/D	Total
Meat and fish	1	25	25	15	20	2	21	13	27	27	19	19	20	19	38	40	16	35	1	41
Women's clothes	1	25	25	13	18	1	21	13	27	27	19	20	20	20	40	40	16	35	1	41
Children's clothes	2	24	25	9	18	2	21	15	27	27	7	20	20	18	39	40	16	36	1	41
School contribution	2	19	25	8	13	1	21	10	26	27	2	20	20	4	37	40	13	34	–	41
Seed	12	21	25	17	19	–	21	17	27	27	1	20	20	8	40	40	22	27	1	41
Fertiliser	–	–	25	–	–	–	21	1	–	27	–	–	20	–	5	40	1	–	–	41
Hiring tractor	–	–	25	–	–	–	21	–	1	27	–	–	20	–	–	40	–	–	–	41
Hiring labourers	1	20	25	12	11	–	21	1	13	27	15	20	20	–	17	40	8	16	–	41

Notes: a. F = Female; b. M = Male or nearest male kin; c. S/D = Sons and/or Daughters of women; d. Total = Total in each case of both men and women, out of the total number of interviews held, as shown in the column.
Source: Field research, October 1978 and April 1979.

the facilities needed: men generally suggested the provision of carpentry
and masonry workshops and women seemed to have a preference for
sewing work, crafts and weaving, and nursing. In one of the villages it
was said that women needed special consideration in the formulation of
employment schemes and the funds for such schemes should be separately administered by women's organisations such as the *Umoja wa
Wanawake wa Tanzania* (UWT, the national women's organisation). In
individual interviews, women were asked what kind of employment-
generating projects they would like in the village. Their answers are
shown in Table 6.8.

Table 6.8: Preference by Women for Types of Projects

Types of projects desired by women	Manzase	Majeleko	Bahi Nagulo	Chifutuka	Haneti	Handali
Agricultural expanding communal farm	10	–	1	4	4	5
Small-scale industries	–	–	–	–	19	4
Keeping livestock, poultry, fish-ponds	–	–	–	3	4	2
Provision of flour mills	15	10	18	–	–	–
Local breweries	–	–	1	1	–	1
Dairies	–	–	–	1	8	–
Sewing/Tailoring workshops	–	2	3	3	3	10
Brick-making	–	–	–	1	–	–
Handcraft/ basketry/pottery	–	10	2	3	–	–
Co-operative shops and hotels	–	–	–	3	1	7
Total no. of interviews	25	21	27	20	40	41

Source: Field research, October 1978 and April 1979.

It is interesting to see how women perceive their own needs and
capabilities. If the inventory shown in Table 6.2 is compared with
Table 6.8, three things emerge:
(i) The women were mainly concerned with labour-saving devices such
as the provision of flour-milling facilities.
(ii) The women in most of these fairly basic villages assumed that the
only way of earning more money was to increase their agricultural
labour on communal farms, and, further, that they would then derive

an independent income from this work.

(iii) In contrast to (ii), the majority of women in Haneti showed a desire for 'small-scale industries'; Haneti is a fairly large village, which is acquiring the characteristics of a rural trading centre.

The availability of labour for employment-generating programmes will depend also on whether the wage offered is considered adequate for the jobs. The criteria used in selecting 'minimum' wages, for example the minimum for subsistence, are sensitive issues in urban areas, where labour is both organised and differentiated. In rural areas, labour is less organised and agricultural work is varied; for instance, people's own estimation of the worth of their labour is unclear, partly because they have only intermittent supplies of cash. Also, what is 'adequate' for one person with fewer family responsibilities may not be adequate for another with perhaps a larger family. There was often prolonged debate about what woud be regarded as an adequate wage for the kinds of job they would choose to do. Usually the consensus was that 380 Tz sh. per month (the national minimum wage at present) was enough for their needs. In some cases 500 Tz sh. per month was mentioned. In contrast, some women who were interviewed individually doubted whether even 500 Tz sh. was enough to feed and clothe a family with many children, without any other means of income or food and cattle. Perhaps men assume and discount the cost of subsistence, including most of the food and all the domestic services provided by the women, and regard the wage as being exclusively for spending on needs other than subsistence.

All the villages have a branch of *Chama Cha Mapinduzi* (CCM, the National Party), though not many have a UWT network. One of the main tasks of both organisations is to mobilise people for development. In response to a question, most women said these organisations did not help in finding employment. Only in two villages did more than two women answer 'yes' to this question: four out of 20 in Chifutuka and 13 out of 40 in Haneti. These institutions assisted mostly by providing an identity through the membership card.

Employment and the Pressure to Move

The nature of growth in the rural areas is circular. Low incomes mean a smaller tax-base on which to levy taxes to finance infrastructural services; inadequate facilities slow down the rate of development which then keeps incomes low. Individuals may try to break out of this vicious cycle by migrating to urban areas to seek employment. In underdeveloped economies such as Tanzania's, urban areas can often not cope with the demands for work and social facilities of large numbers of people from rural areas; which then shifts the burden of unemployment on to the urban areas. The rationale behind providing employment in rural areas is often to reduce migration from the rural areas, rather than to improve the quality of life in the rural areas.

In the village meetings a discussion of the motives behind moving to seek work revealed some of the attitudes which intimidate peasant women from attempting to migrate. For example, whenever the issue of the migration of young people to towns came up in the conversation, it was said that young boys normally sought their parents' permission wher departing to look for work, but that the girls did not. It was clear that they were not likely to get the blessings of their parents because it was always assumed that they would be 'up to no good'. Only in one instance was it mentioned that boys who remain unemployed in towns are just as likely to start pilfering and thieving as girls are to drift into prostitution.

It was pointed out by most villages that married women usually constituted the largest number of migrants from the villages. This is the case in many other parts of rural Africa, especially those where the conditions of life are severe, subject to frequent famine, with shortages of land and so on. It appeared that in Dodoma, children were often left behind in the villages because the women who left usually did not know when they would find a job or whether they would come back. In fact, there has been a growing tendency amongst the women in the villages to migrate in search of wage work over the last ten years, as shown in Table 6.9. For the most part this results from the failure of the domestic economy to provide for basic needs such as food and clothes.

The most heated debate on the motives of men versus the women in migrating took place in Chifutuka, one of the villages more severely affected by famine. Men insisted that married women left for towns because they desired easy lives for themselves which they hoped to get by acquiring wealthy boyfriends in the towns. The men, it seemed, thought it quite reasonable for a man to try for an easier life for himself but wrong for women to do so. The women at this meeting, who were unusually vocal, denied that it was merely the desire for an easy life or any predisposition towards prostitution which caused them to leave. Rather it was the failure of their husbands to provide even essential needs such as adequate food and clothing which forced them to go and find these for themselves, for example by entering domestic service.

Table 6.9: Reasons Why Women Migrate to Seek Wage Employment

Village	Responses to question on whether each woman (interviewed) thinks there are more women leaving to seek work – no. of women in each village answering 'yes'							No. of women answering 'no'	No. of women interviewed
	Total ans. 'yes'	No employ-ment available in village	Prostitutes	To earn money for needs e.g., cloth, food	Husbands failed to provide	Did not like agri-cultural work	Educated women		
Manzase	2	–	–	2	–	–	–	23	25
Majeleko	20	–	3	17	–	–	–	1	21
Bahi Nagulo	21	–	4	3	10	1	5	2	27
Chifutuka	15	–	3	1	12	–	–	5	20
Haneti	23	–	–	19	–	–	–	19	40
Handali	4	3	–	1	–	–	–	18	41

Source: Field research, October 1978 and April 1979.

They said that despite their work on the farms, often their only means of having money at their own disposal was through wage work elsewhere.

It seemed from such meetings that while men who migrate are regarded as being daring and ambitious, and making a rational economic choice in leaving a harsh, unproductive environment, women who do so are resented. The reverse process — that of coming back to the village if they fail to make a living elsewhere — can be more difficult for women migrants, who seem to be subjected to some mockery about their 'failure'. It was not surprising therefore, that villagers said fewer women came back to their own village.

For rural women, therefore, migration may not be just a case of the 'Dick Whittington' syndrome; it is often a matter of economic survival. From a woman's point of view, too, wage employment is a rational choice. It provides direct access to the returns on her labour, whereas this can go unremunerated in the farm and home; and it frees her from the unrewarded drudgery of such work. Many changes are implicit in this freedom: changes in cultural norms, social relationships and so on; and the pros and cons of these changes need careful examination.

Conclusion

The nature of peasant labour is such that it does not easily lend itself to analysis according to yardsticks of employment, unemployment and under-employment which are applied to 'formally' employed urban labour. This is especially so for peasant women's labour, whose variable and overlapping farm and household tasks cannot be compressed into rigid definitions set by planners. It is therefore often discarded as unproductive, inadequately employed labour.

Thus there is a split on the employment issue at two levels: in the differences between the rural/urban sectors; and in the sexual differentiation in the use of labour within the rural sector. It is essential to view any project which has an impact on the development of labour in the rural areas on a sex-differentiated basis. Some of the conceptual difficulties in analysing and quantifying women's labour arise from the tendency to regard their availability for domestic labour in the household as a discrete quantity independent of all other activites. The problem is that while most of rural women's labour is applied to household production, their involvement in development schemes, such as additional income-generating projects, focuses only on their supposed independent activities and assumes that their household activities are unproductive.

When monetary factors are used in defining employment, they lead to the exclusion of women's labour especially because of the role imposed on it historically in providing subsistence. Women in many rural societies, such as Tanzania, are responsible for the production of food for subsistence besides being responsible for all other domestic work; meanwhile men manage and control the cash economy.[5]

The many assumptions are the crux of the problem in quantifying the labour of women. A beginning must be made by recognising that a rural woman's workday constitutes full (or even overfull) employment and that this often involves a sheer waste of human resources, such as long journeys to fetch water, pounding grain by hand, cultivating with outmoded, inefficient implements and so on. The division of labour by sex becomes woven into a social and cultural matrix which makes it difficult to solve any of the problems (or constraints in generating employment) by providing each with a separate solution. If this could be done, then it would be enough to provide technical solutions such as piped water supplies, milling facilities and access to agricultural innovations, which would reduce the treadmill of house and farm work for women and 'free' this labour. The reality is often different: it has been shown that 'employment' issues interchange with other issues, such as the factors which condition access to income and its distribution within the household, changing patterns in job-seeking and expectations, and migration from the rural areas.

The most important factor in shaping policy for the expansion of employment possibilities for rural women is to cease relegating their labour as unaccountable work in the subsistence sector and to begin treating it as a human labour cost in the monetary and production sector. One way being considered for involving rural women in more productive wage-earning jobs is to expand employment opportunities in the public sector. What are the wider ramifications of such programmes? Would they really alter the status of rural women for the better *vis-à-vis* their role in household production? How much employment for whom and for how long should there be? Would such employment disrupt the existing balance in the food economy and, especially, can it trigger the kind of development which will generate and sustain wage-employment opportunities without continuous external aid?

Notes

1. The Arusha Declaration was a major policy directive issued in February 1967, which articulated the type of socialist society envisaged by the Party and the government. The crucial role of agriculture as the basis for development was underlined and *ujamaa* (socialistic living) became the key strategy in the transformation of rural Tanzania.

2. Villagisation: this programme, carried out over a spell of 2-3 years from 1974, attempted the creation of *ujamaa* villages and the resettlement of people from scattered settlements into nuclear villages in order to facilitate the provision of basic services — health, education, transport etc.

3. COMWORKS: Communication and Works, responsible in this case for most of the road maintenance.

4. GAPEX: a state agency, General Agricultural Products Exports, which is the main marketing agency for certain crops such as groundnuts and oilseeds.

5. This has been better described in Boserup (1970).

Bibliography

Boserup, E. (1970) *Woman's Role in Economic Development*, Allen & Unwin, London
Mascarenhas, A.C. (1977) 'Participation of children in social economic activities: The case of Rukwa Region', BRALUP Research Report (Restricted), no. 10, 1 (January)

7 DEMOGRAPHY, POLITICAL REFORM AND WOMEN'S ISSUES IN CZECHOSLOVAKIA

Sharon L. Wolchik

Women's dual roles as workers and mothers have been the subject of a good deal of debate in the Soviet Union and many of the East European countries in recent years. Occasioned in large part by concern over declining birth rates, this debate has focused on the conflicting policy implications of viewing women as primarily economic or primarily reproductive resources. In certain countries, this discussion has led to a re-examination of policy towards women and to a shift in emphasis from women's economic to women's child-bearing potential.

In Czechoslovakia, this process was conditioned by an additional element, the political reform movement which occurred in the 1960s. In this context, debate over the reproductive and economic roles of women soon went beyond the issues which demographers raised to include a basic re-evaluation of the status of women under socialism. The pages which follow examine this process, with the aim of illustrating how this shift in emphasis occurred, the main poles of the debate, and the probable implications of its outcome from the perspective of policy-makers and women.

In order to understand the debate about women's roles which came into the open in Czechoslovakia in the mid-1960s, it is necessary to look briefly at the policy of the elite towards women prior to that time. As in other socialist states, such policy has been determined largely by the relationship between change in women's position and other, higher-priority goals of the elite.[1] In the early post-World War II period, Czech and Slovak elites emphasised women's role as economic producers. The need to mobilise all available labour reserves coincided nicely with the emphasis Marxist writings attached to work outside the home as a precondition for women's emancipation, and the elites used numerous moral and financial incentives to encourage women to enter the labour force. They also urged women to improve their skills and take an active part in political leadership, but little concrete effort was given to overcoming obstacles to greater female activism and advancement. Similarly, although the importance of women's roles as mothers and homemakers was formally recognised, this recognition was not accompanied by measures to facilitate women's performance of these roles or a redistribution of labour within the home.

In the immediate post-World War II years, political leaders sometimes discussed the problems which this assimilationist strategy of sex-role change created for women and called on women to organise to build communal facilities, and to take other steps to alleviate some of these problems. Increasingly, however, women's problems and the conflict between women's various roles were simply ignored. Emulating Soviet practice, Czech and Slovak leaders proclaimed that the institution of a socialist system had solved the basic problems connected with female equality, and discussion of women's issues ceased. In 1952 the women's organisation was disbanded and women became a political 'non-issue'. Women's issues came to be recognised as legitimate topics of political discussion again only in the mid-1960s, when the demographic situation and the reform period brought about a reconsideration of women's actual position in Czech and Slovak society.

Demography and Women's Issues

The original stimulus for a more realistic assessment of women's position under socialism in Czechoslovakia came about as the result of the decline in the birth rate, which began in the mid-1950s. This decline persisted, with slight variations, from 1953 to the late 1960s and occurred despite a sizeable decline in the mortality rate, particularly among newborns.[2] Live births and the natural increase per 1,000 population remained somewhat higher in Slovakia than in the Czech lands, although Slovakia also experienced a decline in both indicators of population growth.

To a certain extent, this decrease parallels that which has occurred in many Western and particularly highly industrialised societies as they have become more developed. However, the decline in the birth rate in Czechoslovakia, as in other socialist countries, has been considerably greater than their level of economic development alone would suggest and reflects the additional impact of several factors peculiar to the region, including the high employment rates of women in the productive ages, severe housing shortages and insufficient child-care and service facilities.[3]

The liberal abortion laws introduced in the mid-1950s have also contributed to the decline in the birth rate. Originally sanctioned as a mechanism to control the population boom anticipated after World War

II, abortion has served as the main means of birth control in many East European countries.[4] The impact of easy access to legal abortion on the birth rate is evident in the ratio of abortions to live births. In Czechoslovakia, this ratio increased from 27.3 per 1,000 live births in 1958, after the liberalisation of abortion laws in 1957, to 57.7 per 1,000 live births in 1967.[5]

The consequences of such low rates of reproduction include those normally associated with a low birth rate, such as ageing of the population and the reduction of the future labour force. The latter possibility has been particularly disturbing to the elites in Czechoslovakia, where there is already a labour shortage.[6] The decline in the birth rate also raised the possibility of upsetting the ethnic balance in Czechoslovakia, for the Slovaks, like the Central Asians in the Soviet Union, continued to reproduce at a somewhat faster rate than the more numerous Czechs.[7]

Early analysis of the causes of the falling birth rate was hampered by the state of demography in Czechoslovakia in the 1950s, and by the widely accepted notion that socialism should be accompanied by spontaneous population growth. This expectation, derived from Marx's analysis of the factors limiting population growth under capitalism, led to the view that the elimination of exploitation and the establishment of a socialist system, with guaranteed work and social security, would be reflected in population growth. Analysts of the population issue in the immediate postwar period therefore emphasised the newly beneficial conditions for families in the new state and urged citizens to fulfil their roles in reproducing the future labour force. The fact that the population was not growing as rapidly as expected was attributed to the continued impact of the poor demographic situation of the interwar period and to the effects of war on the child-bearing population.[8]

The continued decline in the birth rate after 1953, coupled with the change in the political climate after the XXth Congress of the Communist Party of the Soviet Union, led to the establishment of a state commission to deal with population issues and to the first empirical investigation of the causes of the decrease. The earliest of these studies were designed to investigate the factors which influenced population growth and the impact of various population measures.

Although the studies differed to some degree in the focus of their investigations, as well as in the nature of samples used, several common conclusions emerged. First, the number of desired and actual children was influenced by the economic activity of women; employed women at all educational levels were found to plan and have fewer children than those women who remained at home.[9] Secondly, the financial burdens created for families, housing difficulties and problems in finding child-care for the children of employed mothers were identified as the main impediments to increasing the birth rate. These factors, which were most often listed as reasons why couples were unwilling to have additional children, also figured prominently among reasons women gave for seeking abortions.[10]

The connection between women's roles and the demographic problem soon became evident, and early studies of factors which influenced population development were supplemented by others which dealt more specifically with employed women, and their roles as mothers and workers. One of the earliest of these was a study of time-use by employed women conducted in 1959-60. Based on interviews with 80 randomly selected women between the ages of 18 and 44 in a Prague factory, the study illustrated women's continued responsibility for the care of home and children, and foreshadowed the results of more systematic time-budget studies in the late 1960s. The authors noted the disparity between progressive views concerning the use of time and the need for leisure, and women's actual situation, and concluded that stronger efforts should be made to decrease the amount of time spent on housework (Ulrych and Wynnyczuk, 1967, pp. 232-3).

Similar conclusions were reached by one of the most complete of these early studies, an investigation of women's roles conducted in 1962. Based on a representative nationwide sample of 7,955 married women, this study concluded that women's employment outside the home had not been accompanied by a redefinition of roles within the home or by a move away from traditional family structures. Although the husbands of employed women helped in the care of children and housework to a greater extent than did those of women who remained at home, differences between the two categories were minimal, and women retained major responsibility for the care of home and children irrespective of their employment status. The study reconfirmed the role of insufficient child-care facilities in women's decision to remain at home with their children and noted that society had not yet succeeded in creating conditions which would allow women to fulfil their maternal and economic functions without physical and emotional stress. The author linked this situation in turn to the unfavourable population climate and the declining birth rate.[11]

In sum, the early studies illustrated some of the unintended consequences of earlier policies towards women. Scholars found that changes in women's economic activity had not been accompanied by changes in their roles within the home. They also documented the difficulties women encountered in attempting to fulfil their multiple economic and maternal responsibilities without adequate services or child-care facilities, and pointed out the negative implications of these difficulties for the demographic situation as well as for women themselves. The results of these studies, which challenged the prevailing notion that socialism had fundamentally solved the problems of women, were not widely disseminated until the late 1960s. However, they did form the basis for a reconsideration of women's position and a reopening of debate among the elite about women's various roles.

Political Reform: The Renewal of Theoretical Activity and the Women's Organisation

The reopening of discussion concerning women's issues was given added impetus by the revival of the women's organisation. This revival was in turn influenced by new theoretical perspectives on the nature of socialist society and the roles of social groups which were articulated by party intellectuals and social scientists in the mid-1960s. Challenging the prevailing view of social relations under socialism as basically harmonious, certain intellectuals argued that organisations to represent the interests of particular social groups should be recognised as legitimate parts of socialist society.[12] Leaders of the women's movement used these formulations, which culminated in the reform period, to articulate a new approach to women's problems, and, eventually, to establish an organisation to defend women's interests *vis-à-vis* the party and government.

The renewal process in the women's movement actually predated the re-creation of a mass women's organisation and went through several distinct phases. The first of these took place primarily at the elite level and, as in other segments of the population,[13] was led by party intellectuals. Members of the Women's Committee, the commission of prominent women whose main task was to represent Czech and Slovak women at international gatherings, played a particularly important role in this process. Lacking any organisational links to the women's commissions at the local level, certain members of the committee used the mass women's magazines as a forum to raise previously undiscussed issues. First evident in 1964, this changed orientation was reflected in articles in the women's magazines which emphasised women's problems and called for changes in the activities of the women's commissions, as well as a more realistic discussion of women's issues.[14]

The activities of the Women's Committee also began to change during this period. Contrary to past practice, representatives of the committee met government officials to discuss women's needs and grievances. The changing orientation of the committee was evident in the annual meeting of women with representatives of the government on International Women's Day in 1964. In contrast to past years, when this meeting had a largely symbolic character, members of the committee used the occasion to raise a number of unresolved issues which concerned women.[15]

The work of the Women's Committee in 1964 was also characterised by another new feature, an emphasis on a scientific approach to women's issues. This approach, which became more pronounced in the next few years, was evident in effort to use the findings of sociologists and demographers to support women's claims, and in joint discussions and seminars organised in conjunction with members of the State Population Commission and other research groups.

One of the more important of these joint efforts by leaders of the Women's Committee and social scientists was a 1965 seminar organised by the State Population Commission, the Society for the Dissemination of Scientific Information and the Women's Committee. Speakers at this conference criticised previous policy towards women and called for additional investigation of women's actual, rather than legal, position. They also suggested that the local women's commissions pay more attention to working to improve women's position than to carrying out tasks set by the local government. Other issues raised included problems arising from women's low skill levels, unresolved difficulties with services and child-care, and conflicts in women's maternal and economic roles.[16]

This conference was followed by additional studies of women's roles by demographers and sociologists, and increased attention to women's issues in the daily press, specialised journals and women's magazines. Additional seminars were organised to discuss other issues in co-operation with specialists, such as women's lack of leisure time, the placement of 15-year-old girls who had finished compulsory schooling, problems of women working in agriculture and the division of labour within the home.[17]

Leaders of the Women's Committee also took part in the increasingly open debate concerning previously ignored aspects of women's position in socialist society. In the more open political conditions which existed in Czechoslovakia in the mid-1960s, social scientists and women intellectuals discussed the policy implications of the uneven pattern of change in women's roles; they also discussed the consequences of this pattern of change for women. These debates, which illustrated the conflict between women's domestic and economic roles, centred on three related issues.

First, the previous emphasis on women's role as economic producers was criticised for its negative effects on population. Demographers noted the inverse relationship between women's economic activity and number of children, and called for a re-evaluation of the social significance of women's maternal role.[18] Although all parties in the debate took care to note that women's right to work should be respected, certain demographers argued that ways should be found to decrease the high economic activity rates of women in the prime child-bearing years. An article by Milan Kučera in the journal of the State Population Commission provides a good illustration of this position. Arguing that the high employment rates of women led to a 'division of functions among women', that is between those who were employed and those who remained at home, Kučera suggested that the higher reproductive rates of women at home indicated that their social significance was greater than previously recognised. Given the importance of these women in ensuring the reproduction of the population, Kučera argued that they should be rewarded financially for this service. Because all women had the right to work, he continued, the solution to the demographic problem could not lie in sending all young women with children back to the home. None the less, the author concluded his article by suggesting that only women over the age of 30 be encouraged to enter the labour force in the future and that incentives be used to encourage women between the ages of 20 and 30 to leave the labour force.[19] Social scientists, policy-makers and leaders of the women's organisations also discussed other means of encouraging population growth and argued over the potential impact of different measures, such as restricting the grounds for abortion or increasing material incentives for having more children.[20]

The debate over the reproductive consequences of high rates of employment for women in the productive years was linked to discussions concerning the economic utility of women's employment. In connection with attempts to redirect the economy from an extensive to intensive strategy of economic development, certain economists questioned the economic benefit of employing women with small children. Using studies of the value of women's work and the social costs for public care of children, they argued that it would be more efficient, from an economic as well as reproductive viewpoint, to support women to care for their small children at home than to expand the existing network of child-care facilities. Such a solution was held to be particularly rational in the case of unskilled or semi-skilled women with young children.[21]

At the other pole of this debate, members of the Women's Committee, as well as certain demographers and economists, argued that the costs of providing nursery care for small children benefited not only women, but society as a whole. Relying on the importance Marxist ideology attaches to female employment, these women and other specialists called instead for a more rapid expansion of child-care facilities in order to allow women with small children to return to work more quickly. Representatives of this position agreed that greater recognition of women's maternal role would be beneficial, but called on government officials to take measures to allow women who chose to work to fulfil both roles more successfully (Prokopec and Wynnyczuk, 1965; Kont'sekova, 1968). This aspect of the debate, which presaged that which was to occur in the Soviet Union,[22] was reflected in the popular press and resulted in the expression of considerable discontent, by both men and women, with the consequences of women's employment.[23]

Finally, certain intellectuals criticised previous strategy towards women because of its negative effect on women themselves and called for the elaboration of a more appropriate theoretical analysis of women's position. Pointing to studies illustrating the 'dual burden' of women, and the negative impact of household and domestic responsibilities on women's political activism and professional advancement, they argued that earlier approaches to women's issues were inadequate and called for new solutions. These calls were repeated throughout the mid-1960s and were given added impetus by a 1966 statewide conference of women, which proposed the formation of a women's organisation with a mass base to deal with women's issues.[24]

The Central Committee of the Communist Party approved this proposal in 1966. The new women's organisation, which adopted the name of the pre-1952 women's organisation, the Union of Czechoslovak Women (*Československý svaz žen* (ČSŽ)), at first worked through the women's commissions of the local governments. In 1967 these commissions were dissolved, and the union began establishing its own local units.[25] With this step, efforts to improve women's position moved beyond the informal coalition of specialist elites and intellectuals considered most typical of interest-group activity in communist

societies (Skilling and Griffiths, 1973, pp. 335-77), and assumed more of
a mass character. Whereas earlier efforts to promote re-examination of
policy towards women had occurred almost exclusively at the elite
level, leaders of the new women's organisation now sought to involve
broader groups of women.

The work of the new organisation concentrated on several tasks in
1967 and 1968. The leaders worked, first of all, to strengthen the organisation's mass base and reorient the work of the local and district-level
groups. Hampered by the past history of the women's commissions as
well as by the lack of involvement on the part of citizens in the political
process in the pre-reform period, they none the less succeeded in
establishing 8,500 local groups by May 1967.[26] Public opinion surveys
indicate that there was widespread support, particularly among women,
for an organisation to defend women's interests, but this support was
often not translated into active membership. Membership continued to
increase, but efforts to reach broader groups of women remained an
important part of the organisation's work throughout the reform
period.

Leaders of the women's organisation also sought to change the style
of operation of the ČSŽ. Criticising the mobilising functions of the
women's commissions of the local government, they identified work to
improve women's position as the main task of the new organisation.[27]
As in their efforts to increase membership, they had to fight the legacy
of the past when the women's commissions served chiefly to mobilise
women to participate in demonstrations of support for the regime and
take part in voluntary labour brigades. In an effort to increase the
ČSŽ's legitimacy as a representative of women's interests, they urged
members to make their views known to local and central officials, held
numerous discussions of particular issues and commissioned public
opinion polls of members on various topics.

The new approach was accompanied by efforts to develop new
theoretical perspectives on women's situation and define the nature of
women as a social group. Women intellectuals argued that although
different groups of women had many divergent interests, depending on
their age, marital status and education, they were united by their reproductive role, which created certain common problems for their fulfilment in other activities.[28] On the basis of this analysis, women's
leaders called for both a recognition of the different needs of particular
groups of women and action on problems common to most women as
the result of the difficulty of combining maternal and other roles.

Leaders of the ČSŽ also worked to upgrade the authority of the

organisation with state and party officials. Stressing the ČSŽ's orientation as an interest group to defend women's interests, ČSŽ representatives met government officials to discuss women's issues and press for
action to benefit women. The relationship between leaders of the ČSŽ
and the reform leaders, as well as the work of the organisation itself,
was to some extent characterised by a reaction to the difficulties of the
past. Leaders of the ČSŽ expressed support for the reform effort and
saw the continuation of reform as the precondition for the successful
work of their organisation. At the same time, however, they expressed
a certain distrust at assurances by the reform leaders and emphasised
the need for women to continue to take an active part in defending
their own interests.[29]

The activities of the ČSŽ, like those of other social organisations,
changed considerably after the Warsaw Pact intervention in Czechoslovakia in August 1968. Members of the ČSŽ continued to support
the reform process and also to defend women's interests through the
first months of 1969, but the process of consolidation eventually
affected the ČSŽ as well. In November 1969, most of the leaders of
the ČSŽ were removed from office, and the work of the organisation
once again redirected along more conventional lines. The new officials
explicitly renounced the ČSŽ's role as an interest group,[30] and its
activities currently centre on tasks more typical of mass organisations
in communist states, such as political education and mobilising women
for voluntary labour.

Traces of the efforts of women's leaders during the reform years
remain in the work of the women's organisation. The ČSSŽ[31] has not
been disbanded, nor has there been a reversion to the silence of the
1950s concerning women's problems. Official statements concerning
women's position under socialism, while far less critical than during
the reform period, are informed by a more realistic appraisal of
women's actual situation. Leaders of the ČSSŽ, for example, emphasise
the need to approach women's issues in the correct Marxist-Leninist
spirit and often point out the benefits women have received under
socialism. However they admit that certain difficulties remain in the
practical achievement of female equality.[32]

A further characteristic of the work of the women's organisation
in the mid- to late 1960s still evident is the emphasis on a scientific
approach to women's issues. This is particularly the case in Slovakia,
where the women's organisation hired a sociologist in 1973 to direct a
number of studies on women's issues. Proposals made to government
bodies on the basis of these studies have sometimes been adopted, and

it appears that certain leaders of the organisation still have the opportunity to advocate women's interests.[33]

These efforts, in contrast to the reform period, appear to occur solely at the central or elite level. They are also based on different premisses, that is, on scientific expertise rather than on mass action or support by the members of the women's organisation. Individual members of local organisations appear to have little opportunity to take part in the formulation of the organisation's positions, but instead are informed in the mass magazines of measures adopted on their behalf by the government and party.

The end of the reform period has had similarly mixed results for the consideration by the elite of women's issues. Party leaders have emphasised the need to rely on the standard Marxist analysis of women's position and frequently call on women to demonstrate their commitment to socialism by renewed work for the benefit of society as a whole. However, other elements of the discussion of the 1960s have been incorporated into official analyses of women and specific policy measures. Thus, party officials once again acknowledge that certain problems still remain unsolved and note the need to create appropriate conditions for women's fulfilment in socialist society. Party resolutions which promise to improve services for employed women and work to overcome outlived views on women's roles[34] have been accompanied by certain measures to benefit women. The renewed discussion of women's conflicting roles has also been reflected in a reorientation of policy towards women.

Policy Measures and Their Implications

As the result of the debates of the 1960s and a continued decline in the birth rate, the focus of elite policy towards women has changed. In the past decade, such policy has given far more emphasis to women's reproductive than to women's economic role. For the most part, the measures which have been adopted to aid women are those which will also improve the demographic situation.

Beginning in the mid-1960s, Czech and Slovak political elites have enacted a number of pro-natalist policies. These measures include positive incentives to increase the population and to restrict abortion. The political leaders have adopted many of the measures advocated by Czech and Slovak demographers. These include laws to improve the financial situation of young families, to increase children's allowances and to grant tax benefits for families with children.[35] In addition, maternity benefits have been increased and extended to broader groups of women. In 1970, the National Assembly introduced maternity allowances for women who chose to remain at home to care for children up to two years of age. This provision now applies to women who were not employed before the birth of their children as well as to those who were economically active.[36]

The impact of these measures, in conjunction with certain restrictions on the grounds for abortion enacted in 1968, led to a slight increase in the birth rate in the early 1970s. However, this increase was still below the desired rate of 18.1 live births per 1,000 population, and in 1973 Czech and Slovak leaders enacted a law restricting abortions for all but health reasons.[37]

The slow but steady increase in the birth rate since that time indicates that pro-natalist policies are achieving certain desired results. While several of these measures, particularly the maternity allowances, undoubtedly have been beneficial for certain groups of women, their impact is problematic for female equality. Present leaders reaffirm women's right to work and public expression of views against women's employment is not tolerated. In practical terms, however, the policies adopted have emphasised women's maternal role at the expense of all others. Despite the reaffirmation of women's right to work, the elites have opted for a solution which minimises public expenditure for childcare and, in practice, removes large numbers of young women from the labour force for substantial periods of time.

As studies of women in other cultures illustrate, child-bearing not only entails material costs for women from loss of wages and the increased expenses of additional children, but also impairs women's professional advancement (Bernard, 1971, pp. 181-2). Czech and Slovak leaders have called for greater attention to removing the barriers which prevent women from utilising their qualifications and from taking a more active role in economic and political leadership, they have also discussed measures which would counteract the potentially negative professional consequences, including loss of expertise, for women who do remain at home for the full two years after the birth of each child. Very little effort has gone into actually putting such measures into practice, however.

The current solution also carries the danger that it will reinforce traditional views of women's responsibility for the care of the home and children. Emphasis on women's maternal role, coupled with the interruption of employment for several years, is unlikely to foster career orientations in women or, one may surmise, the desire to engage in political leadership. Recent analyses by social scientists of women's position, which confirm the results of those studies discussed earlier, and illustrate the continued conflict between women's family and other roles, have been accompanied by calls for more concerted action to alleviate these conflicts. For the most part, however, these analyses point either to the mechanisation of housework or to the expansion of public services as the solution to the problem.[38] Certain analysts point out the need to change the division of labour within the home, but little action has been taken to change public attitudes or behaviour in this regard (Bauerová, 1974, pp. 142-3).

The expansion of maternity benefits and the lengthy period of time women can stay out of the labour force are also not without their drawbacks for policy-makers. The adjustments required to schedule the permitted maternity leaves and find appropriate positions for women who return to work have been complex, particularly in branches of the economy which employ large numbers of young women. In addition, the emphasis given to women's maternal role does exacerbate, at least in the short run, the labour shortage, for sizeable numbers of women take advantage of the extended leave before returning to their jobs. Eventually, the economic costs of these measures, or their success in achieving a desired level of population growth, may lead to another reorientation of policy towards women and perhaps to more attention being paid to women's potential as economic resources. For the present, however, the elites in Czechoslovakia appear willing to suffer the economic costs, as well as the potentially negative impact on women's equality, of emphasising women's reproductive role.

Notes

1. See Lapidus (1978) for an illustration of this tendency in the case of Soviet women; see Wolchik (1979) for a more detailed examination of elite policy toward women in Czechoslovakia.

2. Infant mortality decreased from 45.1 per 1,000 newborns and 136.8 among children up to one year of age in 1945 to 17.4 and 34.1 respectively by 1955 (Srb, 1967). Live births per 1,000 population decreased from a high of 24.2 in 1947 to 21.2 in 1953 and reached a low of 14.9 in 1968 (Srb, 1967, p. 183; ČSSR, 1970).

3. See Cohn (1973, pp. 41-55); Berent (March 1970, pp. 35-58 and July 1970, pp. 247-50); Heitlinger (1976a); and Feshbach and Rapawy (1976, pp. 113-54) for analyses of the demographic situation in the Soviet Union and Eastern Europe.

4. See Berent (July 1970, p. 278) for the results of studies concerning the use of various birth control devices in Hungary and Czechoslovakia.

5. See Prokopec (1969c, p. 61).
6. See Elias (1972) for a discussion of the labour force in Czechoslovakia.
7. The difference in birth rates between the two main ethnic groups in Czechoslovakia, while not as extreme as that of different nationalities in the Soviet Union, is still substantial. The higher birth rate in Slovakia, coupled with the significantly lower number of abortions, has resulted in a rate of natural increase which is twice as high in Slovakia as in the Czech Lands.
8. See Švarcová (1959) for an early Czech analysis which attributes the departure from the expected population increase in certain socialist countries to these factors.
9. See, for example, Srb and Kučera (1967, pp. 215-18); and Srb, Kučera and Vyšušilová (1967, pp. 228-31).
10. See Prokopec (1964); Kučera (1964a, pp. 9-12); and Srb and Kučera (1967, pp. 214-15).
11. See Prokopec (1962, pp. 60-1).
12. See Remington (1969) for examples of these arguments.
13. See Golan (1971); Jancar (1971); Kusin (1971); and Skilling (1976) for discussions of the renewal process in Czechoslovakia in the 1960s.
14. See, for example, Leflerová (1964, p. 3); Švarcová (1964, p. 6); and also Wolchik (1978, Ch. 7) for a more detailed analysis of this process.
15. See Hajková (1964c, p. 2). See also Hajková (1964a, p. 4; and 1964b, no. 5, p. 5; no. 7, p. 5).
16. 'K postavení ženy v socialistické společnosti', *Zprávy státní populačn komise* no. 4 (1965).
17. See, for example, 'Rozhovor o zamestanosti a materství', *Vlasta*, no. 10 (1964), pp. 2-3; 'Nešidím život dvěma směnami?', *Vlasta*, no. 12 (1964), pp. 4-5; 'Vědci hovoří o zaměstnaných matkích', *Vlasta*, no. 45 (1964), p. 3; and 'Vědci hovoří o starnoucích ženách', *Vlasta*, no. 47 (1964), pp. 4-5.
18. See Čap and Peltrámová (1964, pp. 14-17); Kučera (1964b,pp. 11-13).
19. Kučera (1965, pp. 33-8).
20. See, for example, Prokopec (1966, pp. 29-33); Vítak and Zelénková (1967, pp. 23-5); and Prokopec (1969c).
21. See Plachký (1964, pp. 59-70); and Frejka and Frejková (1965, pp. 169-76) for summaries of these views.
22. See Lapidus (1978, pp. 292-309) for an analysis of recent Soviet debates on this subject.
23. See Scott (1974, Ch. 6); and Heitlinger (1976b) for further discussion of the debate over women's employment during this period.
24. 'Celostátní konference zen – ve znamení aktivniho zájmu o rozvoj naši společhosti', *Vlasta*, no. 6 (1966), pp. 2-3.
25. 'Co chcete vedet o československému svazu zen', *Vlasta*, no. 7 (1967), p. 2.
26. 'V puli dobré cesty', *Vlasta*, no. 23 (1967), p. 3.
27. 'Otevřený list všem československém ženam', *Funkcionářka*, no. 4 (1968), p. 1.
28. 'K postavení ženy v socialistické společnosti'.
29. See 'Z diskuse na krajských konfereních KSČ', *Funkcionářka*, p. 10.
30. 'Komunike zo zasadnutia Československý rady žien', *Funkcionářka*, no. 12 (1969), p. 7.
31. The women's organisation adopted the name Union of Czech and Slovak Women (*Svaz českých a slovenských žen*) in March 1968 the better to reflect its bi-national character.
32. See, for example, *Ženy v boji za socialismus* (MOŅA, Prague, 1971), and *1969-1974, Z činnosti Slovenského zvazu žien* (UV SSŽ-Zivena, Bratislava, 1974).

33. See reports of ČSSŽ influence on the extension of maternity leave and increased pensions in 'Elan, um, schopnost', *Slovenka* (24 March 1972), p. 3.

34. See *XIV sjezd Kommunistické strany Československa* (Svoboda, Prague, 1971), p. 579 for a recent resolution on women in socialist society.

35. See *Population Policies in Czechoslovakia* (Orbis, Prague, 1974) for more detail on the various population provisions adopted in Czechoslovakia.

36. A 1971 law increased the stipend paid to women who chose to remain at home with their children and also expanded the benefits to include women not previously active; 90% of all women eligible are reported to use these benefits: *Population Policies*, p. 61.

37. Radio Free Europe Research, 'Stricter Regulations on Abortion', *Czechoslovak Situation Report/31* (5 September 1973), pp. 9-12. These measures were adopted despite public opinion polls conducted by the State Population Commission which indicated that the vast majority of Czech and Slovak women were against restrictions on abortions. See Prokopec (1969a, pp. 14-24; and 1969b, pp. 3-13).

38. Seé, for example, Magdolen (1973, pp. 45-8; 69-71).

Bibliography

Bauerová, J. (1974) *Zaměstnaná žena a rodina*, Práce, Prague

Berent, J. (1970) 'Causes of Fertility Decline in Eastern Europe and the Soviet Union', *Population Studies*, XXIV, 1 (March) and 2 (July)

Bernard, J. (1971) *Women and the Public Interest*, Aldine, Atherton, Chicago

Čap, V. and Peltrámová, Š. (1964) 'Efektivnost práce žen s dětmi', *Zprávy státní populační komise*, no. 5

Cohn, H. D. (1973) 'Population Policy in the USSR', *Problems of Communism*, XXII, 4 (July-August)

ČSSR (1970) *Statistická ročenka*, p. 91

Elias, A. (1972) *Manpower Trends in Czechoslovakia: 1950-1990*, US Government Printing Office, US Department of Commerce, Foreign Demographic Analysis Division, Washington DC

Feshbach, M. and Rapawy, S. (1976) 'Soviet Population and Manpower Trends and Policies', *The Soviet Economy in a New Perspective*, US Congress Joint Economic Committee, Washington DC

Frejka, T. and Frejková E. (1965) 'O zaměstnaných ženách', *Planované hospodářství*, nos. 7-8

Golan, G. (1971) *The Czechoslovak Reform Movement, 1963-1967*, CUP, Cambridge

Hajková, V. (1964a) 'Musí to byt svátek?, *Vlasta*, no. 4 and 7

—— (1964b) 'Nazory, polemika, kritika', *Vlasta*, nos. 5 and 7

—— (1964c) 'Setkání na hradě', *Vlasta*, no. 12

Heitlinger, A. (1976a) 'Pro-natalist Population Policies in Czechoslovakia', *Population Studies*, XXX, 1

—— (1976b) 'Women's Labour Force Participation in Czechoslovakia since World War II', paper presented at the Symposium on the Working Sexes, University of British Columbia, October 15-17

Jancar, B. W. (1971) *Czechoslovakia and the Absolute Monopoly of Power*, Praeger, New York

Kont'šekova, O. (1968) *Socialno-ekonomicke aspekty zamestnanosti žien*, Prace, Bratislava

150 *Demography and Political Reform in Czechoslovakia*

Kučera, M. (1964a) 'Orientační sonda o přičinách vzestupu porodnosti v roce 1963', *Zprávy státní populacní komise*, no. 1
—— (1964b) 'Ekonomická aktivita žen podle počtu děti' *Zprávy státní populacní komise*, no. 5
—— (1965) 'Zaměstnanost žen a reprodukce', *Zprávy státní populační komise*, no. 2
Kusin, V. V. (1971) *The Intellectual Origins of the Prague Spring*, CUP, Cambridge
Lapidus, G.W. (1978) *Women in Soviet Society*, University of California, Berkeley
Leflerová, H. (1964) 'Problémy nejen předvolební', *Vlasta*, no. 13
Magdolen, E. (1973) *Rodina Její společenský význam a místo v socialistikém způsobu života*, Výskumný ústav zivotnej úrovne, Bratislava
Plachký, M. (1964) 'Populační vývoj a ekonomické problémy, *Planované hospodárštví*, no. 5
Prokopec, J. (1962) 'Vdaná zěna v rodiné a zamestnání', *Zprávy státní populační komise*, no. 2
——(1964) 'Mladé lide ve městě před uzavřením snatku', *Zprávy státní populační komise*, no. 6
—— and Wynnyczuk, V. (1965) 'Věčně o zaměstnanosti žen, o výstavbě jesli polemický', *Hospodářské noviny*, no.1
—— (1966) 'K některým aspektum vývoje potratovost', *Zprávy státní populační komise*, no. 3
——(1969a) 'Současné postoje českých žen k možnosti legálního přerušení těhotenství', *Zprávy státní populační komise*, no. 1
—— (1969b) 'Nažory slovenských žen na interrupční zákon a jeho prováděcí praxi', *Zprávy státní populační komise*, no. 2
—— (1969c) 'Potraty v roce 1968', *Zprávy státní populační komise*, no. 5
Remington, R. (ed.) (1969) *Winter in Prague: Documents on Czechoslovakian Communism in Crisis*, MIT Press, Cambridge, Mass.
Scott, H. (1974) *Does Socialism Liberate Women?* Beacon Press, Boston
Skilling, H.G. (1976) *Czechoslovakia's Interrupted Revolution*, Princeton University Press, Princeton, NJ
Skilling, H. Gordon and Griffiths, (eds.) F. (1973) *Interest Groups in Soviet Politics*, Princeton University Press, Princeton, NJ
Srb, V. (ed.) (1967) *Demografická přírnčka,*Nakladatelství Svoboda, Prague
—— and Kučera, M. (1967) 'Výzkum rodičovství, 1956' in Srb
——, —— and Vyšušilová, D. (1967) 'Průzkum manželství, antikoncepce a potratů, 1959' in Srb
Švarcová, H. (1959) *Populace a společnost*, Státní nakladatelství politické literatury, Prague
—— (1964) 'Jak je to s ženskou otázkou?', *Vlasta*, no. 10
Ulrych, A. and Wynnyczuk, V. (1967) 'Denní režim zaměstrané ženy v Praze' in Srb
Vítak, B. and Zelénková, M. (1967) 'Současné zkušenosti z činnosti interrupčních komise', *Zprávy státní populační komise*, no. 1
Wolchik, S.L. (1978) 'Politics, Ideology and Equality: the Status of Women in Eastern Europe', PhD dissertation, University of Michigan
——(1979) 'The Status of Women in a Socialist Order: Czechoslovakia 1948-1978', *Slavic Review* (December)

8 A HARD DAY'S NIGHT: WOMEN, REPRODUCTION AND SERVICE SOCIETY

Ilona Kickbusch

It's been a hard day's night
and I've been working like a dog
It's been a hard day's night
I should be sleeping like a log
But when I get home to you
I find the things that you do
will make me feel all right.
(The Beatles)

One of the problems with radical feminist theory has been to look at patriarchy as a strong, monolithic and never changing block of power: men will be men. This view is understandable, as we first had to grasp the main structure of our oppression — to re-invent patriarchy so to speak from a feminist viewpoint — after history and the social sciences had taught us at school and university that personal forms of dependency had vanished with the bourgeois revolution. Slavery was outdated and caste was something to be found in India, not in the midst of the American way of life. Only slowly are we beginning to see how patriarchy has changed over the centuries and how it manifests itself in different areas and cultures. Men have exercised power over women in many different ways, some brutal, some subtle, and it is one of the aims of this chapter to put forward some tentative ideas about the reorganisation of patriarchy as we are now experiencing it. Socialist feminism, on the other hand, has fallen into somewhat similar traps when trying to analyse women's oppression in capitalist society, especially in regard to the specific forms in which the state exercises power over women. Too easily — even for the authors themselves — the state would turn into a monolithic block, the explanations would become functional and end up in the circular argument: what exists is functional for capitalist society and forms that are functional for capitalist society will continue to exist.

A theoretical combination of these two approaches can take the form of a simple equation: capitalism equals patriarchy. This then leads to the logical supposition that everything functional for capitalism is also functional for patriarchy and vice versa, which makes the strategic decisions very much simpler than reality tends to be: by abolishing one system you can get rid of the other at the same time.

The view I will take in this paper presupposes (at least) two power systems in present society, one patriarchal and one capitalist, which are by no means always in accordance with each other. This implies that patriarchy is not just a remnant of earlier times still trying to keep a foot in the door but that it has undergone a number of changes these last 200 years that make it quite up-to-date. It is important to stress the point that I am not just talking about a system of norms that await change through the goodwill of all participants: feminists, if they could be a little less radical and take their time over explanations, and men, who are not quite as bad as they seem and only have to start bothering to listen. It is all for our common good. That is the reason why I put the 'at least' into parentheses above, because we are not just fighting systems outside ourselves but systems in our heads as well. That is why so many of us still believe that we (you and I of all women) will find that wonderful exceptional male who will fully understand our feminist uprising and wash our socks and banners while we are out fighting, and who will then take us into his loving arms after a long day of sisterhood-is-powerful: it can kill you. Careful, big brother is loving you.

In what way then can we get closer to analysing changes in patriarchy and its inter-relations with (capitalist) state policies? A starting point is given by Polda Fortunati (1978) who, in a paper presented at the Summer University for Women in Berlin in 1977, put forward the notion that 'it was capitalism that gave patriarchy its proper foundation. Never before in history has the subjection of women to men and their loss of power reached such a peak as with the onset of capitalism.' This of course is provocative — especially for liberal feminists, who like to believe that we have come a long way. Have not women been fighting for their rights as human beings since the onset of the bourgeois revolution, and have not we ourselves been witnesses to changes for the better in women's life conditions, and to more freedom? Things have moved on and we tend to hope that the world gets a better place for women to live in as we continue fighting for more rights, more freedom and more security — which means fighting for more laws, because it is through laws that society defines freedom and humanity. Why then should we be sceptical?

I would like to refer to a statement made by Jacques Donzelot, a French sociologist, about the heart of social democratic politics:[1] the main issue, he says, is how to give the working class more rights, without giving it a right to the state. The main strategy is social policy. Analogously, I will argue that state policies towards women are centred round the issue of 'how to give women more rights without giving them a right to themselves'. The main strategy is reproduction policy — a term which I prefer to use for social policy actions concerned with the organisation of women's lives.

Reproduction Policy

Reproduction policy deals with several aspects of women's lives: the services women produce for patriarchy and the welfare state, for example servicing the adult male and rearing and caring for children, as well as women's biological function as the potential bearer of children. Ideologically they are closely linked, since giving birth to a child implies staying at home and caring for it under very individual conditions, and doing the rest of the family labour as well. Moreover, since women naturally love their children they are predestined to love and care, and not to work — because housework is not 'work'. Women are happy just to be with others, they are just not complete without men or children — no matter what else they do. And as Percy Sledge has sung to us again and again: 'this is a man's world, but it would be nothing, nothing without a woman or a girl'.

Of course it would not, because men would have to work harder. The latest German study on 'working mothers' (working means having a job outside the house as well) comes to the conclusion that three-quarters of these women (from a sample of 400 women with children under the age of 15) had an average workday of seventeen hours. Ursula Baumgärtel, one of the researchers, puts it bluntly:[2] 'It is a fact, that today's model of equal integration of women into the job market does not take into consideration, that the work-resources put into the labour market are not being replaced inside the family.' As the study shows, neither services by the welfare state (who spoke of service society?) nor help by men/husbands eases the lives of these women. So paradoxically we have gained what we have been fighting for: access to the labour market — but with lower pay and fewer opportunities, and family labour as always.

The Rise of the Housewife

Let me touch briefly on some historical issues. The onset of capitalist relations of production created new relations of reproduction. Marxist state theory has contributed to the analysis of this process by showing how the long-term reproduction of the male adult worker was guaranteed by the dialectical tightrope act of social policy, man-oeuvring between legitimacy, loyalty and accumulation. What it did not see was that alongside wage labour a completely new form of domestic labour was coming into existence — unpaid women's work in the home guaranteeing the day-to-day reproduction of the male adult worker and the upbringing of the children while also forcing female wage labour into the factories. State laws regulating family life, working conditions and social relations in general (for example, prostitution) primarily restricted women. Women were not free to move in society even in the sense of the 'free' worker, since by law they were not granted adult status in society.

There was a deal of truth in Engels's remark that, as a woman, the bourgeois wife was even more restricted than her proletarian sister, tied down by the strict set of rules dominating the static family model. Bourgeois women tried to fight the restrictions in the first big upsurge of the women's movement without questioning the family as a mode of patriarchal exploitation; instead they passed it down as a model to their proletarian sisters, for example, as social work or domestic science. Kenneth Galbraith (1974) describes this development as follows: 'The transformation of women into an invisible serving class was an economic achievement of the first order. Servants for work socially not valued had only been available to a minority of the pre-industrial popu-lation, today the subservient housewife is very democratically available to practically the whole male population.' It must be seen as one of the achievements of new feminist theory to have taken the family out of the realm of ideology, where it has been put as a 'socialisation agent', into the realm of work and to have pointed out the relations of production within the home.

Thus the onset of capitalism and the reorganisation of patriarchy created two forms of division of labour: a new sexual division of labour, leaving women responsible for reproduction work in the family, which we can term housework or family labour, and which implies personal services to men and children in a status socially dependent on men, and the division of labour between the services produced by the housewife and the services produced by the state. Thus, for the present, I agree with Polda Fortunati (1978) that women have had to rely on men in a structure of private, isolated dependency at a time when the male working class reached its dialectical freedom from serfdom and independence in wage labour; or as Franco Basaglia put it, 'the new master is nothing but the totality of the serfs'. Patriarchy, itself oppressed through capitalist structures and men oppressing each other, had a new servant class at its disposal: women — who were loved and revered as long as they did as they were told. Feminist analysis has defined housework as patriarchal exploitation, saying that it is not the nature of the work women do that keeps them tied down, dependent and unpaid, but the organisation of its production in the patriarchal family unit. It has shown the historical changes in housework and, in doing so, has developed a new concept of work. Housework, in feminist analysis, is not just washing the dishes and ironing the shirts, it is also consumption work, with women as the central mediators between the profit market, state services and the needs of the family, and it is a human service (*Beziehungsarbeit*) in the form of love, attention, care and sexuality. All the same, feminist analysis has concentrated too much on the static bourgeois family model.

The Onset of the New Woman

Even though much has remained the same since Betty Friedan's brilliant analysis of the 'Feminine Mystique', and even though we may now be experiencing a reversal consisting of renewed praise for feminine/motherly qualities both inside and outside the feminist movement — much else has changed too. The transformation has been marked by the development of the therapeutic welfare state, by the so-called sexual revolution and by changing adult roles, especially for women (which are also closely linked to changes in the labour market, a point which I cannot pursue here). As Laura Balbo (1979) rightly puts it in a recent paper:

> women's situation in these last ten to fifteen years is defined by a 'dual life' which women have not chosen but are forced to lead. The static bourgeois family model has become flexible in a number of respects, bringing with it a woman's role that has changed from one with no alternatives (the static housewife model) to one defined by its own flexibility and compulsive choices, that always end up in a no-win situation, but ideologically suggest a freedom of choice.

The welfare-service state continues to rely on women's family labour and has constructed most of its services on the basis of a subsidiary model which we could term 'women's family labour comes first': this model does not imply lifelong full-time housewives, but flexible women who control their biological reproductive ability, who space their children adequately, who turn in and out of the work force (especially in service oriented jobs), and who manage in spite of the chaos of state services to fill the gaps as best they can. At the same time, new social policy measures (many have been introduced in West Germany during the last few years: abortion laws, divorce laws, motherhood laws) widen the options of women's no-win situations and control the choices through advisory therapeutic services provided by state welfare. It is therefore time that feminist theory reported on this new situation which, at least in the so-called advanced capitalist societies, has out-moded the static 'housewife model' for some time and made women dependent, not only on patriarchy, but directly on the labour market and social security as well — again without gaining any new real power in society. If we accept that women are subject to a dual socialisation (*Vergesellschaftung*), one patriarchal and one capitalist, then women's relationship with the welfare state and social policy cannot be analysed in the same terms as men's (for example, in terms of controlling and reproducing wage labour). Terms like 'reserve army' or 'socialisation through wage labour' are only in part determinants of female life, which is closely linked to patriarchal exploitation as well.

It seems that the welfare state is ready to support the patriarchal exploitation of women as long as its reproductive goals are ensured, and if they are not, it starts 'protecting' them. The definition of the family as a private sphere of life, for example, interestingly enough applies mainly to the way men treat their women and children, but not to bio-logical reproduction and the services supplied by women. The welfare state is in conflict with patriarchy when either accumulative interests (for example, women as a reserve army) or legitimacy (for example, women's claim to equal rights) are at stake. As Mary McIntosh puts it (1978, p. 256), 'the state is always juggling to keep several balls in the air at once', or in terms of state theory, engaging in a 'permanent crisis management trying to discipline conflict potentials'. There seems to be a tendency, as far as social democratic policy is concerned, to make women 'free' adults in a capitalist society (with equal rights, especially in the labour market) without touching very much on women's exploitation by patriarchy. The result is women's dual life, which, as postulated above, has brought women more rights without giving them a right to themselves. In other words, women are being 'integrated' without resolving the problem of personal dependency.

It is important that feminist analysis should ascertain whether conservative policies of pay for housework (as put forward by the Christian Democrats in West Germany) are retrograde or instead a more timely strategy of ensuring women's reproductive potential than labour party policies. Women would thus gain new freedoms in society (for example, spending money or bargaining power) but would not be rid of their social responsibility for reproduction. Indeed the welfare state could then force people even more into the 'normal' family, since wages for housework would be tied to a number of conditions that adults organising their lives in other ways would be unable to meet. The way in which this latter section of the population (such as single-parent families, singles, communes and so on) would receive services (free market?) or supply for themselves has yet to be seen. Here we would probably find another conflict of interest between old patriarchy and new patriarchy; those wanting women's services and offering them patriarchal 'security' and 'protection', and those wanting women, without obligations and conditions, on the basis of a marketplace model (without preconditions).

Our New Humane Oppression

The new feminist movement has put body politics and reproduction politics in the heart of its battle. Body politics means the appropriation of the female body by women themselves — rediscovering it, so to speak, and closely linking female identity to body images. Consciousness-raising groups discussed the historical situation which had severed sexuality from reproduction by the introduction of contraception, but which had not altered heterosexuality. They discovered female sexual pleasure and hoped to prevent reproduction with natural birth control. Feminist reproduction politics began with a battle for the right to abortion and developed more broadly and politically: the search for contraceptives that are not harmful, for new ways of giving birth and the recognition of lesbianism as an acceptable form of sexuality. Contraception, especially 'the pill', brought with it a double-faced revolution, for with it sexuality should always be available; no more 'not tonight dear', but a long explanation of why not. The political objective of the feminist movement that claimed exclusive female responsibility for contraception (who would trust a man, even if male contraceptives were available?), birth or abortion gave men hitherto unknown sexual freedom and freedom from reproductive responsibility. Linda Gordon's (1977) words 'for women heterosexual relationships are always intensive, fear-ridden risks that have to be carefully calculated' are still applicable, perhaps even more so. For with the new freedoms, women have lost old securities. The old double moral standard had implied that men had (in most cases) to marry the woman they had made pregnant, while today there is always abortion and the famous question 'why didn't you take your pill?'. In biological reproduction (and sexuality) women are in a no-win situation similar to that in their dual life situation: to be able to decide does not mean freedom of choice, much less self-determination. Women have the freedom to have to decide all the time: to use contraception or not, and by which method, to abort or not, and how to have a child or a job, to marry or have a career, security, social acknowledgement . . . I believe this to be the crux of women's situation today: not the lack of choice of the simple 'housewife model', but the chronic pressure of decision-making. I do not mean to say that women have not gained new space for manoeuvre, but the consequential problems are now always women's responsibility. For this freedom women are paying in hard currency.

I am sure the overall tendency of social policy for women at the moment will be that the social control and social responsibility of women will be increased while the old forms of 'protection' will be vanquished in the name of equality (for example the West German debate on compulsory military service for women). I also believe this real loss of security, without fundamental new gains, to be the origin of family oriented philosophies that have begun to emerge from the feminist movement recently. We have not yet found strategies for dealing with these new insecurities or new freedoms with any new solidarity. Self-help is just a beginning: women will have to fight against flexible reproductive responsibility, without bringing back the static old form of family organisation and security. Marcuse showed very clearly the cost of the battle for female emancipation, both for women and for men. It seems new and old patriarchy still find women willing to cuddle them after a hard day's night. But who reproduces the new flexible woman?

Notes

1. Jacques Donzelot, unpublished mimeograph.

2. Ursula Baumgärtel and others, unpublished report, University of Giessen, Germany.

Bibliography

Balbo, L. (1979) *The British State and the Organisation of the Family*, mimeograph, Milan

Bock, G. and Duden, B. (1977) 'Arbeit aus Liebe – Liebe als Arbeit: Zur Entstehung der Hausarbeit im Kapitalismus' in Frauen und Wissenschaft, Berlin

Cockburn, C. (1977) 'Capitalist Reproduction: The State and Women', paper presented at the CSE Conference, Bradford

Delphy, C. (1977) *The Main Enemy: A Materialist Analysis of Women's Oppression*, Women's Research and Resources Collective, London

Ehrenreich, B. and English, D. (1979) *For her Own Good: 150 Years of the Experts' Advice to Women*, London

Eisenstein, Z.R. (ed.) (1979) *Capitalist Patriarchy and the Case for Socialist Feminism*, Monthly Review Press, New York

Fortunati, P. (1978) 'Frauen, Staat und Widerstand in den Anfängen des Kapitalismus' in *Frauen als bezahlte und unbezahlte Arbeitskräfte*, Berlin

Foucault, M. (1977) *Sexualität und Wahreit 1: Der Wille zum Wissen*, Frankfurt

Galbraith, J.K. (1974) *Wirtschaft für Staat und Gesellschaft* (Economics and the Public Purpose), München

Gordon, L. (1977) *Woman's Body – Woman's Rights: Birth Control in America*, Harmondsworth

Held, T. (1978) *Soziologie der ehelichen Machtverhältnisse*, Darmstadt/Neuwied

Kickbusch, I. (1978) 'The Political Economy of Personal Services: Women's Paid and Unpaid Labour', paper presented at the 10th World Congress of the ISA at Uppsala

——(1979) 'Weiblichkeit: Sozialgeschichtliche Uberlegungen zur Familie' in *Beiträge zur Feministischen Theorie und Praxis*, Heft 2, Munchen

Lipman-Blumen, J. and Bernard, J. (eds.) (1979) *Sex Roles and Social Policy*, Beverley Hills

McIntosh, M. (1978) 'The State and the Oppression of Women' in Annette Kuhn and Ann Marie Wolpe (eds.), *Feminism and Materialism*, Routledge and Kegan Paul, London

Nagel, H. and Seifert, M. (eds.) (1979) *Inflation der Therapieformen: Sinn und Unsinn der Psychoindustrie*, Reinbek

Offe, C. (1972) *Strukturprobleme des Kapitalistischen Staates*, Frankfurt

Safilio-Rothschild C. (1974) *Women and Social Policy*, Englewood Cliffs, NJ

Starnberger Studien 2 (1978) *Sozialpolitik und soziale Kontrolle*, Frankfurt

Wilson, E. (1977) *Women and the Welfare State*, London

9 TECHNOLOGY, 'WOMEN'S WORK' AND THE SOCIAL CONTROL OF WOMEN

Joan Rothschild

I

A growing body of research and commentary suggests that the effects of technology on traditional 'women's work' in the home are not necessarily the same as technology's effects on the labour process in the paid workplace. Birth control technology decreases, rather than increases, productivity. Although machinery is supposed to save labour time, women in the USA, despite their 'labour-saving' devices, spend at least as much time in housework today as their grandmothers did. Nor are home tasks subdivided and specialised; rather, the housewife takes on more roles, especially those of consumer, and, for the middle-class woman, chauffeur, child-care specialist and family counsellor (Vanek, 1973 and 1974; Hartmann, 1974; Oakley, 1975; Cowan, 1976; Bose, 1979).

What is suggested by these examples? Even though women's domestic work has not lessened over the years, women working in the home appear in some ways to gain, or least retain, control of their own labour process. They can determine pregnancy. They still see many jobs through from start to finish. Their home-related work is still less mechanised, regimented and proletarianised than the work of those — women and men — in the paid labour force. Are women working in the home perhaps the one group of workers left whose labour has not been degraded and increasingly controlled through the technology of industrial capitalism? (Braverman, 1974).

This chapter argues that the apparent control over labour by the home-worker is truly an illusion. Modern technology has aided monopoly capital in further locking women into their traditional roles in the home. Under the guise of freeing women, technology has succeeded in providing an even more subtle masking of the social control of women than the Victorian cult of true womanhood ever did. Technology has succeeded because it serves, in addition to industrial capitalism,[1] a second powerful master: patriarchy.[2] The persistence of the myth that technology liberates women, when it aids both capitalism and patriarchy in controlling women's labour and women, suggests a special relationship of technology to capitalism and patriarchy. This chapter will show how in the USA technology has intersected with capitalism and patriarchy to place women's domestic labour more firmly under the yoke of both, and how in the process the myth of liberation is perpetuated.

The balance of this first section briefly reviews the historical and theoretical place of 'women's work' and clarifies my use of the word *technology*. The second section deals with the question of control of women's domestic labour processes, and what is illusion and what is reality. The third section develops the relationship of technology to capitalism and patriarchy to show how control of women's domestic labour has been affected, and the myth of liberation maintained. A short summary of my thesis concludes the chapter. Examples and documentation will be drawn mainly from experience in the USA since the Industrial Revolution, with particular focus on the twentieth century. Cross-cultural implications of the thesis, while beyond the scope of this chapter, also need to be explored.[3]

Although the sexual division of labour and society predated capitalism, with the rise of industrial capitalism changes in both material conditions and ideology transformed 'women's work' (Sacks, 1974; Baxandall, Gordon and Reverby, 1976; Hartmann, 1976; Kessler-Harris, 1976; Zaretsky, 1976). A key structural change was the separation of home and workplace, men's work moving increasingly outside the home, women's work remaining within it. Although many women worked for wages — either at home, at factory or office, or as domestics in others' homes — women's primary work was located in the home, maintaining the household, reproducing and sustaining family members — without pay. As the middle-class ideal of the two spheres took hold, the 'family' (Rapp, Ross and Bridenthal, 1979)[4] and women's 'proper' role within it developed into a powerful ideology that persists to this day (Welter, 1966; Hymowitz and Weissman, 1978). Under industrial capitalism, 'women's work' became work at home, 'natural' to women because of their biology and, by extension, temperament. To neo-classical economists it was not 'real work' because it was unpaid and did not contribute to the Gross National Product.[5] In the marketplace, the sexual division of labour relegated women to marginal, reserve, ill-paying jobs, or to 'feminised' occupations and professions (Abbott, 1969 ed; Oppenheimer, 1970).

Such characterisation of women's work acts not only to subordinate women but to mask the role that women's domestic labour plays in the political economy. Household labour, although retaining use-value and pre-capitalist elements, also makes it possible for family members to sell their labour power in the marketplace. Thus women's domestic work enters the exchange relations of capitalism. Women's work reproduces the labour force through household labour, and quite literally through biological reproduction. Women's consumer role ties women further into capitalist exchange relations, as women deal directly in the marketplace and in still another way reproduce the social relations of capitalism.[6] Not only is capitalism supported in the process, but men's power over women is strengthened. Women are kept economically dependent, needing men's 'protection' and authority.[7] Patriarchy has provided a cultural and econo-political underpinning for capital's exploitation of women's labour, both domestic and wage. Capitalism and patriarchy join together to perpetuate the sexual division of labour and, through it, to oppress women.

The burden of this chapter is to develop the role that technology has had in the process by which capitalism and patriarchy have combined to perpetuate the sexual division of labour, and to define and control 'women's work' I shall focus on domestic labour because of the way it limits and defines all of women's labour, and thereby women's role in the political economy.[8] In my discussion, I shall include not only housework — the care of household and family members — but also biological reproduction as domestic labour. The concept of technology I start from is Bernard Gendron's (1977): 'A technology is any systematised practical knowledge, based on experimentation and/or scientific theory, which enhances the capacity of society to produce goods and services, and which is embodied in productive skills, organisation, or machinery.'

In working from this definition, I reject the characterisation of technology only as machinery or mechanised processes. Under the Gendron formulation, technology can include such aspects of the organisation of work as scientific management and bureaucratic forms, while under the concept of technology as machines it cannot. It is thus, as David Noble (1977) points out, not just the material products of people, but part of the social relations of production. Technology is a social process that 'must inescapably reflect that particular social order which has produced and sustained it'. While not autonomous, it can have the power of ideology as it 'assumes the particular forms given it by the most powerful and forceful people in society' (Noble, 1977). In this chapter, therefore, technology appears neither as an independent force nor as a wholly dependent one, but rather as an interactive and interdependent variable, tied both to social structure and process, and to ideology, and thus having both material and ideological aspects. Technology is separated out only for analytic purposes. In this chapter, therefore, technology's material and ideological aspects will be explored both as they relate to capitalism and patriarchy, and to the control of women's domestic labour.

II

Industrial technology developed as an integral part of industrial capitalist production.[9] As such, it operated as a tool of management control over the worker and work process (Braverman, 1974).[10] As the scientific-technological revolution advanced in industry from the late nineteenth century onwards, the degree and sophistication of such control also advanced. Designed to increase, or otherwise enhance, productivity, and thus profits, technology has aided in further separating the conception of a job from its operation, subdividing and routinising tasks which are performed now by many persons or automated machinery. Work is designed to become machine-like; human beings are to approximate machines. Skills are reduced and replaced; old skills eventually disappear. Workers are either eliminated or displaced, transferred to less mechanised occupations, and then often displaced anew when automation catches up. Much of human labour becomes 'dead labour', absorbed into capital, and less truly productive. Even more highly skilled technical work becomes subject to the degrading and controlling practices of lower-status work. The technological processes themselves, the regimented and routinised organisation of work and workplace, aid in atomising the work force and isolating workers from each other, discouraging solidarity, and thus enhancing control by management (Ehrenreich and Ehrenreich, 1976).

Do technologies of reproduction and housework produce similar effects? Technologies of reproduction cover three basic areas: birth control, childbirth and regulation of reproductive cycles generally. These technologies are held to enhance women's choice, to free women from pain, discomfort and associated ills. Contraceptive technologies — the pill, diaphragm and IUD being the major ones[11] — promise a woman greater control over her reproductive capacity, including the possibility of remaining childless. Their professional advocates, however, did not seek to free women from child-bearing. Rather, through spacing births, advocates sought to reduce infant mortality, and to create healthier children and mothers who would bear more children, better educated and

cared for. As birth control technology moved out of the private, usually
illegal, realm of knowledge communicated by female networks and
entered the public world dominated by professionalism and the
corporate structure, old skills and knowledge — still practised in non-
industrialised societies — were lost (Himes, 1970 edn; Ehrenreich and
English, 1973; Gordon, 1977; Stanley, 1981). Women became objects
for scientific experimentation; their health and even that of their
children were placed in jeopardy.

Women's choice to use the new contraceptive technologies is limited
in a number of ways. Choice is restricted to products on the market,
and whether or not to use those products. Access may be limited by
class, by education, by law. Women follow doctors' or packaged
instructions which explain end results but do not necessarily enlighten
about the process or risks (unless as now increasingly legally required).
The majority of research in the United States continues to be on
women's reproductive systems, rather than on men's as well (despite
research on the so-called male pill in countries such as China). Women
still bear the major responsibility for contraception. Yet control of
contraceptive technology that should accompany such responsibility
continues to elude them. Birth control technology and through it
women's control over the choice to reproduce — remains a mixed
blessing for women, as the medical and scientific professions, the drug
industry and the state operate to restrict women's choice, and to retain
ultimate control.

The effects of the technologies associated with pregnancy and childbirth exhibit a similar pattern. Advances in medical technology within
the last century have helped overall to reduce deaths from childbirth
and its complications, and the infant mortality rate, as well as to reduce
miscarriages and make for safer pregnancies. But have there been costs
or losses that temper this freedom? As doctors took over birthing from
midwives and childbirth moved from home to hospital, the woman
began to lose control over a process uniquely hers (Ehrenreich and
English, 1973 and 1979; Arms, 1975; Rich, 1976; Wertz and Wertz,
1977; Bogdan, 1978; Rothman, 1979). Use of drugs increased and
mechanisation followed. Drugs relieve pain, but limit or remove participation; surgical procedures are used over which the woman may have
little or no choice; the use of increasingly sophisticated technology such
as foetal monitoring becomes more and more routine, again a medical
decision.[12]

The doctor and accompanying entourage have taken over: the
doctor is conceiver and manager, subdividing the process into numerous

tasks, directing the attendant personnel and use of machinery, so that the woman giving birth is reduced to an almost passive object to be manipulated, responding to orders. The drug known as DES (diethyl-stilbestrol), given to women in the 1940s and 1950s to prevent mis-carriages (its ineffectiveness to do this has since been disclosed), has made recipients' female offspring high-risk candidates for cervical cancer.[13] Amniocentesis, the highly approved and promoted foetal test for birth defects, especially Down's syndrome, can also pose risks for both foetus and prospective mother. It is questionable as to whether technologies that bring health risks or cause illness increase one's control. The medical profession, equipment manufacturers and the drug industry have sought to solidify control over pregnancy and childbirth, replacing and destroying old skills with new but not necessarily superior ones, dehumanising and degrading the worker — in the name of science and technology.

Drugs and new surgical procedures are designed to relieve 'problems' of other phases of women's reproductive cycles: menstrual difficulties, infertility, menopause — all lumped together as pathologies. Again, the pattern is similar. Women are delivered into the hands of corporate medicine. The technology associated with all phases of women's repro-duction has become big business. Far from giving women enlightened control, such technology aids in making monopoly capital's penetration of the intensely private sphere of women's reproduction deep and effective.[14] As we move into new areas of reproductive technology for the future, such as sex pre-selection, *in vitro* fertilisation, as well as various types of *in vitro* gene manipulation, there are strong indications that women will have even less control of such practices because, according to one perceptive analysis, the state will increasingly take over.[15]

Technology and housework present a more complex picture. Although being a housewife is often not a women's sole occupation, we can apply the category housewife to the vast majority of American women. Housewife is not just a work role. Along with motherhood, it is a social role. While all women are not mothers and all women are not housewives, all mothers are women and all housewives are women (Lopata, 1971; Oakley, 1975; Glazer-Malbin, 1976). The work and the person doing it are inextricably linked. Further, in most households, a woman is the family member solely or chiefly responsible for house-work, whether or not she works outside the home, and whether or not she is actually a wife (Berheide, Berk and Berk, 1976). Not only are women thus responsible, they are the ones actually doing the housework (Walker and Woods, 1976). Egalitarian sharing of household tasks with spouse or other family members may make provocative news copy, but in reality describes isolated examples that are the exception to the rule. As Bose (1979) has pointed out, the sexual division of labour in the home, far from diminishing, has even increased in recent years. Nor do servants act as a substitute. In a process that began before World War I, by the late 1920s the middle-class woman was becoming servantless, owing less to technological change, than to changing labour-force opportunities and demands for the working class, and changed ideologies concerning the housewife role (Oppenheimer 1970; Vanek 1973; Cowan, 1976). Today, only the most affluent retain full-time household help; part-time domestic help is basically a once-a-week phenomenon for some of the middle class. Child-care remains inadequate and *ad hoc*, a financial burden for all but the well-to-do and those eligible for whatever limited subsidised facilities are available.

The housewife category cuts across class lines in other ways as well. Although the family consisting of full-time middle-class housewife, with children, and supported by husband represents a shrinking percentage of American households, the image remains a powerful and pervasive ideal. Particularly since the turn of the century, a set of values has been widely diffused, building a cultural ideal of woman as homemaker as her supreme and treasured role. The domestic science movement and the mass media — the latter particularly in developing housewives' consumer role — were instrumental in spreading these values. Technological changes — electrification, gas, running water, indoor plumbing, major appliances, convenience foods, changes in household design, plus the role of the mass media mentioned above — helped to make this ideal a reality. Such technology increasingly became available to more and more women, spreading to working-class women as well (Giedion, 1948; Vanek, 1973; Hartmann, 1974; Cowan, 1976).

According to US Census Bureau reports of purchase and ownership, (US Bureau of the Census, 1978), 98.9 per cent of American households have a refrigerator; 71.9 per cent have a washing machine; 83.8 per cent own one or more motor vehicles; 96.6 per cent own a television set; 61.3 per cent have a colour television; and 33.7 per cent have a freezer. For those households with incomes below the poverty level, 96.6 per cent have a refrigerator; 50.7 per cent have a washing machine; 46.2 per cent own one or more motor vehicles; 89.7 per cent own a television set; 31.6 per cent with a colour television; and 19.7 per cent have a freezer. Figures for all homes wired for electricity (77.8 million in total; the above figures were based on 70.8 million households), and including small appliances (all electric) (US Bureau of the Census, 1979), show 99.7 per cent with a refrigerator; 99.9 per cent with a black and white television (85.2 per cent with colour); 99.9 per cent with toasters, vacuum cleaners and irons (98.6 per cent of the steam/spray variety); 99.8 per cent with coffeemakers; 92.2 per cent with mixers; 60.7 per cent with can openers; 51.2 per cent with blenders; 44.9 per cent with home freezers; 42.9 per cent with food waste disposers; and 41.9 per cent with dishwashers. Although quality and newness of equipment will vary, a very high percentage of US households are equipped with major household appliances, both large and small. The mechanisation of the home now reaches widely across class as well as regional and city/suburban/rural lines.

Finally, the middle-class ideal dies hard because it can be a desirable reality. Half of all married women are now employed outside the home. Women who are single parents hold jobs as well. The vast majority of these women work because they have to — not for 'career fulfilment' or 'pin money'. Many of the jobs available to them, especially the part-time variety, are among the least desirable as regards pay, category and opportunities for advancement. Since she still remains responsible for the housework and can usually ill-afford household help, the employed wife or single parent is in the 'double-bind' of doing two jobs (*New York Times*, 1979). Evidence is conflicting and still scant as to whether, given the luxury of choice, these women would continue to work outside the home (Bose, 1979). Under present work circumstances, however, staying at home and doing only one job can be a preferable alternative. Current inflation trends, which almost compel two-income households, may make that option a moot question.

Thus the category housewife, while hypothetical in some ways, represents a sizeable, real majority of women in the US: a woman primarily responsible for housework, a woman whose household environment is fairly highly technologised, and a woman who at minimum accepts the responsibility for housework(even if resignedly or reluctantly), or who may prefer that role. The category will apply to both middle-class and working-class women, linked together through the work they do, and through the ideological power of the middle-class housewife ideal.

The housework this housewife does consists of two broad areas: household care or maintenance, and care of family members. The technologies associated with housework include: major appliances, such as refrigerators, stoves, washer-dryers; reusable small tools and appliances, such as cleaning tools and small cooking appliances; non-reusable items, such as cleaners and food products; the automobile; commercial services such as dry-cleaners and fast-food establishments; and the organisation of the work processes.

What are the effects of such technologies on housework? On the one hand, technology appears to increase the speed, ease and efficiency of specific tasks. One can wash and dry clothes faster and more effortlessly with a washer-dryer; clean more effectively with vacuum cleaners and spray-and-wipe products; prepare meals more easily with blenders, mixers and convenience foods; sew more quickly with a sewing machine and so on. By rights, then, women should have more control over their time and their work, with an increase in 'free' time in which to do what they wish. Is this, in reality, the case?

Certain factors seem to point to more control. The housewife is not a one-job automaton as the wage worker increasingly is. Her tasks have not been subdivided: she performs many jobs, perhaps a greater variety today than ever before. She operates household tools and appliances herself. Although she has not designed the products, nor does she necessarily know how and why they function, she performs as both manager and operator, as when doing laundry, using cooking tools and so forth. She takes the job through from start to finish, seeing the process completed under her own hand. While some skills are being lost, such as fine hand-sewing, home-canning and baking, and home-devised cleaning compounds, new household skills are required. The housewife is a 'veritable jane-of-all-trades' (Cowan, 1976), with need for expertise in many areas, especially in her consumer role. As a worker, she has not been eliminated or displaced; since automation has not as yet engulfed the home, and new duties have been added. Finally, she appears to have some measure of control over her allotment of time and how she organises her work processes (Oakley, 1975). Popular mythology would have us believe that technology has made the housewife a lucky and free creature, a myth that has just enough reality to help it survive — an issue to be discussed later in the chapter.

Is technology, then, really a tool of control for the home-worker? She is a manager at times, perhaps, but household aids are designed by others. She cannot influence what products shall be made and offered, unless we count marketing polls and the negative sanction of refusing to buy. She is limited by what is available on the market, and by family income. Further, as Baxandall *et al*. point out (1976), products carry minute, step-by-step instructions, leaving little or no room for initiative or ingenuity, and programming women to be docile consumers and workers. Housewives are utterly dependent on the company 'experts'

to deal with malfunctions of the machinery they are expected to
operate but not to understand (and to wait all day for this technician
who never arrives). A consumer oriented economic system and culture
encourage dependency on such tools, products and machinery,
including the seemingly indispensable automobile. She is clearly more
operator than manager (Ehrenreich and English, 1979). While the
housewife has not yet been turned into a machine — and, indeed, her
'human', 'nurturant' attributes are continuously invoked — the degree
to which a push-button quality has entered the homes of the more
affluent gives such women's work a 'make-work' quality, making it less
productive and less satisfying.

The seeming improvements in specific household tasks do not result
in more time available for the housewife. First, 'housework is
inefficient and small scale, because capitalist organisation of industry
has not yet penetrated here' (Hartmann, 1974). Secondly, the content of
housework has shifted, more time now being spent on child-care, as
consumer-shopper, chauffeur, family counsellor, and as husband's
hostess as we move up the class structure. Thirdly, technology has
'freed' women to spend more time and energy striving to meet new,
exacting household standards. Changes in fabrics and advertised norms
lead family members to demand daily clothing changes of outer
garments as well as underwear, and frequent changes of towels and
linen; the complexity of each process increases, as with special wash-
cycles and products such as anti-static sprays; the housewife is to have
spotless, super-polished floors, furniture and windows; meals become
more elaborate, as does entertaining (again, particularly a class oriented
phenomenon) (Vanek, 1973; Oakley, 1975; Cowan, 1976; Bose,
1979). Fourthly, as mentioned above, the housewife gets little or
minimal aid from paid help or family members.

Finally, control over her work processes and the organisation of
her work time are at best only partially retained. As Weinbaum and
Bridges (1976) point out, 'Housewives must work in relation to
schedules developed elsewhere,' schedules which are not co-ordinated
with each other. Weekly paychecks determine when shopping will be
done; husbands' working hours and children's school schedules determine those of the housewives. Her expanded consumer-shopper role
makes her subject to 'changes in the distribution network and expansion
of services [that] demand physical mobility . . . The centralisation of
shopping centres and services may make distribution more efficient, but
at the expense of the housewife's time' (Weinbaum and Bridges, 1976).
This 'rationalisation' of time schedules (e.g., school double sessions,

varied working shifts) and the organisation of systems of distribution — similar to management procedures at the workplace — function to wrest control from the housewife over her time, reducing her further from manager to operator status.

III

Technologies related to reproduction and housework, then, can give the illusion of control by the housewife, when in reality they often aid in reducing her control over her own labour processes. The technologies of reproduction, while seemingly enlarging women's choices, and freeing them from pain and discomfort, have also helped to destroy old skills and knowledge controlled by women, and have delivered women's reproductive systems into the hands of the corporate sector of drugs and medicine, often endangering women's health as well. The tools, machinery and processes which are held to make housewives' work more efficient and convenient, and their time more free, have 'freed' them to do more, if different, work, to have their work processes and time more controlled, and to be delivered up to corporate industry as willing consumers.[16]

In the foreword to David Noble's *America by Design* (1977), Christopher Lasch writes:

> new inventions, new processes, and new applications of scientific discoveries do not in themselves dictate changes in production. Unless accompanied by changes in social relations, especially in the organisation of labour, technological changes tend to be absorbed into existing social structures; far from revolutionising society, they merely reinforce the existing distribution of power and privilege.

In the first section we noted that capitalism and patriarchy have combined to define and control 'women's work'. The analysis in the second section proposes that technology has helped these existing structures of power to reshape and reinforce that system of control so that it is more subtle and pervasive. Yet the myth that technology liberates women persists, effectively making the control exercised. How has this process come about?

Earlier we noted that technology has aided monopoly capital to degrade and proletarianise wage labour through such means as subdividing, routinising and dehumanising the work process, reducing or eliminating skills and turning mothers into machines. Equally, capital needs to control the domestic labour of women at home. What is curious for domestic labour is that technology and capital operate to exercise such control without creating the kind of alienation that exists for wage labour. Housewives are not mechanised, regimented and dehumanised the way wage workers increasingly are. The working conditions and environment for the housewife are perceived as preferable to those of the average wage worker. Why?

In many ways the material conditions of housewives' labour *are* less alienating than those of the marketplace. What helps to make them so is the pre-capitalist character of the household situation and women's labour within it. Although domestic labour is part of the exchange relations of capitalism — reproducing and maintaining workers, consuming, and reproducing the social relations of capitalism — this labour takes place in a pre-capitalist environment. Domestic labour is individual not social production. It has use-value, consumed rather than exchanged directly for pay. Because domestic labour serves human as well as market needs, social relations within the family can retain personal qualities. Much of domestic labour is task oriented. Craft elements remain as the worker uses a variety of skills to take the job through from start to finish (Hartmann, 1974; Strasser, 1977). Technology in the home appears to enhance task orientation and job satisfaction, even at times to encourage creativity, as through the use of blenders, mixers, food processors and other similar appliances in cooking. Preparing meals, cleaning and laundry are whole jobs aided to their completion by tools, products and appliances available to the housewife. Satisfaction can come from elimination of drudgery, the sense of a job completed and well done, and praise from family members. A pre-capitalist work situation appears to help domestic labour to resist the standardisation, regimentation and control of the labour process that obtains when technology is joined to capitalist production at the paid workplace. When technology, however, aids in standardising the housewife's operations through large appliances and convenience products, and in further rationalising and organising her work through service centres for repairs, cleaning, etc., and shopping malls, the housewife progressively loses control of her labour processes. As women's work is brought more directly into the exchange relations of capitalism and into the public sphere, especially in the consumer role, the more control slips out of the housewife's hands.[17]

A curious paradox emerges. It appears that the greater the degree to which housewives can retain their pre-capitalist mode and social relations of production, grafting on all the technological goodies that capitalism and husband can provide, the more free and in control of work and life women are. This is what *McCall's* magazine and the television advertisements argue, and men readily agree to. Logically, they should, for both capitalism and patriarchy benefit from the juxtaposition of the technology of advanced industrial capitalism with pre-capitalist working conditions (Hartmann, 1974).

The woman, performing her labour in the isolated nuclear family, becomes the ideal target for capitalism to penetrate the home through technology, and thus to control women's work. The ubiquitous mass communication medium, television, as well as radio and print media, reach the housewife individually to tell her that each new product will make her work easier, her home a spotless showcase. She is to be persuaded that 'a ring-around-the-collar' brings censure, that Twinkies mean loving children and Geritol a loving husband. The extraordinary inefficiency of the home as a place of work — because it operates on a pre-capitalist model — proliferates almost endlessly the 'need' for consumer items. Each home 'must' be equipped with a stove, refrigerator, freezer, washer-dryer, dishwasher, blender and so forth, and products to make these work, as well as two cars — or more if there are teenagers, and family budgets can afford.

Perhaps most significant is the way that the pre-capitalist work pattern allows capitalism to use technology further to encroach on and control housewives' time. Technological change has relieved housewives of the most back-breaking aspects of housework; from indoor plumbing, gas and electricity to modern appliances, technology, as we have seen, has helped reduce effort and time for major household chores such as laundry, cleaning and cooking. Why didn't this time accrue to the housewife? How did the content and nature of housework shift to take up the slack? Capitalism, which through technology had helped to create this potentially 'free' time, had to appropriate such time. It employed technology to take away what technology had given. New processes and new products were invented; new standards were set; increasingly sophisticated marketing and advertising techniques created new demands: the age of domestic consumerism grew and flourished (Ewen, 1976; Ehrenreich and English, 1979).

Another part of the power structure, too, could not afford to allow housewives *real* free time. That his wife is at home 'doing nothing' can make a man envious, but it also poses a threat. A woman with time to attend to her own concerns might begin to question her position, and his authority and privilege. 'Idle' hands — and brains — must be kept busy in the service of the patriarchal family. The shift in the content of housework from heavy-duty chores to service roles brings husband and children more of the housewife's time.

Men benefit, too, from the juxtaposition of modern technology with a pre-capitalist mode of production. They get the best of both worlds: services improved through the technology of advanced capitalism, delivered in personalised, pre-capitalist style. Through the mediation of personal wife-servant, the washer-dryer cleans clothes for *him*, the refrigerator preserves *his* food, the stove cooks *his* meals, the car delivers and picks *him* up from the station. Contraception, which can free women from fear of pregnancy (but its use still women's responsibility and risk), can enhance a man's sex life by making his wife more available, and by relieving him from any sense of responsibility in extra-marital affairs. The whole arsenal of technological marvels for the home thus operates so that the housewife can render improved services to husband and family members.

A pre-capitalist work situation strengthens men's position in another way. Women are lodged more firmly into the traditional authority structure of the patriarchal family in which status is ascribed, (Phelps, 1975). Under the sexual hierarchy of the patriarchal family, a woman's ability to gain power over her work and self depends totally on being able to please her ascribed superior, on whom she is economically dependent as well, and who can grant or withhold favours at will. The pre-capitalist work situation under capitalism induces economic dependency and thus subjection to patriarchal authority. A woman's domestic labour is seen as not contributing productively, i.e. monetarily, to the household: in reality the woman at home has no money of her own because she is not paid. Economic dependency is masked by a less than absolute patriarchal authority exercised in many households and by a generally favourable level of material well-being.[18] The technology of industrial capitalism provides material advantages. Patriarchy is Catch-22. Women gain materially only if they stay within the traditional system of the patriarchal family. Let a woman step outside and her earning power is less than 60 per cent of a man's. If she has children and is manless, she can become dependent on the state. The economic costs are severe. Technology plays the crucial role of providing the carrot that makes the housewife feel materially fortunate, thus helping to mask the price she pays. Capitalism and patriarchy join to keep women economically dependent, setting the conditions for her work, and locking her more firmly into a system of male supremacy.

Technology, capitalism and patriarchy thus intersect as technology aids in turning women into 'willing slaves'.[19] If it is so rewarding to be a homemaker, if there is such job responsibility, such satisfaction and creativity, why not bear and rear his children, cook, clean and serve one's lord and master — gladly and willingly? Support the family, fight the ERA (Equal Rights Amendment) and a freezer and microwave oven in every kitchen!

The ideological components of technology provide a further link with capitalism and patriarchy to effect control of 'women's work', and to perpetuate the illusion of liberation through technology. I shall discuss two major facets of technological ideology: one is a blind faith in technology that amounts to technology-worship; the other is a value system based on domination of nature and rational objectivity. Technology-worship has strong American roots, tied to American pragmatism, faith in American 'know-how' and American enterprise — and thus, of course, to beliefs essential to capitalism. (Noble, 1977; Ferkiss, 1969; Gendron, 1977; Marx, 1964; Kasson, 1977). Women as well as men, particularly educated and 'enlightened' women, became enamoured of this national faith. By the turn of the twentieth century, the professional women who led the domestic science movement were seeking to apply scientific management techniques to the home. They sought to organise and rationalise housework so that it would match industry's precision and efficiency. But, as Ehrenreich and English point out, their 'feminist' attempt thus to professionalise and upgrade housework — in the service of their scientific and technological ideal — served instead to deliver the movement to industrial capitalism, and to make such work a menial occupation (Ehrenreich and English, 1979: 179-81; Strasser, 1977). The industrial order was only too willing to develop this new market. The domestic science leaders themselves, in the heyday of a faith in American business that equalled faith in science-technology, 'had passed the banner of "right living" on to the manufacturers of appliances, soups, convenience foods and household aids' (Ehrenreich and English, 1979: 180). The legacy of this 'manufacture of housework' is with us today. The 'happy housewife' in her streamlined, appliance-happy home is deemed living proof that technology and American enterprise work. What the picture illustrates is that the combined ideology of a faith in science-technology-cum-American-enterprise is alive and well. Today, the ideology is manifested in the 'technological fix', that technology can solve our most pressing problems. Whether they be crime, poverty, energy, war, peace, they are subject to computerisation, systems analysis, to all the hardware and software systems available. That housewives, along with others of our population, brought up and nurtured in the technological faith, should accept the notion that technology liberates women is not surprising. Despite cracks in the faith in the wake of leaking nuclear power plants, acid rain and toxic wastes, computer errors and appliance breakdowns, the belief is difficult to dislodge. The usefulness of the technology-worship ideology to political and economic leaders – indeed, their own belief in it – and its deep roots in the historical development of the American political economy and its underlying belief system, seem to ensure that the ideology will continue to survive.

Patriarchal ideology also lends its support. If American technology and enterprise can produce such a wealth and variety of consumer goods just for women, and even make the mechanisms simple enough for these limited creatures to operate, then American technological prowess must be advanced indeed. Technology will cure not only broad social ills, but housewives' ills. For depresson, we 'prescribe' a new dishwasher or home freezer, tranquillisers, 'uppers' or 'downers', oestrogen pills, or a new 'miracle' home-care product. The more that women are viewed as subordinate, easily manipulated creatures, the easier it is for technology-worship to flourish in the service of American consumerism, for the myth of freedom to be maintained and for actual control over women to be exercised.

Patriarchal ideology forms an even more explicit link with technology through a shared value system. The underlying belief system of modern technology, that is, rational objectivity and the domination of nature, reflects male values. The domination-of-nature ideology is integral to the science on which much of modern technology is built (Leiss, 1974). Historically, women represent nature; they become synonymous with nature. As such, they are inferior; they must be tamed along with the other natural elements that man can now increasingly control. At the same time, however, nature confers on women a special power – to be both awed and envied – the power to create life. A long tradition of 'scientific' attempts to create human beings, or simulated ones, attests to man's desire to discover and control the mystery of creation. Can we not hold that the drive to control women's reproductive cycles is fed by the need for men to control and subordinate the one 'natural' power women possess exclusively: the power to reproduce the human race (de Beauvoir, 1953; Hays, 1964; Lederer, 1968; Ortner, 1974; Reuther, 1975; Griffin, 1978; Daly, 1979; Gray, 1979; Keller, 1980; Merchant, 1980)?

Modern technology also reflects so-called male values of conquest and dominance, of rationality and objectivity. As corporate capitalism has employed technology to mechanise and rationalise the workplace, personal and subjective values are increasingly shut out. The rational and objective must prevail. Yet critics of modern technological society have pointed to the irrationality of the seemingly rational, which creates further irrationality through its own internal logic (Marcuse, 1964).[20] A technological imperative appears to control, as wielders of power (who are mostly male) ask whether a programme is technologically feasible, and cost-effective, not whether it meets human needs. The human concerns that are thereby suppressed are associated with female values, now conveniently contained as the housewife lovingly whips up her Betty Crocker cake-mix, 'self-polishes' her kitchen floor and 'pampers' her infant. These values, too, become packaged and depersonalised. Are humanising values somehow a threat to the existing order?[21] As the home and 'women's work' within it are mechanised and rationalised in the manner of labour in the paid workplace, and drawn further into the dehumanised exchange relations of monopoly capital, is a technological imperative at work? Does it become necessary, in the name of technological rationality, to suppress women and the values they are said to represent in order to preserve our technological system (Rothschild, 1981)?

Conclusion

I have argued in this chapter that technology has enhanced the power of capitalism and patriarchy to effect the control of 'women's work', and women. A myth has been perpetuated that reproductive and household technologies liberate women, when they have helped to increase women's dependency on capitalist and patriarchal structures of power, and effectively mask the fact that women are thus controlled.

Women's domestic labour under capitalism, performed in an isolated nuclear household, retains pre-capitalist elements despite being part of capitalist exchange relations. The juxtaposition of advanced industrial technology with this pre-capitalist work situation has aided capitalism to penetrate the home with consumer demands and goods. Time saved from drudgery is thus appropriated by capitalism. The level of material well-being which technology helps provide serves to mask such appropriation and control. The price women pay for material advantage is to stay within the patriarchal family where they are economically dependent and under a traditional patriarchal authority structure. Men gain the time and services of a personal wife-servant who employs sophisticated technology to serve men's individual needs.

Technology-worship, part of the econo-political faith in the combined power of technology-plus-American-enterprise, lends credence to the myth that technology liberates women. The domination-of-nature ideology and the commitment to rational objectivity that underlie modern technology reflect male values. Beliefs about women's inferiority become embedded in technological thinking and activity. To the repressive and non-liberating aspects of technology under capitalism is added a male mindset that can bring further entrapment. Continuance of the present technological order may depend not only on suppressing women, but on suppressing human and female-identified values.

The effect of technology's links with capitalism and patriarchy, both materially and ideologically, on women's domestic labour thus opens up new sets of issues about the 'liberating' nature of modern technology, not only for women, but for our whole society.

Notes

1. Capitalism here denotes a system of privately owned means of production for private profit, and includes the supporting social and belief systems.
2. Patriarchy here means a system of male supremacy, rooted in the sexual division of labour, manifested in a given society's practices and institutions, and supported by a self-serving ideology. In this chapter I shall situate patriarchy within the capitalism of American society. The broader framework of patriarchal values and beliefs is that of Western culture. See Eisenstein (1979, pp. 5-40); for further views, see Kuhn and Wolpe (1978) and Sargent (1980).
3. The question immediately arises: what about women under socialism? Don't we find patriarchy here, too? Despite paper guarantees of equality and women's high participation in the labour force, women under socialism have the so-called double-bind of two full-time jobs without the conveniences that American women enjoy. American women and their consumer goods and technology — products of capitalism (see pp. 170-6) — are the envy of their socialist sisters: see, for example, Hilda Scott, *Does Socialism Liberate Women?* (Beacon Press, Boston, 1974).What would happen if technology for the home could be, and were, transplanted to such non-capitalist societies? The Third World is an issue, too. Evidence is accumulating that introducing agricultural and industrial technology into the Third World has not necessarily improved the status of women, as patriarchal attitudes have accompanied such 'development': see for example, Ester Boserup, *Woman's Role in Economic Development* (St. Martin's Press, New York, 1970); Nadia Haggag Youssef, *Women and Work in Developing Societies* (Population Monograph Series, no. 15, Berkeley, Calif., 1974); see also Batya Weinbaum, *The Curious Courtship of Women's Liberation and Socialism* (South End Press, Boston, 1978). Domestic technology and women's status, viewed cross-culturally, therefore raises two sets of questions: (i) it reopens from a new perspective the issue of the relationship of technological development to modes and

ideologies of production; and (ii) it probes further the relationship between women's material condition and women's liberation, i.e., women's right to choose and control their own labour and thus to define their roles in the societies in which they live.

4. Rayna Rapp makes an important distinction between household and family; a household being a 'locus of shared activities' in which people 'enter into relations of production, reproduction, and consumption with one another', and a family being an ideological concept through which 'normative recruitment to those relations' is made. See Rapp (1978) and Rapp, Ross and Bridenthal (1979, pp. 176-9).

5. For Marxists, too, household labour was not 'real work' because it did not create surplus value and therefore was not counted as productive labour. The debate among feminist Marxists as to whether domestic labour is 'productive' or 'unproductive' is a long and continuing one. For a perceptive analysis and critique of the different positions, see Fee (1976); and also Glazer-Malbin (1976, pp. 917-20). Work that moves beyond the debate to create new categories for analysis includes Rapp (1978) and Eisenstein (1979). Other useful works on the role of women's labour under capitalism include Margaret Benston, 'The Political Economy of Women's Liberation', *Monthly Review*, vol. 21 (September 1969), pp. 13-27; Rowbotham (1973); Sheila Rowbotham, *Women, Resistance and Revolution* (Vintage Books, New York, 1974); Joan Landes, 'Wages for Housework: Subsidizing Capitalism?', *Quest: a feminist quarterly*, vol. 2, no. 2 (1975), pp. 17-30; Zaretsky (1976); and Strasser (1977, Ch. 1).

6. As Rapp (1978, pp. 288-9) states:

consumption includes turning an amount of wages into commodities so that labour-power may be reproduced . . . Women experience the pay packet in terms of the use values it will buy. Yet their consumption work is done in the world of exchange value. They mediate the tension between use and exchange . . .

For a similar point made from a non-Marxist perspective, see Galbraith (1973, Ch. IV).

7. Galbraith (1973, pp. 35-6) notes, 'in a society which sets store by pecuniary achievement, a natural authority resides with the person who earns the money . . . The household, in the established economies, is essentially a disguise for the exercise of male authority.'

8. Technology and women's work outside the home is beyond the scope of this essay. The classic text in this area had accepted prevailing stereotypes about women's work aptitudes and abilities: see Elizabeth Faulkner Baker, *Technology and Women's Work* (Columbia University Press, New York, 1964). The new literature, from a feminist perspective, includes Evelyn Nakano Glenn and Roslyn L. Feldberg, 'Degraded and Deskilled: The Proletarianisation of Clerical Work', *Social Problems*, vol. 25, no. 1 (1977), pp. 52-64; Sally L. Hacker, 'Farming out the Home: Women and Agribusiness', *The Second Wave*, vol. 5 (Spring/Summer 1977), pp. 38-48; Sally L. Hacker, 'Sex Stratification, Technology and Organisational Change: A Longitudinal Case Study of AT&T', *Social Problems*, vol. 26, no. 5 (1979), pp. 539-57; *Conference Proceedings: Women and Technology: Deciding What's Appropriate* (Women's Resource Centre, Missoula, Montana, 1979); and Trescott (1979) which also contains a section on technology for the home.

9. Noble (1977, pp. xxii-iii) charts how 'the history of modern technology in America is of a piece with that of the rise of corporate capitalism', resulting in the strengthening of capitalist social relations and ideology.

10. The following is based mainly on Braverman (1974): see especially Chs. 7, 8, 9 and 10. However, Braverman makes a distinction between technology and scientific management which I do not.

11. Abortion, once a major and accepted method of birth control, which has made recent technological advances is not, strictly speaking, contraception. However, its control mechanisms over women are the same as for other forms of birth control discussed. Tubal ligation is not controlled by women either: poor women are sterilised without their consent; middle-class women often find it difficult to get the operation. The condom is used by men and was designed originally for disease prevention, not contraception; it could hardly be said to be under the control of women.

12. As Wertz and Wertz (1977, p. 235) point out, women (i.e., middle-class women) originally co-operated with doctors, endorsing the move from home to hospital birth and the accompanying technology. They add, however, that the 'move into the hospital illustrates how widespread was faith in the practical science of medicine, [and] how cultural, social, and medical motives interacted to medicalise and institutionalise birth'. See also Gena Corea, 'The Caesarean Epidemic', *Mother Jones*, vol. V, no. VI (1980), pp. 28-35 and 42.

13. For an assessment of DES's effects, see Holmes, Hoskins and Gross (1980, *2*, Ch. 1). For an analysis of the effects of technologies associated with both birth control and childbirth, see, by the same authors, the first volume of this two-part work on human reproductive technologies: (1980, *1*).

14. The women's health movement, stressing self-help, demystification of medical practices, home births, licensing of midwives, etc., is providing a long-overdue response. See Boston Women's Health Book Collective, *Our Bodies, Ourselves*, 2nd edn (Simon & Schuster, New York, 1976); Claudia Dreifus (ed.), *Seizing Our Bodies: The Politics of Women's Health* (Vintage Books, New York, 1978); Barbara Rowland and Lawrence J. Schneiderman, 'Women in Alternative Health Care: Their Influence on Traditional Medicine', *International Journal of Women's Studies*, vol. 2 (July/August 1979), pp. 305-10; Sheryl K. Ruzek, *The Women's Health Movement: Finding Alternatives to Traditional Medical Professionalism* (Praeger, New York, 1978). For a theoretical analysis of women and reproduction, see O'Brien (1978).

15. See Rose and Hanmer (1976) who provide an important feminist political analysis of reproductive technologies and women's freedom. On future prospects, see also Amitai Etzioni, *Genetic Fix: The Next Technological Revolution* (Harper & Row, New York, 1975) and Holmes *et al* (1980). My argument does not deny that women's lives have been saved and that reproductive choices have been enhanced through human reproductive technologies. What I question is the degree and kind of control women may exercise over these technologies: over the research, production and marketing, and prohibition and use. If women do not control the technologies or, more accurately, the institutions that make such technologies possible, I question the actual extent of control women can have over their own reproductive processes, now and in the future.

16. While some women do use technology selectively and do not fully buy into consumerism (e.g., job-holding mothers who must cut corners, or the ecologically-motivated woman who has the luxury of choice), such women are responding individually. Their individual actions do not change the system. Betty Friedan's *The Feminine Mystique* (Dell Publishing, New York, 1964), which helped to launch the collective response that became the liberal-reformist wing of the American women's movement, did contain a strong attack on the consumer society and its effects on women. A systematic critique, however, was lacking. While the voices of both socialist feminists and radical feminists are heard, the mainstream thrust of the women's movement continues to lack a

fundamental critique of the capitalist and patriarchal causes of women's oppression. Until the systematic nature of women's oppression is more widely understood, many women will continue to believe in the efficacy of a combination of legal reforms and privatised solutions to women's problems.

17. Landes (1979) points to Marcuse's interpretation that women's home and child-centred experiences develop a social self-ideal that can resist the most oppressive features of late capitalist society. He finds a humanity in women's consciousness that is rooted in their traditional roles, which can lead not only to women's liberation but to the liberation of the whole.

18. Even working for pay, as married women increasingly are in the US, does not necessarily give a woman financial independence. Usually, she works to contribute to family support; nor are her wages enough to support herself or her family on her own. For example, among American families in 1977 in which both husband and wife contributed to family income, the wife's share was one-quarter for white workers and one-third for black workers, with average earnings of $5,683 and $6,257, respectively (US Bureau of the Census, 1979, p. 456).

19. 'All men, except the most brutish, desire to have, in the woman most nearly connected with them, not a forced slave but a willing one, not a slave merely, but a favourite. They have therefore put everything in practice to enslave their minds.' John Stuart Mill, *On The Subjection of Women* (Fawcett Publications, New York, 1971, originally published 1896), p. 30.

20. As Landes (1979) points out, Marcuse in his later work explicitly equates the aggressive and repressive needs and values of capitalism with male-dominated culture. See also Marcuse (1974).

21. See and compare the following psychoanalytic approaches to the development and societal effects of female and male values: Jean Baker Miller, *Toward a New Psychology of Women* (Beacon Press, Boston, 1976); Dinnerstein (1976); and Nancy Chodorow, *The Reproduction of Mothering* (University of California Press, Berkeley, 1978).

Bibliography

Abbott, E. (1969) *Women in Industry: A Study in American Economic History*, Arno and *The New York Times*, New York (originally published in 1910)
Arms, S. (1975) *Immaculate Deception: A New Look at Women and Childbirth in America*, Houghton Mifflin, Boston
Baxandall, R., Ewen, E. and Gordon, L. (1976) 'The Working Class Has Two Sexes', *Monthly Review, 28*, 3, 1-9
——, Gordon, L. and Reverby, S. (eds.) (1976) *America's Working Women: A Documentary History – 1600 to the Present*, Vintage Books, New York
Berheide, C. W., Berk, S.F. and Berk, R.A. (1976) 'Household Work in the Suburbs: The Job and its Participants', *Pacific Sociological Review, 19*, 4, 491-518
Bogdan, J. (1978) 'Care or Cure? Childbirth Practices in Nineteenth Century America', *Feminist Studies, 4*, 2, 92-9
Bose, C. (1979) 'Technology and Changes in the Division of Labor in the American Home', *Women's Studies International Quarterly, 2*, 3 295-304
Braverman, H. (1974) *Labor and Monopoly Capital: The Degradation of Work in the Twentieth Century*, Monthly Review Press, New York
Cowan, R. S. (1976) 'The "Industrial Revolution" in the Home: Household Technology and Social Change in the 20th Century', *Technology and Culture, 17*, 1, 1-23

Daly, M. (1979) *Gyn/Ecology: The Metaethics of Radical Feminism*, Beacon Press, Boston

de Beauvoir, S. (1953) *The Second Sex*, trans. H.M. Parshley (ed.), Alfred A. Knopf, New York

Dinnerstein, D. (1976) *The Mermaid and the Minotaur: Sexual Arrangements and Human Malaise*, Harper & Row, New York

Ehrenreich, J. and Ehrenreich, B. (1976) 'Work and Consciousness', *Monthly Review, 28*, 3, 10-18

Ehrenreich, B. and English, D. (1973) *Witches, Midwives, and Nurses: A History of Women Healers*, Feminist Press, Old Westbury, New York

—— —— (1979) *For her Own Good: 150 Years of the Experts' Advice to Women*, Anchor Press/Doubleday, Garden City, New York

Eisenstein, Z. (ed.) (1979) *Capitalist Patriarchy and the Case for Socialist Feminism*, Monthly Review Press, New York

Ewen, S. (1976) *Captains of Consciousness*, McGraw-Hill, New York, part III

Fee, T. (1976) 'Domestic Labor: An Analysis of Housework and its Relations to the Production Process', *The Review of Radical Political Economics, 8*, 1, 1-8

Ferkiss, V. (1969) *Technological Man: The Myth and the Reality*, George Braziller, New York

Galbraith, J.K. (1973) *Economics and the Public Purpose*, Houghton Mifflin, Boston

Gendron, B. (1977) *Technology and the Human Condition*, St Martin's Press, New York

Giedion, S. (1948) *Mechanization Takes Command*, OUP, New York

Glazer-Malbin, N. (1976) 'Housework', *Signs, 1*, 4, 905-22

Gordon, L. (1977) *Woman's Body, Woman's Right: A Social History of Birth Control in America*, Penguin Books, New York

Gray, E.D. (1979) *Why the Green Nigger? Re-Mything Genesis*, Roundtable Press, Wellesley, MA

Griffin, S. (1978) *Woman and Nature: The Roaring Inside Her*, Harper & Row, New York

Hartmann, H. (1974) 'Capitalism and Women's Work in the Home, 1900-1930', unpublished PhD thesis, Yale University, New Haven

—— (1976) 'Capitalism, Patriarchy, and Job Segregation by Sex' in Martha Blaxall and Barbara Regan (eds.), *Women and the Workplace*, University of Chicago Press, Chicago, pp. 137-69

Hays, H.R. (1964) *The Dangerous Sex*, G.P. Putnam & Sons, New York

Himes, N. E. (1970) *Medical History of Contraception*, Schocken Books, New York (originally published in 1936)

Holmes H. B., Hoskins, B. B. and Gross, M. (eds.) (1980) *Birth Control and Controlling Birth: Women's Perspectives, 1*, and *The Custom-Made Child; Women's Perspectives, 2*, The Humana Press, Clifton, NJ, 2 vols.

Hymowitz, C. and Weissman, M. (1978) *A History of Women in America*, Bantam Books, New York, Ch. 5.

Kasson, J.F. (1977) *Civilizing the Machine*, Penguin Books, New York

Keller, E.F. (1980) 'Baconian Science: A Hermaphroditic Birth', *Philosophical Forum, XI*, 3 (Spring) 299-308

Kessler-Harris, A. (1976) 'Women, Work, and the Social Order' in Berenice Carroll (ed.), *Liberating Women's History*, University of Illinois Press, Urbana, pp. 330-43

Kuhn, A. and Wolpe, A.M. (eds.) (1978) *Feminism and Materialism: Women and Modes of Production*, RKP, London

Landes, J.B. (1979) 'Marcuse's Feminist Dimension', *Telos*, no. 41 (Autumn), pp. 158-65

Lederer, W. (1968) *The Fear of Women*, Grune & Stratton, New York

Leiss, W. (1974) *The Domination of Nature*, Beacon Press, Boston

Lopato, H.Z. (1971) *Occupation: Housewife*, OUP, New York

Marcuse, H. (1964) *One Dimensional Man*, Beacon Press, Boston

——— (1974) 'Marxism and Feminism', *Women's Studies, 2*, 3, 279-88

Marx, L. (1964) *The Machine in the Garden*, OUP, New York

Merchant, C. (1980) *The Death of Nature: Women, Ecology, and the Scientific Revolution*, Harper & Row, New York

New York Times, The (1979) Response to Survey by the National Commission on Working Women (14 July), p. 8

Noble, D.F. (1977) *America By Design: Science, Technology, and the Rise of Corporate Capitalism*, Alfred A. Knopf, New York

Oakley, A. (1975) *Woman's Work: The Housewife, Past and Present*, Pantheon Books, New York

O'Brien, M. (1978) 'The Dialectics of Reproduction', *Women's Studies International Quarterly, 1*, 3, 233-9

Oppenheimer, V.K. (1970) *The Female Labor Force in the United States: Demographic and Economic Factors Governing its Growth and Changing Composition*, Population Monograph Series, no. 5, University of California Press, Berkeley, Calif.

Ortner, S. B. (1974) 'Is Female to Male as Nature is to Culture?' in Rosaldo and Lamphere, pp. 67-87

Phelps, L. (1975) 'Patriarchy and Capitalism', *Quest: a feminist quarterly, 2*, 2, 34-48

Rapp, R. (1978) 'Family and Class in Contemporary America: Notes Toward an Understanding of Ideology', *Science & Society, 42*, 3, 278-300

———, Ross, E. and Bridenthal, R. (1979) 'Examining Family History', *Feminist Studies, 5*, 1, 174-200

Reuther, R.R. (1975) *New Woman New Earth: Sexist Ideologies and Human Liberation*, Seabury Press, New York

Rich, A. (1976) *Of Woman Born: Motherhood as an Experience and Institution*, W.W. Norton, New York

Rosaldo, M.Z. and Lamphere, L. (eds.) (1974) *Woman, Culture, and Society*, Stanford University Press, Stanford, Calif.

Rose, H. and Hanmer, J. (1976) 'Women's Liberation, Reproduction, and the Technological Fix' in Diana Leonard Barker and Sheila Allen (eds.), *Sexual Divisions and Society: Process and Change*, Tavistock Publications, London, pp. 199-223

Rothman, B.K. (1979) 'Women, Health and Medicine' in Jo Freeman (ed.), *Women: A Feminist Perspective*, 2nd edn, Mayfield Publishing, Palo Alto, Calif., pp. 27-40

Rothschild, J. (1981) 'A Feminist Perspective on Technology and the Future', *Women's Studies International Quarterly, 4*, 1

Rowbotham, S. (1973) *Woman's Consciousness, Man's World*, Penguin Books, Baltimore

Sacks, K. (1974) 'Engels Revisited: Women, the Organisation of Production and Private Property' in Rosaldo and Lamphere, pp. 207-22

Sargent, L. (ed.) (1980) *Women and Revolution*, South End Press, Boston

Stanley, A. (1981) *Mothers of Invention*, Scarecrow Press, Metuchen, NJ

Strasser, S.M. (1977) 'Never Done: The Ideology and Technology of Household Work, 1850-1930', unpublished PhD thesis, SUNY, Stony Brook

Trescott, M.M. (ed.) (1979) *Dynamos and Virgins Revisited: Women and Technological Change in History*, Scarecrow Press, Metuchen, NJ

US Bureau of the Census (1978) *Statistical Abstract of the United States 1978*, p. 474
US Bureau of the Census (1979) *Statistical Abstract of the United States 1979*, p. 788
Vanek, J. (1973) 'Keeping Busy: Time Spent in Housework, United States, 1920-1970', unpublished PhD thesis, University of Michigan
—— (1974) 'Time Spent in Housework', *Scientific American, 231*, 5, 116-20
—— (1978) 'Household Technology and Social Status: Rising Living Standards and Status and Residence Differences in Housework', *Technology and Culture, 19*, 3, 361-75
Walker, K.E. and Woods, M.E. (1976) *Time Use: A Measure of Household Production of Family Goods and Services*, Center for the Family of the American Home Economics Association, Washington, DC
Weinbaum, B. and Bridges, A. (1976) 'The Other Side of the Paycheck: Monopoly Capital and the Structure of Consumption', *Monthly Review, 28*, 3, 88-103
Welter, B. (1966) 'The Cult of True Womanhood, 1820-1860', *American Quarterly, 18* (Summer), 151-74
Wertz, R.W. and Wertz, D.C. (1977) *Lying-In: A History of Childbirth in America*, The Free Press, New York
Zaretsky, E. (1976) *Capitalism, The Family & Personal Life*, Harper & Row, New York

10 WOMEN'S EMPLOYMENT NETWORKS: STRATEGIES FOR DEVELOPMENT*

Jeanne Marie Col

> Self-help groups are voluntary, small group structures for
> mutual aid and the accomplishment of a special purpose. They
> are usually formed by peers who have come together for
> mutual assistance in satisfying a common need, overcoming a
> common handicap, or life-disrupting problem, and bringing
> about desired social and/or personal change. The initiators and
> members of such groups perceive that their needs are not, or
> cannot be, met by or through existing social institutions. Self-
> help groups emphasize face-to-face social interaction and the
> assumption of personal responsibility by members. They often
> provide material assistance, as well as emotional support. They
> are frequently 'cause'-oriented, and promulgate an ideology or
> values through which members may attain an enhanced sense of
> personal identity. (Katz and Bender, 1976a, p. 278)

Women are developing themselves and their institutions, and at the
same time transforming their societies. Comprising over 50 per cent of
the population and filling multiple, critical roles, women profoundly
affect their environment when they empower themselves by working
together for their goals. While the goals differ from society to society,
the process of achievement usually involves some co-operative organisational effort by the women. Whether these are organisations of market
women in West Africa or unions of women factory workers in the early
American textile mills, women who otherwise would be divided or
isolated from each other are able to help one another. In the process,
each becomes more powerful and more confident because she has
become part of a group which supports her. With collective strategies
women are strengthened and can effectively assume important
economic, social and political roles.

The data for this study are largely confined to the USA, but some
reference will be made to other countries in order to speculate on how
far concepts can be generalised. A study of such networks has at least
five purposes. The first is to describe and understand what women are
currently doing. The second is to understand and possibly to trace the

links between these networks and political participation, including political recruitment and socialisation. The third purpose is to study the innovative organisational structures and behaviours that may eventually have wider applications. The fourth is to study the extent to which women's networks contribute to the development of a country, both directly and indirectly. Finally, such a study may lead to greater interest in women's networks, and possibly to more and more varied networks being formed.

Although most countries give legal equality to women, the practice is to deny them full participation in economic, social and political institutions through informal means based on traditional male oriented values. In spite of Lionel Tiger's assertion that men, not women, form groups, women realise that their most reliable allies in the struggle for equality are their sisters. Feeling isolated and/or powerless, women are creating groups that meet their needs for contacts for jobs or education, social support, political action and so on. These networks are intentionally inward and need oriented. Past successes need to be developed through hard work, grass-roots organising and setting progressive examples. Many less active women, who feared to become involved in radical feminism in the past, are becoming involved in special interest organisations that relate directly to their needs. Each woman becomes active for her own reasons and only later realises that she is part of an increasingly large network of women.

These women's networks have political consequences not only for the influence on policy that they might exert, but also for the experience of co-operative behaviours, organisational strategies and leadership skills gained by the participants. By reducing their isolation from one another and establishing a mutually beneficial community, women become integrated into a larger society and can imagine participating in society-wide activities and organisations. Through their activities and positions, they can gain visibility that may eventually result in participation in larger, male-dominated institutions.[1] Another important aspect of the women's support networks is that these networks represent innovative methods of aggregating individuals into self-help groups in a decentralised, co-operative, flexible and responsive manner. Even the mostly highly structured corporations are experimenting with project management teams, flexible hours and worker participation. Women's networks serve not only as models of a flexible mode of organisation but also train women in these behaviours. These women will then influence the behaviour of regular employing organisations when women achieve important positions.

A fourth aspect of particular importance to countries which are striving to achieve rapid social and economic change is the ability of women's networks to tap, and even to create, new organisational and individual resources. When relatively powerless individuals join together in a mutual-aid group, they strengthen each other, aggregate resources, heighten awareness of mutual problems and abilities, and create possibilities for future action. Although the mobilisation of previously powerless groups can be disruptive of existing power structures, the process of educating, training and empowering persons ultimately must lead to a stronger political system involving more persons committed to it. Furthermore, such networks link the individual and society as a whole, thereby decreasing anomie. Because women have been victims of isolation and at best tokenism, networks which link women to each other are an important step towards integrating women into the active sectors of society.

The final objective of this study is purely normative and prescriptive. I believe that as more women learn about other women's support networks, they will be encouraged to form such groups themselves, thereby increasing women's capacity for goal oriented, co-operative action.

Methodology

This study is based on a survey of women's support networks in employment. Other types of networks are in health-care, neighbourhoods, social work and amongst senior citizens. Self-help support networks are being formed in all types of employment: white-collar, blue-collar or pink-collar; professional, technical, skilled, non-skilled or clerical, and particularly among minority women, low-income women, women in managerial positions and women in non-traditional jobs; within a job category and across job categories. In each of these cases, women feel isolated and seek strength and help from other women in a similar situation. Within a job category, women are usually seeking advancement; across job categories, they are seeking contacts to help them improve their performance of the job, chances for moving to a better job and the fulfilment of personal-social needs.

A questionnaire was sent to the networks identified. The questions concerned the history, organisation, membership, finances, operation and goals of the networks. Many are very informal and unstructured; others have officers, programmes, staff and so on. Some networks are a dynamic success with an increasingly large membership; others have disintegrated after a short history. This chapter is based on replies from networks concerned with employment, and interviews with members and leaders of such networks. My current list includes at least 100 networks and more than 500 sources of information, such as women's centres and counselling programmes.[2] In addition, I have been an active member of the Albany Women's Forum, one of the first such networks (set up in the winter of 1977), and can draw upon its successful experience and its several 'identity' crises.

Networking and Self-Help Groups

Self-help groups range from *ad hoc*, consciousness-raising meetings to highly organised associations designed to provide specialised training and information for the members. Those concerned with social welfare, widows and battered women have been described elsewhere (Collins and Pancoast, 1976; Katz and Bender, 1976b). All groups help women to see that their problems are not the result of their own personal inadequacy. In employment, self-help groups can help women to deal with quite specific problems. Even when affirmative action has secured a few jobs or higher jobs for a few women, usually in a large hierarchical structure, women find themselves isolated and unable to succeed. One is quoted as saying 'It's lonely being the only woman planner. The secretaries are uncomfortable; the men are uncomfortable (Houyman and Kaplan, 1976, p. 374).

Women who have such 'token' or minority status are developing networks outside their employment. The networks offer moral support by providing regular contact with others similarly placed, the opportunity to compare experiences, learn leadership and management skills, and try out new behaviours. Although much of the content of role (job) definition is learned on the job (role-taking), pre- or extra-employment socialisation can influence how someone adapts the job to herself (role-making).[3] Experience in the women's movement and in support groups of women rather than reliance on referral centres or government agencies can develop an awareness of self, a sense of self-determination and androgynous characteristics, because these groups emphasise both caring for each other and taking responsibility for decisions, planning and the development of the group. However, it is only when women fill more than a token number of the organisation's roles, that they will have an impact on the behavioral norms of their employing organisation, thereby making their non-network environment more hospitable.

These networks are characterised by their spontaneous growth, their development by and for the needs of local, grass-roots women, by their relative self-reliance, flexibility, responsibleness and their participatory style, and by being oriented to change. Among their most influential tenets are an open leadership style, participation, small groups and temporary groupings, such as task forces or consciousness-raising groups. A central aspect is the leaderless group, in which each member learns the skills involved in planning, organising and co-ordinating. Positions of power and the burden of responsibility rotate or are chosen by lot so that the capacity of each member is raised to that of a leader. The group operates in a collaborative, rather than competitive, mode. Not only does such a principle make an individual dispensable but it also represents an investment in the training of every participant (Berger and Neuhaus, 1977). The payoff comes both in the increased collective capacity of the group and in the increased self-confidence of the participants, and their capacity to work effectively in other organisations. This leadership style implies a decentralised mode in which a group is divided into semi-autonomous smaller units. It is anti-hierarchical and anti-authoritarian. In addition, in order to be responsive to their environment and the needs of the members, such groups tend to have a flexible structure, emphasising task forces, project teams and other temporary sub-units.

As a consequence of experience in such groups, women are likely to desire a number of specific reforms in their employing organisations. They will desire more decentralisation, that is, flatter organisations, in which there are more potential leadership roles and more opportunities to advance. They will favour flexible organisational structures, such as project teams or flexi-time, that can help the organisation to respond to environmental and internal demands. They will encourage the internal advertising of jobs, bridges between job-ladders, redesign of jobs, lateral moves, status based on skills and performance rather than rank, as well as open communication about the operations of the organisation (Schwartz and Rago, 1973, p. 75).

Employment Networks

The study focuses on local, grass-roots organisations that are not-for-profit and have no legal status at all. (They are not incorporated and have no written constitution, by-laws or rules.) They usually have little money, few if any staff and borrowed facilities. The leadership is open, but often a few individuals take responsibility for maintaining continuity, serving as role-models and mentors, and recruiting new members and leaders.

The founding of these networks can result from a conference, or a caucus of some larger professional or interest organisation, but most often a few women get together for lunch and decide to institutionalise their meetings, and to open membership to other women. Another model is the group of women who find themselves together in a work-shop or a classroom and then decide to continue to meet as a self-help group (for example, Public Service Women's Studies in Albany and a Mother as Person workshop on Staten Island). Every network thus far responding to the survey began with fewer than 20 women, the average number being seven. Some networks now have mailing lists of several hundred women (up to 1,000 for one network), the average being 546 members. The respondents indicate that members show considerable commitment to the network and have continued to be active for several years or intend to be active for a long time.

Some networks have specialised memberships: women in coal-mining, women in management or women in non-traditional jobs. Others, such as the Albany Women's Forum and the Sacramento Women's Network, are open to all interested women. Their memberships include women working in government, non-profit-making organisations and business, as well as women who own their own businesses. Some groups are open to those seeking jobs and housewives perceiving themselves as only temporarily out of the work force who wish to be integrated into working women's networks. A few networks impose qualifications as to income or job, or recruit members by invitation only. These are gener-ally groups of highly placed women who seek to provide confidential job information and employment help to each other. Two examples of this kind of network are in Denver and Washington, DC.

The members usually come from within a 30-mile radius of a central location, and therefore share an interest in a particular geographical area. Most members are aged between 30 and 39, with many also aged between 40 and 49. A few women are below or above the 30-50 age-range. Networks notice that there is a constant renewal of member-ship as people move into the area, get new jobs, professions or promotions, and realise new aspects of their situation: isolation, alien-ation, discrimination, frustration. Although no network indicated that men regularly attended its meetings, four groups do not exclude men. The programmes and activities are of greater interest to women, and men often feel awkward. One woman interviewed stated that, 'Women have been excluded from men's events for a long time. I enjoy telling men that they cannot attend.'

The most frequently mentioned reason for attending was 'to be involved with other women in their own or other occupations'. Women also mentioned as reasons: to seek employment, to serve as mentors for other women and to meet other women socially. Joining networks is seen as a partial solution to a woman's practical problem. About one-third of the groups responding to the questionnaire include action on issues of public policy in their activities. In contrast another one-third were adamant that their group avoided policy issues; this decision stemmed from a conscious decision to link women with women irrespective of their political preferences. Several networks indicated that they regularly assessed the needs of members through question-naires, thereby responding to changed perceptions of needs and interests.

All networks have some type of steering committee or leadership cadre. Three networks elect leaders and three networks have an open leadership composed of volunteers. Some networks deliberately rotate leadership positions to avoid any member becoming too powerful in the group. In the Albany Women's Forum, whoever comes to the steering committee at any meeting is considered a member for that meeting. While there might be a problem of continuity, women period-ically volunteer to constitute a core group of regular attenders. Thus far we have always had enough volunteers to keep the forum active. The forum attempts to be responsive to members' needs, encouraging every member to be as active as she wishes in planning programmes and activities, and decision-making.

Meetings are most often held monthly, although some networks meet weekly, in restaurants, hotels, women's centres, libraries and local YWCAs. General meetings are open to all members and often to all women. They are usually held in the evenings, after work or at lunch. If there is a cost (for example, luncheon), attendance may depend on ability to pay. The Albany Women's Forum has adopted a policy that those who cannot afford lunch may pay a cover charge for coffee only. Steering committees meet monthly in every case reported thus far. Task forces, committees and staff meet as often as necessary. Sub-units are generally associated with the action oriented groups and have not been formed by groups whose primary function is the provision of contacts and information about jobs.[4]

All networks have some method of mailing details of their activities to members and some include job openings. Some groups also prepare a directory of members in order to facilitate informal communication among members, and to help in finding a 'friend' in a particular government agency, in the insurance business, or with a similar interest or experience.

As a network begins to plan to appoint a director or to programme activities, the inevitable question of money arises. Networks solicit money from their own members, government agencies, private foundations and other voluntary organisations. It is normal for the women's business or agency to contribute postage, facilities or staff time during the initial formation period. Local YWCAs have been very helpful, as have women in insurance and accounting firms. Most of the groups currently collected dues on an annual basis. Except for the most exclusive networks of executive women, the amount is usually small ($5-$15 p.a.) in order that many women can afford to participate. Those networks receiving grants are most likely to be action oriented groups that developed with sponsorship from a larger organisation or agency.

All networks indicate that they have active relationships with other organisations in their relevant professional and/or geographical environment. Those mentioned included: civil rights organisations, labour unions, churches, the YWCA, chambers of commerce, women's centres, educational institutions, and the National Organisation for Women, besides professional organisations such as the American Society for Public Administration, California Elected Women and a Mental Health Association. Women often announce the activities of their other organisations through their networks. Women contacted in this survey mentioned memberships in: the League of Women Voters, Women in Communications, Big Sisters, the National Organisation for Women, Federally Employed Women, women's sports groups, women's religious groups and women's educational programmes. In fact, women's networks are often a means for linking individuals who are members of diverse organisations, and for encouraging women who have not previously been active to join and participate. The women share resources and contacts. Even the most isolated woman finds that after a few meetings she, too, has resources to share with others. This realisation builds confidence and helps the woman to widen her experience further.

Crises in Networking

Networking groups experience predictable crises, relating to the amount of dues, the size of the membership, types of activities and how formally structured they should be. High dues provide funds but exclude potential members who lack the money; effectively this means exclusion on the grounds of class. Limiting the size of the membership may involve restrictions on who can join according to their employment status or type of employer, but increasing size creates purely organisational and logistical problems, for example, handling mailing lists, securing facilities large enough to hold the membership, and creating an atmosphere that appears to be friendly and intimate with 500 women in the room. A great increase in numbers also increases the potential diversity of interests and the possibility for conflict over programme and activities. On the other hand, increasing numbers, increasing diversity, and increasing awareness of each other's problems and concerns can lead to action oriented proposals. Just as networks increase an individual's contacts, they also increase the potential for seeing common problems and collective solutions.

The first decision has to be 'should this network be involved in public policy and action?' or is there a more appropriate group to take action? If the members agree that the network should work actively on some issue, then the members must agree on a means of accomplishing this work. Herein lies the question of appropriate structures. Many networks begin by being open, unstructured groups having no dues, no membership lists, no leadership posts and no rules. When a network embarks on a programme of action, the members must plan for committed and continuous leadership and some means to co-ordinate, finance and organise their projects. The survey and interviews indicate that some groups give in to the 'organisational imperative' while others retain their fluid, non-action oriented structure. Very few unstructured groups engage in public policy actions.

Networks seem to follow a predictable life-cycle. After a period of early informal relationships, permanent rules and organisational structures are created either as a means of developing programmes or as vehicles for the personal fulfilment of the more active leaders. The tendency to develop hierarchical power structures, well-documented by Michels,[5] is in direct conflict with the stated and usually practised value of equality espoused by most women's groups. Placing great value on equality, women attempt to operate networks without leaders and without formal rules. Inevitably women's networks struggle with the conflict between the leaderless ideology and the practical problems of maintaining an organisation. The groups that maintain many innovative organisational techniques already described are providing an important managerial training-ground for women to learn skills and techniques applicable in other organisations.

For those who are accustomed to think of organisational reality in terms of letterhead, office space, leadership roles and organisation charts, these women's networks are a great surprise. The networks are amorphous and exist primarily in the minds of the participants. For men who are excluded or women who choose not to participate, a network is a vague, indistinct, undefinable entity. For those who participate, the network is whatever they happen to get from the network: a new job, new friends, a new skill or just a feeling of the 'existence' of supportive women. The networks are not maintained for their own sake, but only to fulfil the current needs of the members. The networks are of, by and for those that are currently active. Some groups respond to immediate needs and then self-destruct when no longer needed. This 'life-cycle' encourages the long-term expectation that whatever the need, some network will emerge to handle the issues. Only a minimum predictability is necessary: that the network will meet at a regular place, time and date. Women attend because they have current needs and/or because they have a commitment to other women. No-one's ego and self-esteem is committed to 'being' president or chairperson; everyone gives freely and takes what she needs, wants and can find available from the resources of other members.

The Impact of Networks

Women's support networks have a direct impact on the personal development of women. Through participating in networks, women become more self-confident and better able to participate effectively in other organisations. Additionally, the contacts in the network ensure that a woman will have access to other organisations, and to better jobs through the information and support given by other women in the network. Consequently, the networks encourage women to higher achievement. Thus the creative activity of women's support networks extends the possibilities for women's greater participation in policy-making.

Notes

*I owe considerable thanks to the women and men participating in the Round

Table on Sex Roles and Politics, August 1979, at Essex University, who generously commented on the first draft of this chapter.

1. See Wirsing (1977). A sample of candidates reveals that two-thirds hold executive positions in such organisations; high vote-getters even more so.

2. My efforts to locate women's employment networks have been aided by the many Commissions on the Status of Women throughout the USA, the Women's Bureau of the US Department of Labor and Scottie Welch, a freelance journalist studying women's networks. The willingness and openness with which Scottie Welch and the bureau and commissions shared their information is an indication of the co-operation and interest in networking among women.

3. Kanter (1977) discusses these problems very thoroughly on the basis of her research into a large corporation.

4. Information networks and support networks accounted for 50% or more of important activities for most groups.

5. R. Michels (1966) *Political Parties*, Free Press, New York; see references to the Iron Law of Oligarchy.

Bibliography

Berger, P. and Neuhaus, R. (1977) *To Empower People*, American Enterprise Institute, Washington, DC

Collins, A.H. and Pancoast, D.L. (1976) *Natural Helping Networks*, National Association of Social Workers, Washington, DC

Houyman, N. and Kaplan, J. (1976) 'New Roles for Professional Women', *Public Administration Review*

Kanter, R.M. (1977) *Men and Women of the Corporation*, Basic Books, New York

Katz, A. and Bender, E. (1976a) 'Self-Help Groups in Western Society: History and Prospects', *Journal of Applied Behavioral Science* (July/August/September)

————— (1976b) *The Strength in US Self-Help Groups in the Modern World*, Franklin Watts, New York

Schwartz, E.B. and Rago, J.J. jr (1973) 'Beyond Tokenism', *Business Horizons, 16* (December)

Wirsing, R.G. (1977) *Socialist Society and Free Enterprise Politics: A Study of Voluntary Associations in Urban India*, Carolina Academic Press, Durham, North Carolina

11 THE IMPACT OF THE WOMEN'S MOVEMENT AND LEGISLATIVE ACTIVITY OF WOMEN MPs ON SOCIAL DEVELOPMENT

Sirkka Sinkkonen and Elina Haavio-Mannila

Research Problems and Perspective

The focus of this chapter is women's impact on policy formation and outcome. The purpose is to explore how this impact is affected by the various waves or types of women's movement. Our empirical analysis is restricted to the Finnish situation, although these movements have an international character. We hope that our analysis will fill some of the gaps in the knowledge concerning the contribution of women's political activity at the individual and collective level on social development.

The main emphasis of our empirical analysis is on the first stage of the policy process, termed agenda-building or agenda-setting (Cobb and Elder, 1971). In addition, some case studies are presented to explore women's impact on policy outcome. Agenda-building means the process by which the demands of various groups in the population are translated into items vying for the serious attention of public officials (Cobb, Keith-Ross and Ross, 1976, p. 126). The role of agenda-building in the total political process is described in Figure 11.1. This also summarises the research design of our study. Many of the factors presented in Figure 11.1 are used only in the interpretation of the data. Only a small part (mainly parts E and D) of the complex network of factors and political processes described in it are studied empirically in this chapter.

Cobb and Elder (1971) distinguish two types of agendas: public (also called systematic) and institutional (also called formal). If the women's movement has a policy impact, it will occur in the building of the public agenda. According to the framework proposed by Cobb *et al*. (1976), we can conceptualise the role of the women's movement in the agenda-building process as that of articulate demand. This means that the representatives of the women's movement can function as translators of women's problems and grievances into specified demands. The role of women MPs is to feed these demands into the policy process by raising them in the institutional agenda within Parliament (part D in Figure 11.1). This occurs only if women MPs are representing other women substantively as well as descriptively. When studying the policy impact of any representative of a certain group, including women MPs, it is important to distinguish between descriptive and substantive representation.

Figure 11.1: Stages in Agenda-building

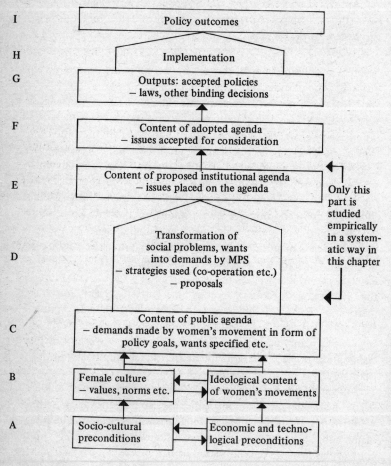

According to Björkman (1979) descriptive representation denotes the situation where an agent, who stands for others, shares at least one significant characteristic with those whom he/she is representing, such as age, sex or race. Substantive representation means that the agent is really serving the interests of the collectivity that he/she stands for. The first type of representation deals with the characteristics of the representative and those of the represented. The second form concerns the activity of the representative in the interests of those represented. The introduction of this form of representation emphasises the importance of evaluating the impact and results of this activity, not its descriptive characteristics.

The claim frequently made, that women's political participation has had no impact in defending specific women's interests or in making feminist policies (Rule Krauss, 1974), might imply that women politicians do not fill the criteria of substantive representation. This problem is expressed by well-known concepts such as false consciousness, co-optation and tokenism. They mean that it is not clear whether a socially descriptive representative really represents the interests of his/her constituency.

On the basis of this discussion, we assume that one impact of the women's movement is to increase the degree of women's substantive representation by increasing women's consciousness of their problems and grievances. In this chapter we explore empirically how different waves of the women's movement are related to the agenda-building activity of women MPs, especially in defending women's specific interests or making feminist policies. Before presenting our factual findings and interpretations we shall describe briefly the demands made by the women's movement, because we assume that they are fairly well-known.

The Content of Public Agenda Made by the Women's Movement

It is possible to distinguish three waves of feminism or types of women's movement. The early women's movement, called here the first wave of feminism, was organised in Finland in 1884, when the first women's organisation was established. The political demands made by this wave can be grouped into four categories:

(i) Equal access of women to all levels and types of education: Finnish women gained full access to universities in 1901.
(ii) Equal access of women to all offices in the civil service (state offices).
(iii) Equal voting rights for women in municipal elections, that is, for tax-payers. Voting rights and political eligibility of women on the same basis as men, for tax-payers. These demands were changed in 1904 to

agree with those of the workers' movement in demands for universal suffrage and political eligibility. Finnish women gained the vote and political eligibility in 1906.

(iv) Demands concerning equal standards of sexual morality for men and women.

In addition, the early women's movement emphasised the solidarity of all women regardless of social status and education (Jallinoja, 1980). The first wave of feminism lost its importance as a social movement by the 1920s. Policy reforms may have undermined its goals, but other factors also contributed to its withering away.

The second wave of feminism began to be organised in Finland in 1966, when a group of men and women founded Association 9. Its major goal was to change the gender-based functional division of labour in society by equalising sex-roles. It emphasised the integration and co-operation of men and women, and not women's solidarity as did the early women's movement. Therefore, an appropriate name for this wave would be the sex-role movement, because it did not fully comply with the principles of feminism. The intellectual basis of this movement lay in the theory of sex-role stereotyping, according to which society creates sex-role stereotypes which oppress both men and women. Thus the oppressive features of the sex-role stereotyping had to be eliminated. Although the radical feminist movement was already active in some countries in the 1960s, the Finnish version of the second wave of the women's movement never used the radical ideas or slogans of the radical feminists, such as sisterhood, sexism and oppression of women by men.

The third wave of the women's movement in Finland first became active in the middle of the 1970s, when the ideas of radical feminists and Marxist feminists reached Finland. In 1974 a few Swedish-speaking women established an organisation based on the principles of radical feminism. The early women's organisations, established at the end of the last century and the beginning of this, have also adopted some of the ideas of radical feminists during the last two or three years.

To summarise, the different waves of the women's movement have raised different issues on the public agenda. They have used some-what different strategies and have worked through different channels to apply influence, for example, by drawing the attention of the mass media to themselves. Many of the women MPs working in the first Diets examined in this chapter were also activists in the women's move-ment (Kilpi, 1953; Noponen, 1964; Jallinoja, 1979 and 1980). Thus the demands made by the early feminist movement were easily integrated into the institutional agenda. The ideas emphasised by the second wave, the sex-role movement, spread widely and quickly through the mass media in the 1960s. The third wave of feminism has, however, not received much attention from the Finnish mass media. It has been somewhat invisible in Finnish society. Consequently, its impact may have been limited so far.

We assume that an organised women's movement forms part of an organisational structure conducive to converting want into demand in order to further women's interests (Figure 11.1). We will examine empirically the influence of different waves of the women's movement in four aspects of legislative activity: how their influence was related to (i) the general agenda-building activity of women MPs and the descriptive representation of women in Parliament; (ii) the forms of agenda-building, and co-operation, and the forming of coalitions among MPs; (iii) the content of policy initiatives of women MPs, especially as regards feminist issues; and (iv) the policy output as exemplified by some case studies of laws and other binding decisions.

Data and Method

Institutional agenda-building has been operationalised by private member bills submitted to the diets by men and women MPs. There are three types of private member bills within the Finnish political system: fiscal, legislative and petitionary. Fiscal bills concern the allocation of government money for certain services, from public resources. Petitionary bills are initiatives to start preparatory work or planning (some issues) for policy reform. Legislative bills differ from the petitionary bills only in that they are more thoroughly prepared and presented in legal form.

The Diet of the year 1907, in which women MPs participated for the first time in the legislative activity of Finland, has been chosen as the starting point for the empirical analysis. After that year every tenth diet was selected for the study and every second private member bill submitted to these diets was included in the analysis. The data were collected from parliamentary documents of the years in question (*Valtiopäiväasiakirjat vuosilta*, 1907, 1917, 1927, 1937, 1947, 1957, 1967, 1977). This procedure produced 2,532 private member bills submitted to Parliament. Their distribution according to the type of bills, legislative, fiscal and petitionary, and their total number in the diets studied are presented in Table 11.1.

Table 11.1: Private Member Bills in the Data According to Year of Diet and Type of Bills

Year of diet	Type of bills			Total no. of bills in these data	Total no. of bills submitted to the diet
	Legislative bills	Fiscal bills[a]	Petitionary bills		
1907	12	—	98	110	218
1917[b]	13	—	53	66	132
1927	14	—	56	70	138
1937	10	91	67	168	335
1947	37	144	201	382	761
1957	62	261	288	611	1,220
1967	84	214	296	584	1,180
1977	76	262	203	541	1,080
Total	308	972	1,262	2,533	5,068
Total with SMP[c]	324	1,127	1,326	2,778	5,556

Notes: a. Petitionary and fiscal bills were not separated in the documents used as data sources before 1937.

b. There were two diets in 1917, these data include the first diet.

c. The bills submitted by SMP (The Rural Party of Finland, a populist party) are excluded from all tables because of the extreme behavior of the MPs of this party. The average number of bills per MP (without the SMP) was 2.9 in 1967 and 2.8 in 1977. The respective figure for the only MP of the SMP (a man) was 68 in 1967: SMP had, in 1977, two MPs (men) who submitted 410 bills.

To measure the strategies used by MPs in submitting bills, and the differences in the legislative activity of men and women MPs, the bills are grouped in four categories according to the gender of the initiator and other signatories in the following way:

(i) Bills initiated by one woman MP, or several women MPs (no. = 47).

(ii) Bills initiated by a woman MP (a woman as first signatory), but also signed by men MPs (no. = 322).

(iii) Bills initiated by a man MP, but also signed by women MPs (no. = 886).

(iv) Bills initiated by one or several men MPs (no. = 1,279).

To operationalise the impact of the two different waves of the women's movement, the period examined is divided into three categories:

(i) The period of the first wave of the women's movement: the Diets of 1907 and 1917. In 1917 there were two diets, the first diet is included in this data (Jallinoja, 1979 and 1980).

(ii) The period of the silence or passivity of the women's movement:

the Diets of 1927, 1937, 1947 and 1957 (Friedan, 1963; Bernard, 1971).

(iii) The period of the second wave of the women's movement or the sex-role movement: the Diets of 1967 and 1977.

Our purpose was to take the Diet of 1977 to present the third wave of the women's movement; but because there was hardly any difference between the Diets of 1967 and 1977 in the aspects examined in this chapter the two last diets were combined. This already indicates that the third wave of the women's movement has not yet had any impact on agenda-building activity. The role of the three waves of the women's movement in building public agenda related to women or feminist issues can be studied by comparing their goals and demands with various aspects of agenda-building.

The Impact of the Women's Movement on the General Activity of Women MPs in Agenda-building and on the Descriptive Representation of Women

We start the examination of the types of impact of the women's movement on the agenda-building activity of women MPs by comparing the number of bills initiated by men and women MPs in Table 11.2. There are no large quantitative differences between men and women MPs in their total activity of initiating new policies. On average, of the 200 members of the Finnish Parliament, 13 per cent were women in the eight years studied. For the same years, initiatives by women constituted 15 per cent of all private member bills submitted to the diets. The legislative activity of women varied with time, however. In relation to their numbers, women were most active in the Diets of 1907, 1947 and 1977, and most passive in the Diets of 1927 and 1957. The higher the proportion of women, the higher their share of initiatives (see differences marked with plus and minus signs in Table 11.2).

Thus women MPs were more active during the periods of the first and second waves of the women's movement and in the postwar Diet of 1947 than in the other diets examined. The passivity of the women's movement during the 1920s, 1930s and 1950s obviously influenced the legislative activity of women in at least two ways. First, the number of women MPs decreased during this period to the lowest in the history of the Finnish Parliament (Table 11.2). Secondly, these few women accomplished far less in terms of policy proposals than even their small number would have suggested. During the election period 1954-7, the

Table 11.2: Proportion of Bills Initiated by Women MPs of All Private Member Bills Submitted to Parliament and Proportion of Women MPs According to Year of Diet

Year of diet	Bills made alone or initiated by women, % of all initiatives	No. of all initiatives	Women MPs, % of all MPs (no. = 200)	Difference in %
1907	13.6	110	9.5	+ 4.1
1917	10.6	66	12.0	− 1.4
1927	5.1	70	8.5	− 3.4
1937	6.6	168	8.0	− 1.4
1947	9.4	382	8.5	+ 0.9
1957	11.1	611	15.0	− 3.9
1967[a]	15.4	579	16.5	− 1.1
1977[a]	24.6	541	23.0	+ 1.6
Total	14.5	2533 (2778)[a]	12.6	+ 1.9

Note: a. The bills submitted by the MPs of SMP have been excluded, see note c. in Table 11.1, p. 200.

proportion of women in Parliament was 15 per cent, but women MPs initiated only 11 per cent of the private member bills in the Diet of 1957. The traditional passive, social and political role of women was adopted even by women legislators at that time.

The data allow us to conclude that the women's movement has had a widespread activating effect on women MPs. The exceptionally high activity of women MPs in the postwar Diet of 1947 is obviously related to the (general) abandoning of traditional feminine roles during the war, owing to the practical necessity of assuming a large number of the customarily masculine tasks in society (Firestone, 1971). The silence of the women's movement is reflected also in the decrease of women's descriptive representation in Parliament during this period (Friedan, 1963; Bernard, 1971).

The Impact of the Women's Movement on the Strategies Used by Women MPs in Agenda-building

Figure 11.2 allows us to study the impact of the various waves of the women's movement on the strategies or forms of politics used by women and men MPs in submitting bills. It is possible to distinguish four types of strategies used in making the policy proposals: (i) single member bills, that is bills submitted alone by one man or woman MP; (ii) co-operation and stable coalitions between several women or

between several men from the same or different parties; (iii)
co-operation between men and women MPs where women MPs
take the lead in taking the initiative and mobilising other male support
(co-signatories) at the stage of submitting the bill; and (iv) co-operation
between men and women MPs where men have the initial lead and
women a supporting role as co-signatories.

**Figure 11.2: Number of Private Member Bills Per Women and Men MPs
According to Gender of the Initiator and Signatories in Different Years**

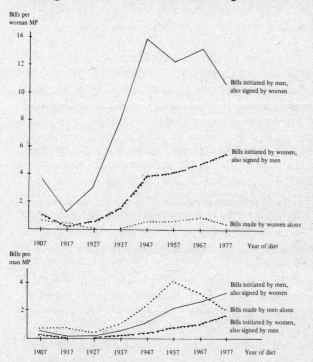

The emphasis on women's solidarity in the first wave of the women's
movement is clearly visible in the large number of block bills of women
MPs during the first period. Block bills are those initiated by women
all from the same party or by women from several parties. These bills
indicate that women's solidarity can overcome party loyalty in some
cases. The second wave of the women's movement emphasised the integration and co-operation of men and women. We interpret the low
degree of co-operation among women MPs, as compared with that
between men and women during the last period (Figure 11.2), as being

a reflection of this. There is a definite change in the patterns of MPs submitting bills during the period examined. In the first six Diets examined (1907-57) there were only five single member bills initiated by women MPs, while in the last two Diets (1967, 1977) the number of single member bills of women increased considerably, being 22 altogether. From the bills submitted by women MPs alone, 12 per cent were initiated by one woman during the first period; the figure was 4 per cent in the second period, and 50 per cent in the third period. In 1967 and 1977, women worked individually or in co-operation with men MPs, not in a women's block, as was the case in the first two periods.

The number of bills initiated by men and signed by women rose rapidly until 1947, when a decline began. This shows that earlier on men MPs had a strong leadership role in agenda-building. In the postwar diets, however, women MPs became active in assuming leadership to a larger extent than before. The only group of bills, of those compared in Figure 11.2, which shows a steady increase over the period is that of those initiated by women and supported by men. The number of bills introduced only by men (*pro rata* of men MPs) reached its peak in 1957, after which a decline began. Thus, the number of shared-gender bills has been increasing. This is in accordance with the ideology of the second wave of the women's movement in the 1960s.

Women's ability to mobilise male support for bills initiated by them may also be influenced by the changes in the policy content of the bills. The differences between the policy content of bills proposed by men and women MPs have decreased as will be seen in the next section.

On the basis of the data above we can conclude that both the first and the second waves of the women's movement have influenced the types of strategy used by MPs in their agenda-building activity. Solidarity among women regardless of social class and education was the goal of the first wave of the women's movement. The major goal of the second wave of the women's movement in the 1960s was a greater integration of women and men.

The Impact of the Women's Movement on the Content of Institutional Agenda in Parliament

The sex-based division of labour and the different value orientations of men and women, based partly on this division of labour, is clearly reflected in the contents of their legislative activity (Table 11.3). The

most noticeable sex differences are the extent to which women MPs
concern themselves with bills related to social legislation, and to
cultural and educational policies, whereas men MPs concern themselves
with transport, public utilities and economic policy. The institutionalised role of women in society as care-taker, educator, consumer of
culture, and supporter and protector of underprivileged groups is
visible also in the legislative activity of women MPs. Of the total number
of bills initiated by women MPs, 44 per cent concerned social legislation and 28 per cent educational or cultural policy. The corresponding figures for bills initiated by men were 19 and 16 per cent. Of
the bills introduced by men alone, 22 per cent concerned economic,
energy or regional policy. The corresponding figure for women was 2
per cent. One-third of the bills introduced by men alone concerned
transport and public utilities; only 5 per cent of bills introduced by
women alone, and 14 per cent of bills initiated by women and co-signed
by men, were related to policies on these subjects.

There are considerable changes in the content of the bills between
the three periods examined. In all, these changes mean some decrease in
gender-based specialisation in legislative activity. The proportion of bills
concerning social policy initiated by women was higher in the first and
third periods than in the second. During the first period, bills introduced
only by women all concerned social legislation. The content and bene-
ficiaries of these policy proposals differed from those of the second and
third periods, however. In 1907 and 1917 policy initiatives from women
alone intended to improve the position of women or children, especially
underprivileged mothers and their children (lonely, unprotected,
unmarried and widowed mothers with their children). Many of these
bills concerned marital law and family matters and aimed at increasing
the autonomy of the wife, and giving equal rights with the husband in
respect to property and children. In the second and especially in the
third period, the bills introduced or initiated by women on social legislation concerned more general matters within social policy: working
conditions, pensions, health services and family counselling.

In the second period between 1927 and 1957, women became active
in educational and cultural policy (Table 11.3). In 1907 and 1917
women MPs made no initiatives concerning educational and cultural
policy. Over the period as a whole, the largest group with this slump is
general and vocational education, which was the topic of 19 per cent of
all bills initiated by women. Of the bills initiated by men, only 12 per
cent were aimed at further education. The number of all policy
proposals concerning education and culture has steadily grown, and

Table 11.3: Content of Private Member Bills by Men and Women MPs According to Year of Diet (%)

Content	Bills by women alone				Bills by men alone				Bills initiated by women, signed also by men				Bills initiated by men, signed also by women				All bills			
	1907 1917 57	1927-57 1977	1967-1977	Total	1907 1917 57	1927-57 1977	1967-1977	Total	1907 1917 57	1927-57 1977	1967-1977	Total	1907 1917 57	1927-57 1977	1967-1977	Total	1907 1917 57	1927-57 1977	1967-1977	Total
Social policy	100	67	46	62	17	12	17	15	63	33	45	41	35	23	26	25	28	18	26	22
Educational and cultural policy	–	33	29	24	13	14	18	15	–	32	29	28	19	20	18	19	13	17	21	18
Public safety and justice	–	–	–	2	5	1	1	1	13	1	2	2	4	1	2	2	6	1	2	2
Support of interest groups and minorities	–	–	–	–	–	0.8	2.0	1.3	–	–	1.5	1.2	7.5	1.6	1.4	1.8	2.6	1.1	1.8	1.5
Environmental and consumer protection	–	–	–	–	–	0.4	0.2	0.1	6	3	–	1.2	–	0.3	0.9	0.6	0.5	0.3	0.7	0.6
Development of administration and political system	–	–	4	5	10	5	4	5	–	2	2	2	22	5	8	7	12	5	5	5
Taxation	–	–	8	5	2	4	4	4	–	3	3	3	–	4	8	6	1	4	5	4
Transportation and public utilities	–	–	8	8	25	35	34	34	19	18	11	14	4	24	22	21	17	29	24	27
Economic, energy and regional policy	–	–	4	2	28	26	18	22	–	7	5	6	9	22	12	16	19	22	13	18
Foreign policy and defence	–	–	–	–	0.9	2.2	1.2	1.7	–	0.9	1.5	1.2	–	1.5	2.1	1.8	0.5	1.8	1.5	1.6
Sum	100	100	99	100	101	99	99	99	101	100	100	100	100	102	100	100	100	99	101	100
Number of bills[a]	9	12	24	45	110	734	447	1,291	16	123	198	337	54	392	424	870	189	1,261	1,093	2,543

Note: a. Some bills have been included in several categories; bills by SMP excluded (no. = 239), see note c. in Table 11.1, p. 200.

their proportion to all other bills has remained fairly constant. These results are similar to those of Paula Tuomikoski-Leskelä (1977, p. 164) concerning art policy in Finland in the years 1917-47.

Among the bills initiated by women MPs, there was a relatively large number related to research and development included in the category of educational and cultural policy, and their number has increased over time. This may indicate the different decision-making behaviour of men and women. Women politicians seek more information and are more careful in political decision-making than men.

The decrease in gender-based specialisation in legislative activity is also shown in the fact that men have become more active in cultural policy: the proportion of bills introduced by men alone increased from 13 per cent in the first period to 18 per cent in the last period (Table 11.3). Correspondingly, there has been a decrease in the proportion of bills introduced by men alone concerning economic policy, from 28 per cent during the first period examined to 18 per cent during the third period. Twenty per cent of bills introduced by men alone concern economic policy, whereas 2 per cent of bills introduced by women alone are on this subject. One-third of the bills introduced by men alone propose improvements to transport and public utilities, while only 5 per cent of bills initiated by women alone belong to this category, and 14 per cent of those bills initiated by women and co-signed by men. Most of these bills propose the construction of local roads to areas which the MPs themselves represented.

Bills related to foreign policy and defence are initiated more often by men than by women. No clear change in their proportion over time can be seen. Women MPs proposed more bills than men concerning public safety and justice, interest groups and minorities, and environmental and consumer protection. This is in accordance with the assumptions concerning the different orientations of men and women as political decision-makers. Women MPs have been more active than men in relation to the humanitarian values emphasised by the new feminist movement.

These changes in the subject matter of bills are in accordance with the goal of the second wave of the women's movement to decrease sex-role stereotyping in society. Women MPs have worked more than men MPs for the interests of women. Of the bills from women alone, 35 per cent concern specific interests of women, while among those introduced by men alone, 0.6 per cent belong to this category. The role of women MPs as representatives of the interests of their own gender was particularly evident at the beginning of the century. In the first diets studied, those of 1907 and 1917, every second bill of the 22 introduced alone or initiated by women MPs was of specific interest to women. In the period 1927-57 a much lower proportion, 12 per cent, of the 131 bills initiated by women alone concerned women's issues, and in the two last diets studied, in 1967 and 1977, the proportion was only 5 per cent (no. = 225). The role of women MPs as defenders of the interests of their sex-group was clearly more pronounced in the years immediately after women's suffrage than it is at present. This can also be related to the strong feminist movement at the beginning of the century, in which the first women MPs had participated actively.

The Impact of the Women's Movement and Women MPs on Policy Output and Outcome

So far we have examined only how and which issues are raised from the public agenda to the institutional agenda. In order to find out what the contribution of the women's movement and women MPs is on the final policy content, and thus on the social development of society, one also has to study the other stages in policy processes in order to see how the initiatives made by women MPs are transformed into accepted policies. To find out how responsive and successful the policies are from the women's perspective, one has to go even further and analyse the consequences of the policies implemented (Figure 11.1). In this section we try to see how some of the bills have been adopted and acted upon in the later stages of policy processes.

It is possible to estimate, although very roughly, some of the types of the policy output on the basis of Table 11.4. We do not have any systematically collected information on the impact of women MPs in policy output. Therefore the data in Table 11.4 has to be taken only as an example to show specifically that women's united efforts can produce results in terms of policy output, in spite of a strong bias in favour of male values, beliefs and interests in the policy process (Bacharach and Baratz, 1971). Our examples are limited to two types of bill. First, bills which were submitted jointly by women MPs in the first diet in which women were represented. Only in these cases can we be sure that the bill was the first occasion on which the issue was raised by women MPs. In other cases, because of our method of sampling the diets (every tenth), we cannot be sure that a similar bill had not been introduced already in a previous diet. In addition, we have taken five policy proposals made in the later years as examples which have been

Table 11.4: Summary of Some Case Studies on Policy Proposals (Bills) and Output

Content of policy proposal and type of bill	Year of policy proposal: Proposal	Output (laws, etc.)	Time lag in years (proposal - output)	No. of parties in Bourgeois block	No. of parties Socialist block	No. of parties in bourgeois socialist block
Legislative and petitionary: concerning marriage						
— equal rights of spouses (2 bills in 1907)	1907 1917	1929	22	1 3	1 1	
— increase of women's marriage age from 15 to 18	1907	1908	1	1	1	
Petitionary: position of children born out of wedlock	1907	1922	15	1		
Petitionary: equal access of women to all state offices	1907 1917	1925	18	1 1		
Legislative: to strengthen the penalty for rape and sexual abuse of young girls	1907	1908	1	1		
Petitionary: home for poor, unwed mothers with small children	1907	1942	35[a]		1	
Fiscal: research on the value of women's work to national economy and private households (made by all 19 women MPs)	1947	1978	31			6[b]
Fiscal: higher education in nutritional physiology and in applied nutrition (name of the field since 1973 is nutrition)	1937	1947[c]	10			6[b]
Fiscal: higher education in household technology (2 bills) (professorship, University of Helsinki)	1957 1957	1969	12			3[b] 6[b]
Fiscal: government founding of nursing research institute	1977	1978	0[d]			6[b]

Notes: a. The first home for unmarried mothers and their children (Ensikoti) was established in Helsinki in 1942. Now there are such homes all over the country. After the first bill in 1907 several bills were made by women MPs concerning these homes.

b. Only six parties had women MPs in these diets. Thus women MPs from all parties co-operated in initiating this successful bill.

c. Education in home (household) economics began at the University of Helsinki in 1946 as a consequence of a bill introduced by women MPs in a Diet not included in the data in our sample.

d. There has been at least one previous fiscal bill proposing the same thing, made in 1966 by all MPs from the liberal party.

successful in terms of policy output, even if we do not know whether similar bills had been introduced in some previous diets. These bills are interesting because they reveal the strategies used by women MPs to introduce successful bills. All these bills were introduced in co-operation with women MPs from opposing ideological parties, that is across the bourgeois-socialist line. Four of them were made by women MPs from all six parties with women MPs in Parliament during the years in question. The content of bills made by the united women's front is also revealing. They all concern research and the development of higher (university) education in typically women's subjects: home economics, household technology, housekeeping, nursing and nutritional chemistry. An interesting bill, introduced jointly in 1947 by all the 19 women MPs then in Parliament, proposed government funding for research to investigate the value of women's work in the home and in wage labour outside the home in the nationalised and private sectors of the economy.

Women MPs have thus made efforts to put together information on which to define women's contribution in society. The activity of women legislators in developing higher education and research in typical women's subjects can be interpreted as efforts to increase women's resources. It is worth noting that there are no corresponding bills related to typically male subjects. Because of the inherent mobilisation of bias in the political system favouring the power-holders, that is to say because of sexism, there is no need to use private member bills. The typical male subjects are automatically funded. In the Finnish political system the private member bills are considered to be additional agenda-building. The main agendas are built outside Parliament in the cabinet, and at the higher hierarchical levels in public administration and the trade unions (Nousiainen, 1961; Heiskanen, 1975; Karvonen, 1979), where women are present in limited numbers or not at all (Sinkkonen, 1977).

A good example of what women can achieve through united effort is the intensive activity of women MPs in the reform of marital legislation beginning from the first Diet of 1907 (three women's block bills), and continuing until a liberal marital law was enacted in 1929. This activity was successful in securing a policy output. The new marital law of 1929 established the equality of husband and wife in property, children, and rights in divorce. In some respects it is more favourable to the wife than to the husband.

As a consequence of the sex-role movement of the 1960s three important laws affecting women's position were enforced, i.e., the abortion law legalising abortion on social grounds, the children's day-care law, and the law removing the last restrictions from women's access to state offices. The sex-equalising measures at the beginning of the 1970s are examples of inadequate policy reform. A government commission was established in 1966 to plan reforms concerning the position of women. The commission introduced a reform proposal in 1970 for the establishment of a government Council for Equality, which was realised in 1972. The task of this council, a consultative body in matters concerning the equality of the sexes, and especially the position of women, is to take initiatives. Much of its work consists of gathering information and research. It has made many recommendations for increasing women's representation in important policy-making bodies. If evaluated only in terms of policy output, these measures have been successful and many recommendations have been made; but if we apply an outcome criterion and examine what consequences the policy has had in improving women's position, the conclusions are quite contrary. These policies have been inadequate because they are very superficial reforms.

Their influence in changing women's position towards greater equality has been minor, if any. This is indicated, for example, by the fact that there has been no increase in the proportion of women in important policy-making bodies, regardless of the various recommendations (Sinkkonen, 1977). For example, in the new research councils appointed in 1979 for the three-year period, there are fewer women than in the two previous periods of 1974-6 and 1977-9. Another example is the government commission appointed in 1980 to plan policy proposals for working hours.

According to time-budget studies, the uneven distribution of household tasks between the sexes leads to very different working hours for women and men (Szalai, 1972). Preferences for the shortening of working hours also vary according to gender: women prefer shorter daily working hours (SITRA, 1977; Flick, 1980) and the opportunity to be absent from work when the worker him/herself chooses, whereas men prefer an extension of annual holidays and an earlier retirement age (SITRA, 1977, p. 94). The sex-roles are very relevant to solving problems connected with working hours. Despite this, a government committee, which at first included only one woman member and 22 men, was appointed in 1980 to investigate the alternatives for shortening working hours in Finland. Later, one other woman was appointed to this committee when a man retired from it.

Conclusion

It is possible to make the following conclusions on the basis of this study concerning the contribution of women MPs in building the institutional agenda. Women MPs have made a definite contribution by politicising the wants, needs and demands of women, and the women's movement, by transferring them to the institutional agenda. The content of bills proposed by them, as well as strategies used, have been influenced by the first and second waves of the women's movement. The different goals and demands of these two waves of the women's move-ment, the early feminist movement at the beginning of this century and the sex-role movement in the 1960s and 1970s, are reflected in the content of policy initiatives of women MPs, but also in those of men MPs. The first movement increased the substantive representation of women MPs directly, for example, by making MPs aware about women's problems and demands, and indirectly by specifying the demands, and by making the legislative activity of women MPs easier with respect to feminist policies. The second movement furthered policies of equality for both men and women, and tried to integrate the sexes. These aims are also reflected in the agenda-building activity of MPs and in policy output.

The impact of the first and second waves of the women's movement on the agenda-building stage in the policy-cycle can be summarised as follows. Both have activated women generally, and influenced the content of bills and the strategies used in submitting bills. The early feminism increased co-operation among women, while the sex-role movement has increased collaboration between the sexes and especially encouraged women to take the lead in this co-operation, as was shown by the increasing proportion of bills initiated by a woman and co-signed by men.

The influence of these movements in the content of proposed policies can be seen, first, in the large number of proposals made by women MPs concerning women's specific interests at the beginning of the century and, secondly, in the variety in initiatives from women in the last two diets. These tendencies are consistent with the goals of the two waves of the women's movement: feminist policies during the first wave and integration of the sexes in policy-making during the second wave. Drude Dahlerup's study (1980) shows that similar trends have occurred in Denmark with respect to women's movements, policy processes and output.

The observed lack of impact from the third wave of feminism in public policy-making is consistent with its strategies. It is less articulate in its political demands than the first and second waves. It has a definite mistrust of the willingness and ability of government bodies to improve women's position in those matters which it considers vital. Therefore, its strategy is not so much to get changes through public policy but through consciousness-raising among women. It also emphasises the importance of sharing women's common experiences by making them public. It has assumed the ideology and practice of self-help and grass-roots movements by providing some of the services itself (homes, refuges for battered women, self-help clinics and so on). It is not expecting government intervention in the production of these services. Its activity is oriented to a large extent against the sexual oppression of women (the use of women as sex-objects) and the isolation of women in the private sphere, the family. In this respect it is closer to the first wave of feminism, which also raised issues concerning relationships between men and women (prostitution and penalties for sexual crimes, e.g., rape). There are however greater differences in the content of issues raised by these two movements and their strategies. The first movement had connections with the legislative bodies through women politicians, and women politicians had close relationships with the movement. This is not so much the case at the moment, as may be understood, for example, from an interview with the 52 women MPs elected in the last Parliamentary elections in Finland, in 1979 (Myllymäki, Peutere, Sormunen and Vehkaoja, 1979).

These interviews reflect the invisibility of the third wave of feminism very well and, at the same time, the visibility or impact of the sex-role movement. The answers given by the women MPs to the question of whether they were ready to work together across party lines on issues concerning interests specific to women is revealing. The answers often indicated that there were no 'women's issues', but only issues concerning all human beings. The issues mentioned on which women were prepared to co-operate across party lines related mostly to aspects of general social policy, but their willingness was conditional on the party programme. Party loyalty among the new women MPs was very visible in their answers, especially in the case of women MPs from the two socialist parties. Other women were less articulate in this respect, or they did not express their party loyalty as clearly as their socialist women colleagues (Myllymäki *et al.*, 1979).

The argument that women have had no policy impact (for example in Rule Krause, 1974) is not justified on the basis of this data. Our results indicate that utilitarian arguments for increasing the proportion of women in policy-making bodies are also justified on empirical grounds. In addition to feminist issues, women MPs have proposed more policies based on humanitarian values, aiming at reforms to solve problems of deprived and disadvantaged groups, than have male MPs.

Thus, it is worthwhile to get more women into the policy-making process. At the same time, however, it is very important to guarantee that they fulfil the criteria of substantive representation of women. For this purpose, alerting social movements and good contacts between women legislators and other women are necessary.

A critical note on the research perspectives and methodology used in this study is in place. This analysis clearly shows that a conceptual framework and methodology are needed which allow the impact of women's collective and individual political activity on the agenda, as well as on policy output and outcome, to be distinguished. The agenda by itself is not enough. The political influence of women can best be measured by identifying those proposals made by women which are adopted and also have desired policy outcomes in terms of improving women's position. When examining the lack of women's political influence, concepts such as non-decisions and mobilisation of bias add to the usefulness of the agenda perspective (Bacharach and Baratz, 1971). The conclusions concerning the political impact of women MPs and the women's movement are our interpretations of the observed co-existence of the phenomena studied. It is of course possible that the data could be interpreted differently.

Bibliography

Bacharach, P. and Baratz, S. (1971) *Power and Poverty: The Theory and Practice*, OUP, New York

Bernard, J. (1971) *Women and the Public Interest: An Essay on Policy and Protest*, Alan Atherton, Chicago and New York

Björkman, J.W. (1979) 'Representation and Decentralisation in the Health Sector: Principles, Performance and Paradox in Public Policy – Preliminary Observations on Sweden and the United Kingdom', paper at the workshop 'The Health Services – Its Politics and Economics', ECPR, Joint Sessions, Brussels, 17-21 April

Cobb, R.N. and Elder, C.D. (1971) 'The Politics of Agenda-Building: An Alternative Perspective for Modern Democratic Theory', *The Journal of Politics, 33*, 892-915

Cobb, R., Ross, Jennie-Keith and Ross, M.H. (1976) 'Agenda-Building as a Comparative Political Process', *The American Political Science Review, LXX*, 1, 126-38

Dahlerup, D. (1980) 'Approaches to the Study of Public Policy towards Women', paper at the workshop 'Women and Public Policy', ECPR Joint Session, Florence, April

Firestone, S. (1971) *The Dialectic of Sex*, Jonathan Cape, London

Flick, M. (1980) 'Preferences for Sex Equalising Measures', paper at the workshop 'Women and Public Policy', ECPR, Joint Sessions, Florence, 24-29 March

Friedan, B. (1963) *Feminine Mystique*, Random House, New York

Heiskanen, J. (1975) 'Valtioneuvoston asema Suomen poliittisessa järjestelmässä', *Eripainos. Valtioneuvoston historia 1917-1966, III*, Valtioneuvosto insti-tuutiona, Valtion painatuskeskus, Helsinki

Jallinoja, R. (1979) 'Suomen varhaisen naisasialiikkeen synty', *Tiede ja Edistys, 4*, 4, 34-41

―――― (1980) 'The Women's Liberation Movement in Finland', *Scandinavian Journal of History, 5*, 37-49

Karvonen, L. (1979) 'Om policy-källor och anhängiggörande av policy-processor Politiikka', *Valtiotieteellisen yhdistyksen julkaisu, 1*, 33-48

Kilpi, S.K. (1953) *Suomen työläisnaisliikkeen historia*, Kansankulttuuri, Helsinki

Myllymäki, H., Peutere, R., Sormunen, H. and Vehkaoja, H. (1979) 'Millaisia ovat uuden eduskunnan 52 naiskansanedustaja?', interview in a woman's magazine *Anna, 13*, 42-6

Noponen, M. (1964) *Kansanedustajien sosiaalinen tausta Suomessa*, WSOY, Helsinki

Nousiainen, J. (1961) *Eduskunta aloitevallan käyttäjänä*, WSOY, Porvoo

Rule Krauss, W. (1974) 'Political Implications of Gender Roles: A Review of the Literature', *The American Political Science Review, LXVIII*, 4 1706-23

Sinkkonen, S. (1977) 'Women's Increased Political Participation in Finland: Real Influence or Pseudodemocracy?', paper at the workshop 'Women in Politics', ECPR, Joint Sessions, Berlin 27 March-2 April

Szalai, A. (1972) *The Uses of Time*, Mouton, The Hague and Paris

SITRA (1977) 'Suomalaisten vapaa-aika ja lomanvietto vuonna', *Sitra Sarja* B 32, Helsinki

Tuomikoski-Leskelä, P. 'Taide ja politiikka. Kansanedustuslaitoksen suhtaut-uminen taiteen edistämiseen Suomessa. Historiallisia tutkimuksia', *Julkaissut Suomen Historiallinen Suera, 103*, Pohjolan Sanomat

Valtiopäiväasiakirjat vuosilta (1907, 1917, 1927, 1937, 1947, 1957, 1967, 1977) Liiteosat, Valtion Painatuskeskus, Helsinki

12 WILL WOMEN JUDGES MAKE A DIFFERENCE IN WOMEN'S LEGAL RIGHTS? A PREDICTION FROM ATTITUDES AND SIMULATED BEHAVIOUR

Beverly B. Cook

The efforts of feminist organisations in the USA to secure the appointment of women to new judgeships and to vacancies indicate their expectation that women judges will act to improve the legal status of women. Judges, depending upon court jurisdiction, have the opportunity to establish legal principles on equal access to employment, insurance, abortion, education, welfare, and to social resources unevenly distributed by sex. The question which this chapter raises is: Are judges' attitudes about sex-roles and simulated behaviour on women's issues related? How new women judges think and behave can be projected from the responses to a survey of female judges sitting on major state trial courts in 1977. Whether the women will make decisions more supportive of sex equality than the men can be predicted from a comparison of responses from a matching sample of male judges.

The organised campaign to place more women on the bench rests on the hope that women judges will seize decision-making opportunities to liberate other women. The conventional but different approaches to the explanation of the behaviour of political women do not predict pro-feminist decisions. One approach fits an organisational and the other a biological theory of behaviour (Gehlen, 1977). In the organisational model, the common professional training and identical constraints imposed by the rules and customs of the organisation overcome any biological, psychological, or experience-based differences between the sexes. The self-interest of the women lies in accommodating to the males higher in the hierarchy who control their working conditions, income and career development. Women would lack the motivation or incentive to behave any differently from men in respect to women's rights.

The biological model suggests that women will exhibit a different style of decision-making and emphasise different substantive goals, compatible with certain intrinsic characteristics of the sex. The stereo-typically passive and home oriented woman in the office, however, is likely to have conventional rather than radical views of women's social

216

role and rights. The organisational woman who identifies with men in the same position would not be motivated to help her sisters outside the organisation, but the biological woman with emotional, indecisive, dependent and unsophisticated qualities would not be equipped to help other women. Even the positive qualities which are defined as 'feminine', for example understanding, pacifism, unselfishness and patience, imply the acceptance and support of an existing culture in which most women are treated as subordinates and inferiors. The qualities of invention, bravery and energy which would allow officials to introduce fundamental social changes favourable to women are attributed by the stereotype to the male sex, which has little incentive to liberate women from housework and other traditional roles.

An inventive explanation for the behaviour of a female elite is not rooted in an organisational or biological but in a socialisation framework. In this model women act differently from men in public office to the extent that their socialisation varies. The participation of women neither depresses nor uplifts society, since women are no better or worse and, particularly, no less self-interested than men, but have different skills, interests and conflicts stemming from their sex-specific socialisation. The assignment of women to court specialities, such as domestic relations or juveniles, fits the biological proposition, but the socialisation approach explains why women satisfied with family court work in one generation now demand transfer into other divisions. The socialisation model sees the failure of token women judges to eliminate sexist laws in terms of their training in chauvinistic law schools.

A feminist political philosophy assumes that the sex of the judge would not relate to the performance of public roles, if both sexes received the same social treatment from cradle to old age. The feminist rationalisation for the sex integration of public offices is not the unique but the cumulative contributions of individuals given equal opportunity to participate in a democratic society. The inclusion of women in government, during a period when this right to choose social roles free from sex discrimination is only partially recognised, means that women officials will make different decisions in policy areas salient to sex-roles. The research findings reported here indicate that during a period when sex identity still has tremendous cultural salience, male authorities do not feel for or act for women's interests, and women authorities largely do.

Women on US Courts

The judgeships in the hierarchies of US courts have historically been male monopolies. Even at the lowest level of factotum women gained jobs in courts later than in business or the executive branch of government. Until recently the primary consumers of the court product, e.g., the legal counsel, civil plaintiff and criminal defendant, were male. The major female role in court was passive spectator until active participation as juror was finally legitimated by the Supreme Court in 1975.[1] Women on the bench today are as much the subject of surprise, admiration (or the reverse) and curiosity as when the first woman won election to a major state trial court (Ohio) in 1920 and the first woman was appointed to a federal appellate court (6th Circuit) in 1934 (Allen, 1965). The overall percentage of judges who are women in all US courts is about 4 per cent (Cook, 1978a: 84 and 89-90). Since the percentage of women in the pool of legal eligibles has increased rapidly since the barriers to law school entrance have broken down, the percentage of women on the bench should double early in the 1980s.

The judiciary in the US is a dual system. The national government includes as its third branch the federal courts, a three-tiered hierarchy, with a single Supreme Court in Washington, DC, 11 regional appellate courts, and 90 trial courts located within the 50 states (Schmidhauser, 1979). The number of women in the federal courts is too small (only 4 in 1980) to support data analysis or generalisations. Half of the women selected as district judges by President Carter to date moved up from the state courts. Women are more likely than men to come from the state pool of eligibles, since an administration can afford mistakes in selecting a member of the dominant white/male elite, but will insist on proven performance for nominees who will be highly visible products of an affirmative action policy.

Table 12.1 describes the inclusion of women among the life-tenured judges on the federal bench since 1789. Of the 101 Justices of the Supreme Court not one has been female (Schmidhauser, 1979); however, the number of promising candidates for the next vacancy has increased suddenly with the selection of women to other appellate benches. On the regional federal appellate courts, called the Courts of Appeals, one woman served on the Sixth Circuit for 25 years prior to 1960; and one woman served on the Ninth Circuit from 1968 to 1979. (She is now Secretary of the new Cabinet Department of Education.) Each woman constituted less than 1 per cent of the judicial personnel appointed during her respective period. Under the Omnibus Judgeship Act of

Table 12.1: Women Appointed to the Federal Bench, 1789-1980, by Court Level[a]

	Supreme court		Circuit court		District court	
	Total	Female	Total	Female (%)	Total	Female (%)
1789-1932	75	0	190	0	640	0
1933-60	17	0	120	1 (0.8)	402	1 (0.2)
1961-76	9	0	119	1 (0.8)	200	4 (2.0)
1977-9						
turnover[b]	0	–	15	0 (0)	60	10 (16.7)
omnibus[b]	0	–	35	11 (31.4)	117	19 (16.2)
Total	101	0	479	13 (2.7)	1,419	34 (2.4)

Notes: a. The total number of judges appointed to the circuit and district courts in the four time periods are approximate and based on John Schmidhauser, *Judges and Justice: the Federal Appellate Judiciary* (Little, Brown and Company, Boston, 1979), Table 3.15; and Harold W. Chase *et al.* (1976) *Biographical Dictionary of the Federal Judiciary* Table 1; and *The Third Branch* (1976), vols. 9-12 (Federal Judicial Center, Washington, DC).
b. The Omnibus Judgeship Act of 1978 created 152 new positions for President Carter to fill, in addition to the normal turnover which creates vacancies. Nominations for some of the new judgeships have not been announced as of May, 1980; the final number of women appointed after Senate confirmation may be larger.

1978, President Carter chose 11 more women for these courts, to sit on the Second, Third, Fifth, Sixth, Ninth, Tenth and DC circuits, each woman from a different state. Except for those in the DC and Ninth Circuits, women judges will not sit together on a panel or *en banc*. They may meet occasionally at a national judiciary seminar or a bar association meeting. These women are as unusual and highly visible as the one woman judge before 1978.

The first woman appointed to the district court in 1949 continues as a senior (semi-retired) judge in 1980. The presidents between Eisenhower and Carter selected four more women, 2 per cent of those appointed, and 1 per cent of the entire active bench (Goldman, 1965 and 1974; Cook, 1978). President Carter used ten vacancies and 19 omnibus seats to raise the proportion of women trial judges. (He elevated one woman trial judge appointed by President Nixon to the circuit level (Goldman, 1978).) Two women are in active service in the same, large New York City courthouse; two in Detroit; two in Los Angeles; and three in DC. Over the country's history 2 per cent of the federal trial judges have been women; of those serving in 1980 about 6 per cent are women.

Each of the state governments has its independent and unique court structure composed of at least one trial court level located by county, and one appellate court usually at the state capitol. Before court reforms simplified and unified the structure, the states provided special courts for specific localities and/or areas of law, such as juvenile, probate, domestic relations, small claims, traffic and limited jurisdiction courts for the least populated areas. The number of judges and courts is unrelated to population or caseload, a product of historical, political accommodations. The state appellate courts, which are collegial, are 4 per cent female; but the women are scattered among the 52 highest courts and 31 intermediate courts to the extent that only two have any routine likelihood of sitting together on a case. The highest percentage of women serve in appellate courts on the east coast, followed by the west, the midwest and the south (Cook, 1978a: 85-8).

The proportion of women on important state trial courts (general jurisdiction covers serious crimes and civil matters involving substantial sums of money or basic rights) is about 3 per cent. The east coast cities have a larger percentage of women on the bench than the west, and over twice the percentage in the south and midwest. Almost half of the 59 states are without a single woman on a major court. California, New York, Pennsylvania and Illinois have the largest contingent of women, but some states with smaller judiciaries have a larger percentage (Cook, 1978a).

In the state court systems, service on the limited jurisdiction courts is one stepping stone to the major courts, but less than 4 per cent of the judges in the pool of eligibles are women. The west coast has over twice the proportion of women on minor courts than the other regions, which may indicate that in the future that region will have more women elevated to higher courts (Cook, 1978a).

The special courts were once considered the only appropriate 'place' for women judges, because of the nature of the cases — marriage, children and inheritance. Twice the percentage of women serve on these courts as on the generalist minor courts. Modernisation of court structures involves the absorption of these special courts into divisions of other trial courts, thus eliminating a former avenue of access for women into judicial office. A larger percentage of women serve on these courts in the east and west than in the midwest and south. Justice courts still operate in many rural areas and may employ 10 per cent or more females. Since the officers of these courts do not need law degrees and control small resources, they are not linked by an ambition ladder with the other courts.

The dual court system does not mean that the state and federal courts are isolated from each other. They are linked by personnel since state court judges move by presidential appointment to the federal bench. They are also linked by the movement of cases on appeal from the state appellate to the federal appellate courts. The interpretation of the US Constitution by the federal court binds the state courts to certain minimum standards; and the interpretation of the US Constitution in state court opinions can be persuasive to federal judges. Federal courts may make legal interpretations but send cases back to the state courts for application of the law to specific facts. The federalism of the courts has implications for the legal status of women. A sympathetic state judiciary can influence the federal courts to some extent but more importantly can set higher than minimum standards for sex equality and for distribution of social goods to women. On the other hand, a pro-feminist appellate federal judiciary can have a profound impact upon all 50 of the state court systems or upon the state courts in the geographical region of a circuit. A pro-feminist federal trial judiciary can raise the consciousness and legal standards of the parochial state courts (O'Connor and McGlen, 1978). The introduction of women on the state or the federal bench can have an impact on the legal status of women throughout the dual court system.

Affirmative Action for Women Judicial Candidates

The affirmative action plan to recruit women for the federal bench emerged from the interplay of American group politics. Women's organisations want women judges who will improve the condition of women; and women lawyers want the judgeship as career goals (Griffin, 1979). Politicians respond to their mutual demands by measuring out patronage according to their estimate of the political clout of women in the next electoral contest (Lipschutz and Huron, 1979). The political and personal motives of all the participants are cloaked in the symbolic garb of equality and representation values (Goldman, 1979). The shared values allow those with different material interests to make exchanges. The women's movement has given impetus to the ambitions of women lawyers but expects some *quid pro quo* for their pressure upon federal and state officials to choose women for judgeships.

The major focus of feminists, lawyers and politicians in 1979-80 was on the selection of judges for the 152 new positions in the federal courts created by the Omnibus Judgeship Act of 1978 (Cohodas, 1979). Federal judgeships are the highest prizes for lawyers because they carry prestige, life-tenure and opportunities to handle important social issues (among the more numerous routine controversies). Federal judicial salaries are not competitive with income from private practice in urban areas, but for lawyers who savour the excitement of politics and the challenge of making policy, judicial office offers more security than legislative office (Diamond, 1977). For women not admitted to exclusive firms and not yet competitive in legislative or executive political races, judgeships offer upward mobility.

The competition among politicians to control the patronage, and among lawyers to gain these offices, makes the federal bench highly visible both in the states and nationally (Jackson, 1974). Placing women in federal judgeships is psychologically more advantageous to the women's movement than placing them in state or local positions. The availability of 117 trial and 35 appellate judgeships at one point in time also gave the pressure groups some leverage. Politicians respond more favourably to a request by less powerful groups for a slice rather than for the whole of the patronage pie. When only one job is available, it is likely to go to the traditional candidate backed by the entrenched (male) groups. Women's groups asked for one-third (or 50) of the omnibus positions and had received 30 up to the end of 1980. Working on sporadic vacancies in the state courts requires accurate information gathering and fieldwork, which these groups cannot afford, in the face of a lower probability of payoff. The concentration of their efforts, however, during a two-year time span on a large pool of national judgeships is showing impressive results. Women's bar associations in states and cities, and local feminist groups are working on state court vacancies.

President Carter has firmly supported the movement to place women on the federal courts through campaign promises, executive orders and appointments. Although the President has constitutional authority to make the nomination, he does not have complete control over the selection of appellate judges and can only veto the senatorial choice of trial judges. He can exert influence through the Department of Justice and through political connections, but cannot coerce senators to select or support a woman candidate.

President Carter firmly supported the movement to place women creating nominating commissions to present five candidates for each vacancy. Before the passage of the Omnibus Act he issued an executive order requiring these commissions 'to make special efforts to seek out and identify well qualified women and members of minority groups as potential nominees' (Berkson, 1979).[2] In his 1978 Law Day address Carter said that the Omnibus Act would be a unique opportunity to make the judiciary more representative of the US population. In February 1979 Carter sent a letter asking each senator with new district positions to fill to 'redouble your efforts, whether personal or through a nominating commission, to find qualified lawyers among women'. He approved the idea of White House legal counsel placing an article in *Judicature*, a journal widely read by judges and lawyers, to explain how the use of sex as a criterion for judicial selection was appropriate in a democracy in order to secure a diversified judiciary. Carter's argument was that merit and representation (or quality and equality) could be found in the same nominee (Lipschutz and Huron, 1979).

The Justice Department has working responsibility to produce the appropriate names and to develop supporting information for their recommendation to the President, and then to the Senate. The Attorney-General implemented the affirmative action policy by designating the head of his civil division, Barbara Babcock, as his agent and by assigning a full-time assistant to the search for women candidates. Babcock encouraged women's groups to send names directly to the department. Attorney-General Bell, himself a former circuit judge, wrote letters to senators of both parties asking them to establish merit commissions for the district jobs. He personally consulted with senators who submitted white/male lists in an effort to persuade them to add women.

As part of the Omnibus Act Congress took 'notice of the fact that only one per cent of federal judges are women . . . and suggests that the President, in selecting individuals for nomination . . . give due consideration to qualified individuals regardless of race, color, sex, religion, or national origin' (Tydings, 1977). Congress also asked the President to establish guidelines for merit selection of district judges, even though the adoption of a merit procedure was voluntary to the senators. Under pressure from the President and fellow legislators in the House, a substantial number of senators did create their own nominating commissions; others were not inclined to relinquish direct personal control over patronage.

Women members of the bar and on the lower courts have a direct interest in gaining access to more prestigious and better-paid positions. In their organisations they are not as centrally focused upon helping women as a class as pressure groups formed for that purpose. Women lawyers' organisations at the national and state level are undergoing a renaissance, in recognition of the existence of both new opportunities and new resistance to women in significant legal positions. The Federation of Women Lawyers (FWL) created its own judicial screening panel to rate nominees for federal judgeships and to check on candidates' commitment to the improvement of the status of women. The FWL has a weaker role than the American Bar Association, the only private organisation which monitors candidates at the crucial stage for the Department of Justice. The FWL examines the credentials of the final nominee before the Senate Judiciary Committee at the stage of advice and consent. Women judges only now exist in sufficient numbers to form their own organisation. The first national conference of women judges met in Los Angeles in October 1979 under the sponsorship of the Judges' Committee of California Women Lawyers and created the National Association of Women Judges (NAWJ). This group unanimously passed a resolution in favour of the nomination of a woman to the next US Supreme Court vacancy.[3] The central although not the only concern of these professional activities is to open doors to women at the elite level.

The women's organisations expect the women they help into authoritative positions to be more sensitive than men in creating legal remedies against discrimination. The two largest associations open to laypersons, the National Organisation of Women (NOW) and the National Women's Political Caucus (NWPC), both developed projects to place more women on the bench. NOW's Legal Defense and Education Fund (LDEF) received a grant from the MS Foundation to prepare informational handouts on the under-representation of women on courts for the mass media, and women's groups at the state and local level. Local chapters of NOW encouraged women lawyers and state judges to submit their names as candidates for the new federal positions and sometimes made endorsements to US senators and to the Attorney-General. NOW groups also monitored the nominating commissions and expressed to media reporters their approval or disapproval of the sex composition of the lists of recommended candidates. Newspapers and news magazines reached the general public with editorials and feature stories extending consciousness of the male monopoly of the courts, and aggravating feelings about the unfairness of such skewed representation.

The NWPC formed a Legal Support Task Force with a continuing concern for judicial appointments and co-ordinated publicity efforts with NOW-LDEF. The 1978-9 chair of NWPC gave high priority to the project of placing women in omnibus poisitions by testifying before the Senate Judiciary Committee about the historic opportunity to rectify the under-representation of women. The organisation proposed names directly to senators or to commissions and actively sponsored particular

women, such as the first woman nominee for the Fifth Circuit Court of
Appeals. When the list of candidates for four district judgeships in
Virginia turned out to be all male and white, the NWPC sent its own list
of names to the Attorney-General.

Besides the two major national organisations, smaller, *ad hoc* groups,
alone or in coalition with minority groups, introduced and sponsored
candidates. The Judicial Selection Project took the responsibility of
reaching out to identify and assist at least 100 women to apply to the
advisory nominating commissions, and to campaign for appointment.
This coalition was composed of leaders from public interest, racial and
ethnic, and women's legal defence societies. The project contacted state
civic groups and urged them to select and lobby for candidates who
would increase the diversity of the federal bench, and who were sensitive to the needs and problems of minorities and other groups that
traditionally have not enjoyed full access to the legal system. The
project also successfully objected to a circuit nominating commission
guideline of 15 years of legal experience, which had the effect of
reducing the pool of eligible women, since admission barriers to law
school were reduced only in the last ten years.

Although women's organisations purport to be dissatisfied with the
results, the affirmative action achievements in filling the omnibus
judgeships during the Carter Administration are entirely without precedent. The large percentage of women appointed to circuit seats (31 per
cent) in contrast to district positions (16 per cent) shows that
President Carter contributed more to court integration than the US
senators. The impact of the political process of judicial selection has
been to legitimise the inclusion of women and to pronounce their
exclusion as contrary to American ideals. The combination of old
values of equality with new attitudes towards women and positive
lobbying action may be a turning-point in the struggle for integration of
the court elite. Whether the new judges will behave as anticipated by
feminist groups will become evident in the near future. The proba-
bilities of pro-feminist judicial decisions will be discussed in the next
section which reports the empirical findings about women state judges.

Differences Between Women and Men on the Bench

The data for this research are the responses of 170 state trial judges to
questionnaires mailed in 1978. The women judge respondents are 68
per cent of the female universe sitting on state courts of general juris-

diction at any time during 1977 (excluding New Jersey which has a rule against surveys). The male judge respondents are a sample of the large male universe (approximately 5,655) selected to match the female judges in court location. The women respondents are representative of the female universe in respect to age, race, place of birth, party, career pattern and region (Cook, 1978b). Answers to the question about the different perspectives and decisions by women and men in office were necessarily speculative until a large enough universe of women gained political positions to allow this kind of data collection and quantitative analysis (Kritzer and Uhlman, 1977).[4]

The research reported here uses the individual judge as the unit of analysis. The independent variables are the sex, the political philosophy and party affiliation of the judge. The intervening variables are the judge's attitude towards job/home role conflict and commitment to feminism. The dependent variable is the simulated decision in a women's issue case. The indicators for the variables are the judge's self-report on sex, party membership and political philosophy (liberal, moderate or conservative). The attitude towards sex-roles was operationalised by constructing an index which will be explained in detail below. The commitment to feminism was treated as dichotomous, i.e., those who did and did not describe themselves as feminists, and also as trichotomous, i.e., feminist, non-feminist who supports the Women's Liberation Movement (WLM), called sympathisers, and non-feminist/non-supporters, called disapprovers. The vote in the hypothetical case was for or against the woman plaintiff.

These variables can be used to describe the state judges serving on major trial courts (see Table 12.2). More of the women judges belong to the Democratic party (65 per cent) than the men (45 per cent). What is more surprising is the very small percentage of women compared to men who declare membership in the Republican party. Women are more likely to prefer third parties or to assert their independence of party affiliation. This rejection of partisanship would exclude them from gaining access to appointing authorities and collecting political debts which come from active party work in states or counties controlled by one party. Although it is possible in some states to gain judgeships without paying political dues, in many states and in the federal courts the political party credential is essential for nomination. More women (36 per cent) than men (25 per cent) also claim to be liberal. In their membership of the Democratic party and their liberal ideas, women judges are similar to women elected to office in the other two branches of government (Lynn, 1975).

Table 12.2: Party, Philosophy, Attitude to Role Conflict and Feminism by Sex of State Trial Judges

	% Female (no. = 85)	% Males (no. = 85)
Party:		
Democrat	65	55
Republican	18	41
Other	17	4
Philosophy:		
Liberal	36	25
Moderate	47	52
Conservative	17	23
Work/Home index:		
Liberated	65	32
Unliberated	35	68
Commitment:		
Feminist	49	11
Sympathiser	39	73
Disapprover	12	17

The women judges have strong attitudes in favour of new social roles for women in comparison to the weaker and sometimes antagonistic attitudes of male judges. There is a difference in attitude towards job/home role conflict by sex of judge within both parties but not by party within each sex. Even among liberals the female judges have a significantly different attitude towards sex-roles than male judges. Although the difference among moderates and conservatives by sex is less, over half of the non-liberal women judges nevertheless approve of new work-roles for women. Within the male-sex sample there are strong differences by ideology. Less than half of the males of both parties and of non-liberal temper favour the liberation of women from old definitions of domestic responsibilities.

The women judges are much more openly committed to the liberation of women than the male judges. As Table 12.2 shows, almost half of the women and only one-tenth of the men are willing to label themselves as feminists. Men, of course, do not have the motivation of self-interest, and their comfort in the *status quo* provides a strong incentive to oppose new roles for women outside the home. However, only 5 per cent more of the men than women disapprove the movement entirely. Those judges who are liberal in political philosophy and members of the Democratic party also tend to take a feminist posture. Only 10 per cent of the Democrats but 24 per cent of the Republican judges disapprove of the movement; and almost three times the proportion of Democrats to Republicans are feminists. Feminism, however, is not a plank of the Democratic party, but cuts across party lines. Liberals are stronger feminists than Democrats and conservatives less supportive than Republicans. Since feminism challenges the traditional social institutions, it is not surprising to find it rejected by judges with non-liberal ideologies.

Judicial Attitude toward Job/Home Role Conflict

Women have moved into non-domestic roles in industrial societies by small increments. Women living at the level of subsistence took work offered at pay rates which men would not accept throughout the nineteenth century. During periods when men were not available, such as wartime, women handled more demanding and better-paid technical jobs. Generally, however, the expansion of the female role outside the home into permanent, sex-segregated jobs has depended upon new social needs, e.g., for teachers to provide literate labourers, and upon new technologies, e.g., for typists, at a point in time when men with the appropriate abilities could be employed at better-paid jobs (Whitehurst, 1977). The cultural approbation of the woman in paid work covered first the young single woman, then the married woman without children, and only in the period of the contemporary women's movement the woman with young children. The relaxed divorce laws and the inability of men to support separate households, as well as the increasing cost of public welfare for women with children but without a male wage-earner contributed to the social acceptability of the mother in paid work. The price of keeping the female in the domestic role was too costly for the individual ex-husband and for the public budget (Lewis, 1978).

A judge's attitude towards the female role is of particular concern because the traditional female roles are legal as well as cultural. Through marriage women took on obligations for household tasks, which were balanced by the income-producing duties of the husband. American law has not treated the wife/mother as a producer of goods in its tax or retirement laws. (Brown, Friedman, Katz and Price, 1977). In a society where public value is measured by ownership of goods and/or by salary for producing goods or services, the wife/mother had only personal value. Without a legal male cohabitor she had no personal value which could be translated into legal entitlements. Although law reflects culture, law also educates to new beliefs, introduces new ideas and establishes rewards. The extent to which women can risk new roles depends upon the interpretation of laws relating to marriage, credit, inheritance, health insurance, social security and so on. Judges are in a position to encourage or discourage the assumption of the risk of non-domestic roles through their decisions.

   The job/home role conflict variable was operationalised by the judge's response to eight provocative statements, intended to reveal the judge's perspective towards family responsibilities of American women and towards their importance relative to obligations outside the home. The respondents agreed or disagreed with the following statements which describe a belief, norm or policy preference commonly held now or in the past about women's social roles. Each statement has been given a cryptic title for identification on the list.

	Female %	Male %
1. *Nocareer*: If a woman's family needs her at home, she should give up her career. (Norm) No. = 135 Total disagree: 50%	64.5	38.4
2. *Homebody*: Most women are happiest taking care of home and families. (Belief) No. = 125 Disagree: 64%	76.5	49.1
3. *Noname*: It is silly for women to use different last names from their husbands, particularly if they have children. (Belief) No. = 155 Disagree: 64%	78.4	49.4
4. *Daycare*: Government or business should make available adequate day care facilities for the children of working parents. (Policy) No. = 157 Agree: 75%	84.2	65.4
5. *Mother*: Women who have school-age children should not work outside the home unless absolutely necessary. (Norm) No. = 160 Disagree: 79%	93.6	64.6
6. *Eschare*: Wife and husband should share the economic responsibility of supporting a family. (Norm) No. = 157 Agree 84%	92.1	76.5

7. *Priority*: It is more important for a wife to help
her husband's career than for her to have a
career herself.
(Belief) No. = 148   Disagree: 86%   94.1   80.0

8. *Nonite*: A married woman should not
accept a job that would require that she be
away from home overnight.
(Norm) No. = 159   Disagree: 94%   100.0   89.0

Both sexes had the fewest feminist responses to the *Nocareer* statement. A majority of women judges disagreed that a woman should give
up her career to meet family 'needs' and a similar majority of male
judges thought that she should. There was disagreement by sex on the
Noname and *Homebody* questions, with a majority of male judges
taking the non-feminist position. Men were a great deal more disturbed
than women judges about a married woman taking her own name and
more certain that women are happy at home. On the other five
questions a majority of the male judges gave a pro-liberation response
but the number of women judges was significantly higher. The most
significant difference was on the question of whether women with school-
age children should go out to work if not necessary. There was complete
agreement among all the women judges that the convention against
married women working away from home, particularly overnight, is
dead. Only a quarter or less of the male judges accepted old norms and
beliefs about the importance of the husband's career and his primary
responsibility for breadwinning. The differences in response by sex was
significant for every statement using both chi-square and T-test
analyses.

The consensus among judges on the last three statements was too
high (over 80 per cent) to allow further analysis. The other five statements are examined separately and together as an attitudinal index, in
relation to sex and other variables. To ascertain that the five statements
belonged on the same attitudinal dimension, they were factor
analysed. The factor loading matrix had an eigenvalue of 1.98 and
accounted for 40 per cent of the variation in the response pattern. The
factor score of each judge provides a measure of the complex attitude
on the interface of the home and employment duties of women.
Eighteen of the male judges had low scores, below 1.0, which indicates
their traditional attitude that women should concentrate their
activities in the home and subordinate career interests to the family

needs for unity and service. Only one woman had a score just below 1.0. The simple correlation between sex of the judge and the job/home role conflict score was .434. Sex is strongly related to this attitude.

Table 12.3: Support for Public Roles for Women: State Judges With High Scores on Work/Home Role Conflict Index

	% Females	% Males
Party:		
Democrats	67	33
Republicans	60	30
Philosophy:		
Liberals	87	66
Moderates	50	22
Conservatives	57	15
Commitment:		
Feminists	79	67
Sympathisers	55	31
Disapprovers	40	14

Within both parties, Table 12.3 shows a clear difference in attitude towards job/home roles by sex of judge. The difference is significant for Democrats, but on either party ballot the selection of the female would offer a higher probability of selecting a judge with a progressive attitude towards women's social roles. Among liberals the female judge is also significantly different from the male on the role index. Although the difference among moderates and conservatives by sex is less, over half of non-liberal women judges approve new roles for women, while over three-quarters of the males want women to stay in their 'place' at home. The sex-role attitude in turn related strongly to the degree of commitment to feminism. Over half of those with high scores on the job/home index were feminists; only 5 per cent were disapprovers. None of those with a low score on the index were feminists.

Explaining Decisions in Women's Cases

The judges 'decided' simulated cases which described factual situations commonly encountered in trial courts today. To control for the different law and precedent in the 50 states, the judges were asked to assume 'that the law would support a decision for either party'. It is realistic to recognise that trial judges do enjoy a great deal of discretion in a period of cultural change, when the settled law no longer fits human experiences nicely. The two cases which follow concern the modern woman's social roles.

232 Women Judges and Women's Legal Rights

Case 1. A young woman in a divorce suit asks for temporary alimony to pay for a degree in physical therapy. She argued that she worked to pay for his computer technical training. The husband agrees to child-support payments but refuses to pay for his wife's schooling. Would you award enough temporary alimony to cover her school costs? (no. = 155: yes = 92 per cent; no = 8 per cent)

Case 2. A married woman with two children files a petition to change her last name to her maiden name. Her husband disapproves and argues that it will be embarrassing to him and their two school-age children. Would you approve the name change? (no. = 155: yes = 63 per cent; no = 37 per cent)?

There was a strong consensus favourable to temporary support for a woman who wanted to prepare herself for an occupation, so that ultimately she could carry her burden of child-support as well as child-care. There was no significant difference between the way women and men judges would decide the alimony case, or the way feminists and non-feminists would decide. Of course her self-sufficiency was to the long-term advantage of the ex-husband.

More disagreement appeared over the right of a woman to take a name which gave her an identity separate from her husband. The symbolic issue may generate stronger feeling than the bread-and-butter issue because of the family unity implicit in the common name. The use of a name is more than symbolic, of course, with practical implications for career development and recognition. A decision not to allow the woman a different name should relate to judicial attitudes on women's domestic and career roles.

The name-change case raises in symbolic form the conflict between the domestic and the public roles of women. Should a married woman devote herself to organic family interests or to the development of her own personality? The adoption of the husband's name at marriage is a custom with heavy implications of ownership and control by the husband, and subordination and service by the wife. Only one state — Hawaii — translated the social custom into law (repealed in 1975), but other states established elaborate legal procedures for name change based on the universal practice of the custom.[5] The change of name at marriage is symbolic of loss of individuality and can be viewed as the antithesis of ERA (Equal Rights Amendment) as a symbol of the recognition of women's value as a person equal under the law to men.

The name case is useful to elicit simulated behaviour across state lines because there is no US Supreme Court precedent binding upon state judges which declares woman's right to her own name. The Supreme Court has not considered the name problem important enough to hear oral arguments or to write a full opinion.

State trial judges have enjoyed a great deal of discretion in deciding how to deal with married women who have been using their husband's name and decide to re-establish their own individuality by taking their own name. State supreme courts, following common-law principles, unlike the federal court in *Forbush*,[6] usually allow a woman to retain her own name without a formal proceeding if she rejected the custom at the time of marriage and continued the consistent, non-fraudulent use of a different last name.

Law reform has been initiated in a number of states to clarify name choice at marriage, and for driver's licence and voting registration. But even where the law is sex-neutral, trial judges have interpreted the law to the disadvantage of women's choice of identity. Many trial judges throughout the country still persist in refusing to allow a woman to relinquish her husband's name, although their decision may be reversed if the plaintiff can afford to press her demand to the appellate level.[7] Appellate state courts generally but not always find the denial of petitions for name change by women, even with minor children and husband's opposition, to be an abuse of discretion. Trial judges have wide discretion to follow their own notions of priority, particularly when a 'transitional' woman decides after some years of marriage to take a symbolic step toward individuality.

The instruction in the questionnaire gave the judges in the study full discretion to apply their own sense of the fitness of things to the hypothetical case facts. The sex of the judge related significantly ($< .05$) to the decision to approve the name change. Barely half of those judges who asserted sympathy with women's liberation were supporters of the woman's request for separate identity. An abstract approval of the ideals of a movement is not easily translated into action. Only feminists can be relied upon to give both real and symbolic resources to women.

In order to understand how the sex of the judge relates to a judicial decision, the method of path analysis is employed in this hypothetical case. Path analysis is appropriate where a number of explanatory factors can be arranged in a time series. Biological sex is a part of the individual's identity from birth and so can be treated as the first variable in the series. Sex identity in society colours daily life and almost every experience which contributes to the development of personality. The next factor is political party identification, which is usually accepted as a family inheritance during childhood. There is no relationship expected between sex and party, since children of both sexes usually join the family party and neither party has given adult feminists an incentive for allegiance.

The third variable in terms of time is the attitude which the individual forms towards women's conflicting home and work responsibilities. The expectation for a relationship between the independent variables of sex and party, and the job/home attitude rests on the supposition that women more than men recognise the potential benefits of wider social roles, and that Democrats more than Republicans accept change and approve equal opportunity.

An attitude favourable towards expanding women's work roles contributes to the individual's active commitment to a feminist lifestyle. This commitment to feminism, as an intervening variable, relates most strongly to actual behaviour, such as judicial decision-making, while the factors which appear earlier in a life-history, i.e., sex and party, have less direct effect.

The path programme on Figure 12.1 shows that the coefficient which relates the sex of the judge to the work/home attitude is .378.

Figure 12.1: Causal Explanation of Judges' Feminism and Case Decision

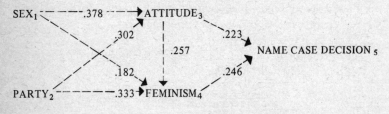

Path to Feminism		Path to Decision	
F-ratio	= 26.96	F-ratio	= 9.39
Sig @	.000	Sig @	.000
R	= .572	R	= .431
R^2	= .328	R^2	= .185

Note on variables:

Party: Self-identification as Liberal Democrat, Liberal Republican, Moderate Democrat, Moderate Republican, Conservative Democrat, Conservative Republican in rank order.

Attitude: Index of responses to five sex role statements.

Feminism: self-identification as feminist, favourable to women's movement but not feminist, and unfavourable to women's movement, in rank order.

Name case decision: Judges' vote on hypothetical case: 'A married woman with two children filed a petition to change her last name to her maiden name. Her husband disapproved and argues that it will be embarrassing to him and their two school-age children. Would you approve the name change?' Yes or No.

Controlling for party, the correlation is even higher (.400). The path coefficient between party membership and attitude is .302 (.330 when controlling for sex). Commitment to feminism can be explained by the relationship with the judge's sex, party and attitude. The strongest path is between political party and feminism (.333); the next strongest between attitude and feminism (.257); and the least strong but most significant is between sex and feminism (.182). The multiple correlation of the three variables with feminism is .572; they explain one-third of the variation in the degree of judges' commitment to feminism.

The decision which the judges indicated they would make in a case of name change is directly affected by the attitudinal and feminism variables. The path between attitude and behaviour is .223, and between feminism and behaviour .246. The factors of sex and party which were established more remotely in time do not have any direct impact upon decision. The direct influence of sex identity or of party loyalty would also be contrary to the ethical expectations for judicial behaviour. On the other hand, as Justice Cardozo and many other judges have admitted, no decision-maker can avoid the unconscious biases which spring from life experience. These life experiences depend upon basic ascribed and achieved characteristics, such as sex and party associations. The indirect effect of these variables can be calculated. Sex works through three paths, through attitude ($p_{31} p_{53} = .0243$), through feminism ($p_{41} p_{54} = .0448$), and through attitude and feminism ($p_{31} p_{43} p_{54} = .0239$), for a total indirect influence of .153. Party works through the same three pathways ($p_{32} p_{53} = .0674$; $p_{42} p_{54} = .0820$; and $p_{32} p_{43} p_{54} = .0191$) for a total indirect influence of .169. The effect of party affiliation is slightly larger than that of sex, indicating the continuing salience for judicial decisions of both identifications at a hidden level.

The intervening variables in the analysis, attitude and feminism, only explain 18.5 per cent of the variation in case outcome. A path analysis for only women judges explains somewhat more of their decisions (22 per cent). In a legal model of judicial decision-making, the fact that such variables explain any part of court output would be surprising. The behavioural model would predict that these factors would be even more powerful, particularly where the law is in flux. The modest explanatory power of attitudes and commitments indicates that legal organisations are a constraining force but not a straitjacket. Sex-related variables do explain about one-fifth of the variance in the women's issue case.

Conclusion

A question which has been raised with respect to choosing among candidates for legislative office can also be asked about judges: is a vote based on the sex of the prospective judge a better guarantee of performance than a vote based on other cues? The answer depends of course on the type of selection process and the amount of information available on the viable candidates.

Those who participate in the appointment of federal and state judges work with almost full information. The political elite — lawyers in bar associations, members of *ad hoc* lobby groups and nominating commissions, task-force leaders of women's groups, advisors to the President or Governor, the staff of senators and congressional committees and attorneys at the Justice Department — know a great deal more about the candidates than sex and party. Party is not even a useful cue, since the President's (or Governor's) party will take at least 95 per cent of the available patronage seats. With party fixed, it is sensible to bet on the female over the male candidate. The female Republican is obviously different from the male in attitude and behaviour. Although the male Democratic judges seem to have the same attitude as females towards the women's movement, the research findings show that their simulated behaviour is quite different. This research establishes the utility of the criterion of the Judicial Selection Project — proven commitment to equal opportunity — for their approval of judicial candidates.

Voters operate with imperfect and, in fact, minimal information, often acting on the basis of salient cues like party. Where voters select judges as well as other office-holders, party is a useful indicator only in districts which are competitive or where judges are selected on a nonpartisan ballot. In districts dominated by one party, a choice based only on sex would be reasonably predictive of attitude and behaviour. Sex is usually apparent from the name of the candidate. Such identification in the past has damaged candidacies of women (Hedlund, Freeman, Hamm and Stein, 1979), but with positive expectations associated with female identity, voters could use the cue in a positive way. While political reformers would prefer voters to study the promises and records of candidates carefully, and then vote in the general interest, the political realist will settle for a turnout based on self-interest and will hope for cues to illuminate that self-interest. Women voters can vote for women judicial candidates with as much profit as men have

voted party.[8] And women's organisations can continue to encourage
and support women with feminist attitudes and records, with a high
probability of getting egalitarian public decisions for women from the
bench.

Notes

1. *Taylor* v *Louisiana*, 419 US 522 (1975).
2. Executive Order no. 12059, 4(d), 11 May 1978; Berkson (1979).
3. The author was an observer at this organising meeting.
4. The first study testing the hypothesis that women judges behave differently from men had an inadequate balance of male and female judges: Kritzer
and Uhlan (1977) report no information on the number of women judges
or the number of cases per individual judge; however, during the period of
their study (1968 – 74) about four women and 50 men were assigned to
trial divisions. The women judges heard only 4.5% of the sample of over
43,000 criminal cases in their data base. The authors' conclusions that the
'female judges in Metro City behave no differently than their male
colleagues' does not flow from their findings. A more accurate interpretation
is that on a court with a token number of women, the small decisional output
of women judges is indistinguishable from the large output of the male judges.
There was no basis for discussing possible explanations for the behaviour of
judges as individual decision-makers, since the unit of analysis was not the
average sentence of each judge but the average sentence of the male pool
and the female pool of cases. Nor could their conclusion apply to courts with
different sex compositions, in which female judges decide a larger proportion
of the cases.
5. Useful reviews of the common law of names are found in the
Maryland Supreme Court opinion, *Stuart* v *Board of Supervisors, Howard
County*, 295 A2d 223 (1972) and in the Wisconsin Supreme Court opinion,
Kruzel v *Podell*, 226 NW2d 458 (1975). Also see *Krupa* v *Green*, 177 NE2d 616
(1961).
6. *Forbush* v *Wallace*, 405 US 910 (1972), affirming 341 F. Supp. 217
(1971), without oral argument.
7. In the following cases the state appeals court reversed the trial judge who
insisted that the woman use her husband's surname: Texas, *In re Erickson*, 547
SW2d 357 (1977); West Virgina, *In re Harris*, 236 SE2d 426 (1977); Maryland,
Klein v *Klein*, 373 A2d 86 (1977); Michigan, *Protrowski* v *Piotrowski*, 247 NW2d
354 (1976); California, *Weathers* v *Superior Court*, 26 Cal Rptr 547 (1976);
Florida, *Davis* v *Roos*, 326 S02d 226 (1976); New Jersey, *Egner* v *Egner*, 337
A2d 46 (1975); Tennessee, *Dunn* v *Palmero*, 522 SW2d 679 (1975); Virginia, *In
re Strikwerda*, 220 SE2d 245 (1975); South Dakota, *Ogle* v *Circuit Court*, 227
NW2d 621 (1975); Missouri, *In re Natale*, 527 SW2d 402 (1975); Wisconsin,
Kruzel v *Podell*, 226 NW2d 458 (1975).
8. However, the non-feminist woman voters may not consider the sex cue to
be legitimate: see Perkins and Fowlkes (1980).

238   *Women Judges and Women's Legal Rights*

Bibliography

Allen, F.L. (1965) *To Do Justly*, The Press of Western University, Cleveland, Ohio, pp. 41-6; 93-7

Berkson, L. (1979) 'The U.S. Circuit Judge Nominating Commission', *Judicature, 62* (May), pp. 466-82

Brown, B., Friedman, A.E., Katz, H.N. and Price, A.M. (1977) *Women's Rights and the Law*, Praeger, New York, Ch. 5.

Cohodas, N. (1979) 'Merit Selection Diversifies Federal Bench', *Congressional Quarterly Weekly* (27 October), p. 2418

Cook, B.B. (1978a) 'Women Judges: the End of Tokenism' in W.L. Hepperle and L. Crites (eds.), *Women in the Courts*, Williamsburg, Virginia, pp. 84, 89-90

—— (1978b) 'Women Judges and Public Policy on Sex Integration', paper delivered at the annual meeting of the American Political Science Association, New York City, September

Diamond, I. (1977) *Sex Roles in the State House*, Yale University Press, New London, Connecticut

Gehlen, F.L. (1977) 'Legislative Role Performance of Female Legislators', *Sex Roles, 3*, 1, 1-18

Goldman, S. (1965) 'Characteristics of Eisenhower and Kennedy Appointees to the Lower Federal Courts', *Western Political Quarterly, 18* (December) 755-62

—— (1974) 'Judicial Backgrounds, Recruitment, and the Party Variable: The Case of the Johnson and Nixon Appointees to the United States District and and Appeals Courts', *Arizona State Law Journal, 2*, 211-22

—— (1978) 'A Profile of Carter's Judicial Nominees', *Judicature, 62* (November), 247-54

—— (1979) 'Should There Be Affirmative Action for the Judiciary?', *Judicature, 62* (May), 488-94

Griffin, M.K. (1979) 'Women Judges Would Balance Bench', *National Law Journal* (2 July), p. 17

Hedlund, R.D., Freeman, P.K., Hamm, K.E. and Stein, R.M. (1979) 'The Electability of Women Candidates: the Effects of Sex Role Stereotypes', *The Journal of Politics, 41* (May), 513-26

Jackson, D.D. (1974) *Judges*, Atheneum Publishers, New York

Kritzer, H. and Uhlman, T.M. (1977) 'Sisterhood in the Courtroom: Sex of Judge and Defendant in Criminal Case Disposition', *Social Science Journal, 14*, 77-88

Lewis, G.L. (1978) 'Changes in Women's Role Participation' in I.H. Frieze *et al.* (eds.), *Women and Sex Roles*, W.M. Norton & Co., New York

Lipschutz, R.J. and Huron, D.B. (1979) 'Achieving a More Representative Federal Judiciary', *Judicature, 62* (May), 483-5

Lynn, N. (1975) 'Women in American Politics' in Jo Freeman (ed.), *Women: A Feminist Perspective*, Mayfield Publishing Co., Palo Alto, Calif., pp. 364-79

O'Connor, K. and McGlen, N.E. (1978) 'The Effects of Government Organisation on Women's Rights: An Analysis of the Status of Women in Canada, Great Britain, and the United States', *International Journal of Women's Studies, 1* (November-December), 588-601

Perkins, J. and Fowlkes, D.L. (1980) 'Opinion Representation versus Social Representation; Or, Why Women Can't Run as Women and Win', *American Political Science Review, 74* (March), 92-103

Schmidhauser, J.R. (1979) *Judges and Justices: the Federal Appellate Judiciary*, Little, Brown & Co., Boston, pp. 44-9

Tydings, J.W. (1977) 'Merit Selection for District Judges', *Judicature, 61*
    (September), 113-18
Whitehurst, C.A. (1977) *Women in America: the Oppressed Majority*,
    Goodyear Publishing Co., Santa Monica, Calif., pp. 55-63

13 FUTURE PERSPECTIVES

Margherita Rendel

The preceding chapters have shown the relevance of a study of women to political scientists. They have also shown that many of the traditional ways of studying women can be misleading. Asking questions about women that have not usually been asked (and indeed asking questions of women) can lead to an examination of issues that are central to political science. The study of women may therefore be one of the more fruitful ways of developing the discipline. Scholars have for long studied women from certain perspectives, however. The developments that are now proving most fruitful are those developed by feminist scholars during the last decade.

The chapters have also demonstrated ways in which knowledge and understanding can be enhanced by the use of data developed in other disciplines. This has implications for teaching and for students. There is often little training given to students to encourage such an approach. I am suggesting that interdisciplinary studies require both an openness of mind that distrusts disciplinary boundaries and a willingness to learn, understand and respect unfamiliar ways of thinking, and of collecting and analysing data.

Political scientists have now begun to turn their attention towards the questions raised in this book. Is it possible to indicate priorities or preferences among the problems to be tackled? It has been shown that the presence of women themselves in sufficient numbers in positions of power assists the devising and executing of measures that take their interests into account, and that the absence of women leads to their own interests being neglected and the demands of the work they do to be overlooked. The consequences are that governments and planners have not been entirely successful in achieving their ostensible aims. Research into the factors which facilitate women's entry into positions of power, and enable them to be effective once there, would therefore be valuable. Such research should also include ways of deliberately increasing women's promotion and of helping men to share power. Research on these topics bears directly on public policy; it would

240

include all levels of education, employment and conditions of work, child-care facilities, care of the disabled and elderly, insurance, family law, relationships, reproduction and sexuality, as well as women in the public service, political parties and trade unions.

A more theoretical approach lies in considering the gains and losses arising from the sexual divisions of labour, and the type of society which those divisions entail. Or is it the type of society which imposes the divisions of labour, and the tensions and frustrations that these divisions cause? In the first two chapters, questions were asked relating to competition and protection as factors making for hierarchy, authoritarianism and sexual divisions. If we want a more peaceful society, do we need first to destroy sexual divisions?

APPENDIX ONE: PAPERS PRESENTED TO THE ROUND TABLE OF THE IPSA STUDY GROUP ON SEX ROLES AND POLITICS HELD AT THE UNIVERSITY OF ESSEX, 6-8 AUGUST 1979

Berenice Carroll, University of Illinois at Urbana-Champaign: 'Patriarchy and Political Philosophy'

Jeanne Marie Col, State University of New York at Albany: 'Theoretical Perspectives on Women's Actual or Potential Participation in Organisations'

Beverly B. Cook, University of Wisconsin-Milwaukee: 'Women Judges, their Role as Representatives of Women's Interests'

Eleonore Eckmann, European University Institute, Florence: 'Women and Work: Law, Reality and Movement in Italy'

Ilona Kickbusch, Free University of Berlin: 'Political Theories of Women in the Service of Society'

Haing-ja Kim, Ewha Women's University, South Korea: 'A Comparative Role Analysis of Female Legislators: US House of Representatives and the National Assembly of Korea'

Shoshana Klebanoff, The Harry S. Truman Research Institute, The Hebrew University of Jerusalem: 'The Political Manipulation of Israeli Women'

Linda Layne, University of Cambridge: 'Algerian Women's Social Networks'

Susan Mezey and Michael Mezey, De Paul University, Chicago: 'Feminist Attitudes and Government Policy'

Christine Obbo, University of Wisconsin-Madison: 'Victorian Laws, Ganda Women and Development'

Helen Place, University of Waikato, New Zealand: 'Sex Roles in Employment'

Joan Rothschild, University of Lowell, Mass.: 'Technology, Patriarchy and the Social Control of Women'

Sharon Wolchik, George Washington University, Washington, DC: 'The Status, Liberation and Mobilisation of Women in Czechoslovakia'

APPENDIX TWO: PAPERS PRESENTED AT THE FORMAL AND INFORMAL SESSIONS OF THE STUDY GROUP ON SEX ROLES AND POLITICS AT THE MOSCOW CONGRESS OF THE IPSA, 12-18 AUGUST 1979

Nermin Abadan-Unat, Ankara University, Turkey: 'Women in Government as Policymakers and Bureaucrats: the Turkish Case'

Keziah Awosika, Nigerian Institute of Social & Economic Research, University of Ibadan: 'Women's Education and Participation in the Labour Force: the Case of Nigeria'

Minoti Bhattacharyya, Bijoy Krishna Girls' College, Howrah, University of Calcutta: 'Politicisation of Indian Women'

Frank R. Boddendijk, Vrije Universiteit, Amsterdam: 'Alice in Weimar, or the Rising Waves of Feminism'

Deborah F. Bryceson and Marjorie Mbilinyi, University of Dar es Salaam: 'The Changing Role of Tanzanian Women in Production from Peasants to Proletarians'

A.G. Kharchev and M.S. Matszkovski, Institute for Sociological Research, Academy of Sciences of the USSR, Moscow, USSR: 'Problems of Combining by Women the Occupational, Family and Social Roles'

Haing-ja Kim, Ewha Women's University, South Korea: 'Role of Women in the Change Process in Korea'

Linda Layne, University of Cambridge: 'Jordanian Government Policy in Regard to Women Wage-earners'

Margaret Leahy, University of Southern California: 'Equality and Inequality in Capitalist and Socialist Societies: Women and National Development'

A. Norikova, Highest School of Trade Unions, Moscow, USSR: 'Development of Women's Social Activity in Soviet Society'

M.G. Pankratova, Institute for Sociological Research, Academy of Sciences of the USSR, Moscow, USSR: 'Uzbekistan Women'

Joan A. Rothschild, University of Lowell, Mass: 'Technology, "Women's Work" and the Social Control of Women'

Najma Sachak, University of Dar es Salaam, Tanzania: 'Employment Opportunities for Rural Women; Some Issues Affecting Attitudes and Policy'

Sirkka Sinkkonen, University of Kuopio, Finland and Elina Haavio-
  Mannila, University of Helsinki, Finland: 'Impact of Women MPs
  and the Women's Movement on Agenda-building'
Judith H. Stiehm, University of Southern California: 'Citizenship;
  Mobilisation, Participation, Representation'
Fanny Tabak, Pontifícia Universidada Católica do Rio de Janeiro,
  Brazil: 'Women's Role in the Definition of Public Policies in Brazil'
Tsveta Vasileva, Institute of Marxism-Leninism, Sofia, Bulgaria: 'The
  Participation of the Women in Bulgarian Political Life'

NOTES ON CONTRIBUTORS

Nermin Abadan-Unat, PhD, Professor of Political Behaviour, Chairperson for Political Behaviour, Faculty of Political Science, University of Ankara; Awarded Order of Great Merit Cross by German Federal Republic, 1979; President of Turkish Social Science Association, Vice-President of Turkish Association for Political Science; visiting professor at German and American universities; formerly senator in the Turkish Parliament; author of numerous books and articles on migration, especially Turkish workers in Germany, and the status of women, including *Women in Turkish Society* (E.J. Brill,Leiden).

Georgina Ashworth, MA (Edin.), founder CHANGE International Reports Women and Society, Research Adviser to UK Refugee Agencies, former Assistant Director, Minority Rights Group, London; editor of *World Minorities*, vols. I, II and III, Quartermaine, and of numerous articles on human rights, minorities, refugees and imperial history.

Keziah Awosika, BA (Durham), D Phil (Oxon.), Research Fellow, Nigerian Institute of Economic and Social Research, Ibadan; Assistant Secretary, Nigerian Economic Society, member of Western State Marketing Board, 1975-7 and of Ondo State Economic Advisory Council; principal research interests: women and development; money, banking and international finance; inflation; author of reports and articles on these subjects.

Jeanne Marie Col, Associate Professor in Public Administration at Sangamon State University, Illinois; served as Assistant Professor, State University of New York at Albany (1977-81), and Lecturer, Makerere University, Kampala, Uganda (1972-76); edits the quarterly newsletter of the Research Committee on Sex Roles and Politics of the International Political Science Association; her books *Uganda: A Profile* (Westview Press) and *Women's Support Networks* (US Department of Labor) will be available in 1981; her survey of women's networks include international and local women's organisations throughout the world.

Beverly B. Cook, BA (Wellesley College), MA (University of Wisconsin-Madison), PhD (Claremont University; Professor, University of Wisconsin-Milwaukee; fellowships/grants: Ford Foundation Faculty Fellow; Social Science Research Council; American

245

Philosophical Society; Center for the American Woman and Politics.
Research interests: judicial behaviour; selection and specialisation of
elites; law and equality. Author of numerous articles published in
political science and law journals. Publications include *The Judicial
Process in California*, and chapters in *Women in the Courts, The
Study of Criminal Courts,* and *Women in Local Politics.*

Elina Haavio-Mannila, Associate Professor of Sociology at the University
of Helsinki, Finland since 1971. She has conducted research work in
medical sociology and immigration problems, but her main specialisation is in women's studies. Since the publication of her book on
Finnish women and men in 1968, she has written several articles in
Finnish and in English on the position of women in comparative
perspective. Recently, she has completed a book on afternoon
dances in Finland. She began to study women in politics in 1970,
with the publication of 'Sex Roles in Politics' in *Scandinavian
Political Studies.*

Ilona Kickbusch, MA (Konstanz), Consultant, Health Education, WHO
European Office; formerly Research Assistant, University of
Konstanz; Chairperson, Women's Concerns, Sektion Frauen-
forschung of the German Sociological Association. Research
interests include self-help in health care. Publications include *Self-
help and Health in the Federal Republic of Germany.*

Margherita Rendel, MA (Cantab.), PhD (London), Research Lecturer in
Human Rights and Education, University of London Institute of
Education; Chairperson, Research Committee on Sex Roles and
Politics of International Political Science Association; Consultant
for UNESCO on Women's Studies; has given invited evidence to
parliamentary and official bodies; member of Editorial Advisory
Board of *Women's Studies International Quarterly*; Convenor of
postgraduate courses in Rights in Education. Books include *Advisory
Committees in British Government* and *The Administrative
Functions of the French Conseil d'Etat*; numerous articles on public
law and women in education.

Joan Rothschild, Associate Professor of Politics and Co-ordinator of
Women's Studies at the University of Lowell (Lowell, Massachusetts,
USA). Born and raised in New York City, she is a graduate of Cornell
University and holds a doctorate in politics from New York
University. Prior to her academic career, Professor Rothschild was a
professional writer in newspaper and magazine publishing. Her
recent work in feminist theory, and women and technology has
appeared in *Quest: a feminist quarterly* and *Women's Studies Inter-*

national Quarterly.

Najma Sachak, BA (Manc.), MA (Dar es Salaam); Research Fellow, Bureau of Resources Assessment and Land Use Planning, University of Dar es Salaam. At present on leave of absence and at the Institute of Social and Economic Research, University of the West Indies, Kingston, Jamaica; has worked on numerous projects on agricultural resources. Publications include articles and papers on these topics and women's control of food resources.

Sirkka Sinkkonen, MA (Helsinki), PhD (Johns Hopkins), Professor in Public Health and Nursing Administration, University of Kuopio; previously Professor of Planning, technical expert for World Health Organisation in nursing research; Member of IPSA Executive Council 1974-6; Research Fellow of the Finnish Academy of Science, 1977-9. Research interests in sociology: medical sociology, health-care and marriage; and in political science: women and politics, and in public administration.

Judith Stiehm, PhD (Columbia); Associate Professor of Political Science, University of Southern California; since 1975, Director of Programme for the Study of Women and Men in Society; member of Defense Advisory Committee on Women in the Services and of California Postsecondary Education Commission; Convenor of three panels at IPSA Moscow Congress. Books include *Nonviolent Power: Active and Passive Resistance in America; Bring Me Men and Women: Mandated Change at the US Air Force Academy*; numerous articles on nonviolence, women and equality, and women and the military, including 'Women and the Combat Exemption' in *Parameters* (1980).

Fanny Tabak, PhD (Lomonosov University), Senior Lecturer in Political Science, Pontifícia Universidada Católica, Rio de Janeiro; research interests: women's studies, environmental and urban studies, science and technology and national development, and local government; numerous articles on these topics.

Sharon L. Wolchik, PhD (Michigan), Assistant Professor of International Affairs and Political Science, George Washington University; member of the Institute for Sino-Soviet Studies; research interests: role of specialists in policy-making and the policy-making process in communist states; currently completing a book on women's status in Eastern and Western Europe; articles in *Slavic Review, Comparative Political Studies* and *Women & Politics*.

INDEX

Abadan-Unat, Nermin 39
abbesses 16
abortion 20, 25, 45n30, 137-8, 141, 145-6, 149n37, 156-8, 179n11, 211, 216
absence from home 104, 230
absolute, absolutism, absolutists 24, 37, 43n7; less than 137
academic disciplines 33-4, 41, 71-3, 240; interdisciplinary, multi-disciplinary studies 33-6, 39, 240; tunnel-vision, disciplinary boundaries 33, 41-2, 132-3, 240; see also humanities, sciences, social sciences, demography, etc.
access: to education 37, 95, 98, 103, 112-14, 163-4, 197, 216; to positions of power 16-17, 21, 24-30, 39, 216, 223, 240; to resources 34, 164, 216; see also education, employment paid, powerful positions
accumulation 154, 156
achievement 25-6, 95, 103, 184, 193
Adam 17, 43n7
Adelman, L. and Morris, C.T. 96
affirmative action 98, 104, 187, 218, 221-5; guide-lines 223, 225; sex discrimination legislation 42
Africa 91, 130; Accra 55, 88; Uganda 46n35; West Africa 88, 148; see also Nigeria, Tanzania
age 63, 189, 196; and educational level 88-9; and participation in labour force 100, 141, Ch. 4 passim
agenda-building Ch. 11 passim
agriculture 19, 34, 70, 72, 81, 84, 90, 96, 98, 140; agricultural innovation, modernisation 35-7, 70, 90, 133; agricultural produce 97; Agricultural Revolution 17; agricultural work 28, 34-7, 124, 128-33; crop-buying centre/marketing/export 37, 117, 120, 134n4; see also farms, food, subsistence

aid, in development 117, 133, 191, 224
Albania 94, 95
alienation, anomie 27, 41, 163, 165, 168-9, 170-1, 176, 186, 189
advisory posts 24, 45n28n29, 111, 236
American Civil War 61
anti-authoritarian 188
apolitical 31-2
apprenticeship 100, 110, see also vocational training
Aristophanes 61
Ataturk, Kemal 39, 94
attitudes 35, 39, 78, 95, 98, 108, 112, 216, 229, 237
authority 33; authoritarian attitudes 36, 38, 41; authoritarian regimes 74, 78-9; authoritarianism promoted by competitive values 241: changing patterns of 95; governmental 18, 24; patriarchal 162, 172-3, 176
automation 163, 168
Awosika Keziah 39

Bacon, Francis 19, 45n25
Balbo, Laura 155
Bandaranaike, Mrs 43n4
Basaglia, Franco 155
basic need 120, 125, 130
battered women 187, 213
Baumgärtel, Ursula 153, 159n2
Beaud, Mary 38
Beziehungsarbeit 155
Bills, Private Member 199-215 passim; content 204-10, 212; 'fiscal', legislative, petitionary 199, 209; men and women co-signatories to 203-5, 207, 212; single member 202, 204
birth control 20, 136, 147n4, 157-8, 160, 163-4, 173, see also fertility
birth rate 137-8, 145, 147n2, 148n7; declining 135-8, 145; increasing 146; policies 19, 145-6; see also birth control, mortality rates,